WYCLIF IN HIS TIMES

WYCLIF
IN HIS
TIMES

EDITED BY

ANTHONY KENNY

CLARENDON PRESS · OXFORD
1986

Oxford University Press, Walton Street, Oxford OX2 6DP

Oxford New York Toronto
Delhi Bombay Calcutta Madras Karachi
Kuala Lumpur Singapore Hong Kong Tokyo
Nairobi Dar es Salaam Cape Town
Melbourne Auckland
and associated companies in
Beirut Berlin Ibadan Nicosia

Oxford is a trade mark of Oxford University Press

Published in the United States
by Oxford University Press, New York

British Library Cataloguing in Publication Data
Wyclif in his times.
1. Wycliffe, John
I. Kenny, Anthony
274.2'05 BX4905
ISBN 0-19-820088-9

Library of Congress Cataloging in Publication Data
Wyclif in his times.
Includes index.
1. Wycliffe, John, d. 1384. I. Kenny, Anthony
John Patrick.
BX4905.W93 1986 270.5'092'4 86-8805
ISBN 0-19-820088-9

Set by Joshua Associates Ltd.
Printed in Great Britain
at the University Printing House, Oxford
by David Stanford
Printer to the University

Preface

JOHN WYCLIF died on the last day of the year 1384. He had been–by one count–the thirteenth Master of Balliol in 1360 and for a year or two thereafter. Balliol in 1984 was anxious that his sexcentenary should be appropriately celebrated in Oxford. Accordingly, the Faculties of Theology, History, and English and the Sub-faculty of Philosophy were invited to co-operate with Balliol in funding a series of commemorative lectures in Michaelmas Term of 1984. The faculties accepted the invitation and each of them invited a lecturer to elucidate the importance of Wyclif for their own branch of studies. The theologians invited Professor Gordon Leff, the philosophers invited Professor Norman Kretzmann, the historians entrusted the task to Dr Maurice Keen, and the Faculty of English commissioned Dr Anne Hudson.

The commemorative lectures delivered in Balliol provide the core of the present work. Three of the lectures–Keen on 'The Bible and Transubstantiation', Kretzmann on 'Continua, Indivisibles, and Change', and Hudson on 'Wyclif and the English Language'–are here reproduced with the minimum of alteration. To avoid overlap, Professor Leff's Balliol lecture is here replaced by an updated version of his much-admired paper in the *Bulletin of the John Rylands Library* (50. 387ff.) on the doctrinal relationship between Wyclif and Hus. Two other papers which were read in Oxford during the Wyclif centenary year have been added to the collection: Anne Hudson's paper on 'Wycliffism in Oxford' and my own paper on Wyclif's realism were both read to the Oxford Medieval Society during its 1984-5 session. To round out the volume two papers have been included which deal with Wyclif's posthumous influence: Maurice Keen describes the first four decades after the reformer's death, and I have attempted to describe the way in which the condemnation of Wyclif at Constance influenced the course of Catholic and Counter-Reformation theology before and after the Council of Trent.

Introducing the centenary lectures as Master of Balliol, I remarked that when I was a child there were two facts about Wyclif which were supposed to be known to every schoolchild. One was that he was the first to translate the Bible into English; the other was that he was the theorist responsible for the Peasants' Revolt. Learned spoilsports, I observed, had now called both of these facts into question. None the less, it seemed to me, Wyclif was a person well deserving of the attention of historians, theologians, philosophers, and students of the English language. The present volume, I believe, confirms this judgement. It shows also that Wyclif was a genius who can interest scholars of very various background and expertise. The contributors to this volume belong to diverse faculties and contrasting schools of thought. They would select quite different aspects of Wyclif as matters deserving of continuing concern. They would disagree about the interpretation to be put upon fundamental doctrines of the reformer, and the weight to be attached to the several evidences of his life and teaching. But all would agree that Wyclif was a metaphysical thinker of compelling power, and a historical figure of far-reaching influence.

ANTHONY KENNY

Balliol,
November 1985

Contents

Abbreviations

CHLMP	*The Cambridge History of Later Medieval Philosophy*, ed. N. Kretzmann, A. Kenny, and J. Pinborg (Cambridge, 1982)
CPR	*Calendar of Patent Rolls*
CT	*Concilium Tridentinum, Diariorum, Actorum, Epistolarum, Tractatuum Nova Collectio*, ed. Societas Goerresiana (1896-)
EETS	Early English Text Society
FZ	*Fasciculi Zizaniorum*, ed. W. W. Shirley (Rolls Series, London, 1858)
ICAMT	*Infinity and Continuity in Ancient and Medieval Thought*, ed. N. Kretzmann (Ithaca, NY, 1982)
MCW	*The Yale Edition of the Complete Works of Sir Thomas More* (New Haven and London, 1963-)
SCH	*Studies in Church History* (Cambridge, 1962-)
U	John Wyclif, *De Universalibus*, ed. I. Mueller (Oxford, 1985); trans. A. Kenny, *On Universals* (Oxford, 1985)

I

Wyclif, the Bible, and Transubstantiation

MAURICE KEEN

IN this paper I shall attempt to trace the stages in the development of Wyclif's thought that turned him from a radical critic of his contemporary church, into what he is remembered as, a heresiarch. The formal turning-point in that development is quite clear; it is the moment at which he began to maintain in the schools views concerning the Eucharist which were directly at variance with the orthodox doctrine of the Church of his day. It is equally clear that his decision to determine on this topic, and his refusal to retract his opinions or to keep silent in the face of condemnation, were individual decisions; that his heresy, that is to say, has to be explained in terms of his personal circumstances and convictions. For that reason I must start with a brief review of what we know about his life and the general development of his ideas—in order to provide a context for what I want to say about this central moment in his life and thought.

Wyclif's life was not one fraught with drama. His career was as a don, who was never formally anything greater than a don. We do not know precisely when he was born, but it must have been about 1330. A Yorkshire man, he was probably supported in his early days at Oxford by a local patron; when he is first heard of, in 1356, he was a fellow of Merton.[1] By then he had incepted in the Faculty of Arts. He was elected Master of Balliol in 1360, an office that he filled only briefly;[2] later he became Warden of Canterbury Hall, an office which involved him, a secular, in wrangles with the regulars (the masters and students belonging to regular religious orders), which culminated in his losing the post, an experience that probably left its mark.[3] He held a minuscule series of livings, being presented ultimately, in 1374, to the

---

[1] J. A. Robson, *Wyclif and the Oxford Schools* (Cambridge, 1961), 10.
[2] Ibid., 13.
[3] Ibid., 15-16. Robson quotes Woodford's belief that Wyclif was marked by the experience.

crown living of Lutterworth in Leicestershire. But he was never, until his very last years, resident in any of his livings, and after leaving Canterbury Hall he had rooms in Queen's College (a foundation with Yorkshire connections). At the university he seems to have waited longer than the average–among scholars of distinction at any rate–before proceeding from the Faculty of Arts to that of theology: he probably incepted as a BD in 1368/9 and as a Doctor of Theology in 1372/3.[4] Though the bulk of his time was spent in Oxford, he was, on a number of occasions between 1372 and 1378, employed by the government and by men in high places as a polemist whose criticisms of contemporary ecclesiastical privileges could be made useful for political purposes.[5] The last occasion on which we know that he was so employed was in the Gloucester Parliament of 1378, where he spoke to justify the right of the royal officers to enter the Westminster sanctuary in order to arrest two squires who were crown debtors. That was just a year before he began to defend in Oxford those views of his on the Eucharist which were to be condemned as heretical. As a result of their initial condemnation by a university commission he left Oxford in 1381 and took up residence at his rectory at Lutterworth. About the same time he seems to have suffered from a stroke; and at Lutterworth he died, of another stroke that paralysed his body and his tongue, in the last days of December 1384.

To complete the introductory picture, I must say a little about the professional academic works that Wyclif produced in his career as a don. First I need to say a word (briefly since more will be said elsewhere in this book) of his philosophic works, commenced while he was an artist and completed, almost certainly, before he incepted as a Doctor of Theology–about the tracts that, gathered together, are known as his *Summa de Ente*.[6] These reveal him as an uncompromising opponent, in philosophy, of the dominant school of his day–that of the *moderni*, the nominalist disciples of William of Ockham. Ockham taught that all human knowledge was, ultimately, experientially acquired, as a result of acquaintance (essentially through sense data) with singular objects. For him and his school, abstract concepts had no demonstrable existence outside the mind. This philosophic

---

[4] H. B. Workman, *John Wyclif* (Oxford, 1926), i. 201 n. 1, 203.

[5] On Wyclif's political employments, see K. B. McFarlane, *John Wyclif and the beginnings of English nonconformity* (London, 1952), chapter 3.

[6] On the *Summa de Ente*, and on Wyclif's own part in putting together the tracts that are included in it, see Robson (above, n. 1), chapter 5, 'The Structure of the *Summa de Ente*'.

approach had implications for theology, it should be noted. We cannot see or touch or taste God; so our knowledge of him, and of his eternal verities, is not knowledge in the ordinary sense, nor are he and his truths susceptible of logical discussion: the eye of faith may discern or know them, but not the eye of reason. Wyclif was one who reacted against this fashionable teaching. In his views on cognition he was avowedly Platonist. We know things, he taught, not because we touch or see them, but because they *are*, because of something about them and in them that renders their being intelligible. Abstract concepts, being intelligible, have reality–otherwise the mind would not be able to grasp them. This approach to cognition, equally with Ockham's, had implications for theology. On this view by peering behind the surface of things to the reality underlying them–to what makes them what they are–we can peer forward towards an understanding of God, who makes all things and whose universal knowledge of all things makes knowledge of some things in a degree accessible to men who are made in his image. This is a teaching which, obviously and explicitly, allows significant room for human speculation in the field of theology. Its truths are not 'unknowable'; if they were, nothing would be knowable.

Wyclif's philosophical views–his realist or Platonist metaphysics–are in consequence the key to much of his theological work. In particular they are the key to his views on a number of subjects which have–or rather had–very practical applications: lordship, the Church, the papacy, the office of kingship, and above all the authority of the Bible. These topics are the themes of a series of works which date, in the form in which we have them, from the years 1374-9. I will not attempt to do more than summarize, very succinctly, some of the central views that they relay. Wyclif's belief that all human knowledge depended on God's eternal foreknowledge naturally made him a radical predestinarian. This coloured his view of the nature of the Church.[7] None but those with a standing in grace were in a true sense members of the Church: hence the Church was the body of the elect, among whom the pope and his clergy might, or might not, be numbered. It coloured also his view of lordship, or possession.[8] Following and adapting the opinions of Giles of Rome and Fitzralph

[7] On Wyclif's views on the Church see for a summary Workman (above, n. 4), ii. 6-20; and G. Leff, *Heresy in the Later Middle Ages* (Manchester, 1967), ii. 516-46.

[8] For Wyclif's views on lordship and Church endowments, see for a summary Workman (above, n. 4), i. 217-30, 257-66: and Leff (above, n. 7), ii. 546-9.

of Armagh, he argued that lordship depended on grace and that therefore righteousness was the only genuinely valid title to lordship. All lordship depends on God: therefore, only those whom he justifies can be said to have a valid right to lordship: those in sin forfeit their right, since right cannot be justified by a merely human instrument, by a foundation charter or papal decree, but only by that justification which declares that the righteous possess all things. This enabled him to embark on a radical critique of ecclesiastical endowments. But above all his philosophical stance coloured his view of Scripture. In scholastic terms, he believed that the divine truth articulated in it had of itself intelligible being: in Robson's words it was 'an emanation of the supreme being, transposed into writing'.[9] The Bible, said Wyclif, was God's book, a summary of truth in a more important sense than a mere matter of words on a page: it was the testament of the Father,[10] a 'charter written by God', 'the mirror of eternal truth'.[11] As such, it was the key to human understanding of truth, and the 'logic of Holy Scripture', as Wyclif called it,[12] was superior to all human logic. It was the key to human understanding of the divine, because it came direct from the source of that understanding; and the key also both to Christian doctrine and to Christian living–the full and perfect guide, that is to say, to human social and political association. What could not find foundation in Holy Scripture had no real foundation (the word 'pope' was not used therein, Wyclif pointed out).[13] The whole law, the truth, the life were to be found there, and any addition thereto could only detract from its perfection, never enhance it. True, its understanding required the exegesis of the scholar, to bring truth within range of the unlettered and to clarify obscurities of language: and for ordinary men it must be translated–by scholars. But its truths, he claimed, were not beyond their understanding, and the obscurities in it were only apparent, not real. There could not, ultimately, be obscurity in the source of light itself. This was the trend of the views that Wyclif expounded *in extenso* in the *De Veritate Sacre Scripture*, the last major work that he completed before he began to tackle the question of the mass.

It was in the summer, probably, of the year 1377 that Wyclif first

[9] Robson (above, n. 1), 146.

[10] *De Veritate Sacre Scripture*, i. 100.

[11] B. Smalley, 'The Bible and Eternity: John Wyclif's dilemma', *Journal of the Warburg and Courtauld Institute*, 27 (1964), 81, quoting from Wyclif's sermon at his inception as DD.

[12] *De Veritate Sacre Scripture*, i. 29, 50, 53, 195.

[13] *De Potestate Pape*, 165.

began to determine–to give his view in public lectures–on the Eucharist. In doing so, he entered a new area of debate. He had already, it is
true, gone very far in the statement of a radical position on ecclesiastical endowments, on papal power, on the right of the secular
authority to reform ecclesiastical discipline; and he had in consequence attracted hostile attention both from the English bishops
and the *curia* of Gregory XI.[14] But the questions that he had raised to
date were mainly concerning authority and administration in the
Church, on which matters the fourteenth century was used to hearing
radical opinions. He still had, apparently, numerous academic
disciples and sympathizers, and among regulars as well as seculars,
especially among the friars–those mendicants whom a little later, in
his *De Apostasia*, he called 'my most dear sons among the mendicant
orders, who are not among the apostates'.[15] We still have the notebook
in which one of them, Adam Stocton, copied 'twelve points to show
the Pope is anti-Christ' from Wyclif's *De Potestate Pape*, with the
approving comment, 'hec venerabilis doctor magister JW in quadem
sua determinatione, anno 1379'. Probably within the year, perhaps
only a few months later, Stocton crossed out the words *venerabilis
doctor* and substituted *execrabilis seductor*.[16] Those who had followed
Wyclif as long as he was talking of the nature of the Church, of the
authority of the pope, and of the evangelical path to perfection, could
not follow him any longer when he rounded upon a central Christian
doctrine, and they sheered away. For a little while some, apparently,
hoped he would withdraw from his new extreme position. 'I do not call
him a heretic', wrote the Oxford friar Dr Thomas Winterton 'seeing
with tearful eyes the many errors and heresies of the famous doctor
John Wyclif, since I do not know whether he has the intention of obsti-
nately defending his errors, or is ready to be corrected . . . submitting
as is his duty, to ecclesiastical authority.'[17] Wyclif, however, was not
ready to submit to that authority, whose claims he had already torn to
pieces in works which men like Stocton, and perhaps Winterton, had
seen no cause to quarrel with. Winterton's hopes for him proved
empty: he stood by his Eucharistic teaching, and that put him beyond
the pale of orthodoxy and in 1381 drove him from Oxford. That for
Wyclif was the final turning point, and the turning point for those who

---

[14] See Workman (above, n. 4), i. 284-8, 293-9.

[15] *De Apostasia*, 44.

[16] A. Gwynn, *English Austin Friars in the Time of Wyclif* (Oxford, 1940), 238-9.

[17] Introduction to Winterton's *Absolutio*, printed in *Fasciculi Zizaniorum*, ed. W. W.
Shirley (Rolls Series, 1858), 182 (henceforward quoted as *FZ*).

cared to follow him too. Henceforward they would be heretics, not just the sympathizers with a radical anticlericalism they had been able to call themselves hitherto.

The question is, therefore, what it was that turned Wyclif decisively at this particular point. What was it that led him, over the years 1379-81, to call in question the teaching of the Church on the central sacrament of the Eucharist, to flout authority, and to devote himself in the remaining years of his life to reiterating, with increasing vehemence, his denunciation of that teaching, in the works that he penned from his rectory at Lutterworth? In order to attempt an answer to this question, it is clearly necessary to say a little bit more of what the debate was about and just what teaching it was that Wyclif rejected.

Transubstantiation, the doctrine with which Wyclif quarrelled, had been given the stamp of orthodoxy by a decretal of Innocent III in 1215.[18] It is a doctrine whose medieval philosophic implications are not easy to understand—at any rate for one, like myself, who is untrained in scholasticism. It claims that, at the mass, there is a change of substance in the consecrated host, and to understand that, one must understand also what substance technically means. For the medieval philosophers, following Aristotle, substance was what differentiated things or stuff of one kind from things or stuff of another kind. Substance was thus something to be differentiated from accidents in descriptive statements. Socrates is a man, he is white, he is clever, he is old. 'White', 'clever', 'old' are predicates about accidents—the whiteness and cleverness and age of Socrates; his humanity, however, is not accidental but substantial. It tells you what kind of thing Socrates is and that he is not another kind of thing that might also be white, clever, and old—say, a horse. At the Eucharist, according to the scholastic interpretation of transubstantiation, it is the substance of the consecrated host that changes, not the accidents; the whiteness and roundness of the host remain, but the substance is not bread any more—it has changed from that kind of stuff into stuff of a quite different kind.

This explanation of the mass is one which poses a number of problems. There is for instance the one that others had raised and that Wyclif crowed over: if a mouse eats the consecrated host, do we say that it has eaten—substantially—the body of Christ?'[19] Or again, and less flippantly, are we to say that at the mass the priest *breaks* what is in

[18] 4th Lateran Council, Decree I, *De Fide Catholica*.
[19] Anselm had discussed this problem; see Wyclif's *De Eucharistia*, 130, and references there cited.

substance the body of Christ? But the most important and obvious difficulty, which logically precedes these, is this: what are we to say about the accidents of what was once bread, which most certainly have not changed? Changes of substance posed no problem for the scholastic: Aristotle had explained such change in terms of the components of substance, matter, and form, and substantial change was, observably, common enough. What was milk becomes butter; a dead body decomposes, and becomes carrion, then clay. But when these changes occur, not only does the substance change, but the accidents also–or enough of them to register the alteration. In contrast, in the case of the consecrated host there is nothing to register the change; and an ugly philosophical problem arises. We have a small, round, white object and we are told that its smallness, roundness, and whiteness (its accidents) are not the roundness and whiteness of bread as they seem to be. We also know that they cannot be the roundness and whiteness and size of Christ's body–if we say that Christ's body is round and white and two inches across we shall patently be blaspheming, as Wyclif triumphantly pointed out.[20] But if the accidents are not the accidents of bread and are not the accidents of Christ's body either, what are they? An accident is a quality of something else, of a substance: accidents without substance are a contradiction in terms. Surely we do not say that the host that we see elevated at the mass is a contradiction in terms?

Two explanations of what happened at the mass were offered by scholastics of earlier generations than Wyclif's. Aquinas suggested that the substance of the bread was changed and that the accidents that remained were upheld by what he called 'quantity'. This is not an easy argument to follow. Dziewicki explains it thus:

Quantity is not a mere substance, not a mere mode of being; it is different from extension for it is what makes extension, and may be defined as a force that extends material substance. Thus, after the words of the consecration, the substance of bread is no longer there, but quantity takes its place naturally, being itself upheld by God's supernatural power: and therefore whatever the bread could do, even to feeding the body, is now performed by the quantity that remains.[21]

I am not sure that this is a very clear explanation, but it has been quoted by historians more learned than I as the best they can offer.

---

[20] *FZ* lx; 120-1, 129 (Wyclif's *Confessio*): compare *De Apostasia*, 57; *De Blasphemia*, 20-5.
[21] M. H. Dziewicki, in his introduction to the *De Apostasia*, xv.

Actually, I think St Thomas's suggestion is perhaps a better one than he himself could have realized. Take two statements which appear at first sight parallel: 'Socrates is white' and 'the sky is blue'. Socrates is a substance all right and whiteness is an accident of that substance: but is the sky a substance? Surely it is not, and to describe it we shall have to say something like that it is 'the appearance of depth in space'—in other words we shall arrive at saying that its blueness is an accident of a phenomenon that we have to describe in quantitative terms. Aquinas, dependent on an Aristotelian cosmology, could not of course have quoted this example, and nor could Wyclif—but it is a good reminder that what Aquinas said was not by any means absurd, or a quibble, as one might at first be tempted to think.

The other scholastic explanation of what happened at the mass, and which was much more widely adopted in Wyclif's day, was that of Scotus, in which the majority of the *moderni* (the followers of Ockham) concurred. Scotus, in order to explain a problem that seemed insoluble, fell back upon the omnipotence of God's will. He held that the substance of bread was not changed at the consecration of the host, but 'annihilated'—that it simply ceased to be. In the place where it had been there was now the body of Christ: there was not substantial change, but substantial substitution. The accidents of the bread remained, Duns taught, as what he called 'verities without substance', maintained by the unlimited and unlimitable power of God. Thus, as Workman put it 'the eucharist is the constant repetition of a stupendous miracle'.[22] The Ockhamite explanation of what happened at the mass was, as I have said, substantially the same as Duns's. To this school, this explanation posed no philosophical problems. Christ's body, after his Ascension, was not something that we can see or touch: the ordinary rules of logic therefore did not apply to statements about it. The will of God, Ockham's disciples taught, is a *potentia absoluta*,[23] a power unconditioned by the rules of reason (or any other rules). He can annihilate substance and uphold accidents at his will, because he can do anything. Men cannot fully understand what has happened; but the accidents are, according to this teaching, no longer the accidents of bread, in consequence of a great miracle whose working is not susceptible of logical explanation, but whose verity we accept on the basis of faith.

[22] Workman (above, n. 4), ii, 33. I have followed Dr Workman's summary of the Scotist view.

[23] See on this matter G. Leff, 'The Changing Patterns of Thought in the Earlier Fourteenth Century', *Bull. John Rylands' Library*, 43 (1961), especially 356-64; and his *Richard FitzRalph: Commentator of the Sentences* (Manchester, 1963), 5-7.

This Scotist explanation of the mass was, however, quite irrecon-cileable with Wyclif's teaching. All knowledge, he believed, was of God; we perceive things only because he has made them intelligiible. Wyclif must almost certainly at some point have come across the famous passage in Ockham's *Summa Totius Logicae* in which he rejects the Platonist view of universals. If one believes that a universal is something that really exists in singulars, Ockham says, 'it would follow that God cannot annihilate one singular of a given substance without annihilating all the others; for if he annihilated the singular thing he would annihilate that which is the essence of the singular in question, and consequently would annihilate the universal that is in it and in other singulars of the same substance, and so they would not remain either.'[24] Ockham's logic was, as usual, flawless. If, as Wyclif believed, the substance of bread had intelligible being which was imparted to every singular piece of bread, then if the substance of bread was annihilated in one piece of bread it would be annihilated in all pieces of bread. He had therefore to deny the premiss that God could annihilate substance. There was a common-sense strength in this argument, even though it did pose some theological difficulties, for annihilation, as he pointed out, made nonsense of sense data. The host which we see consecrated and receive at the mass becomes, on that view, the appearance of nothing. To accept that would undermine the basis of any theory of cognition, realist or nominalist, and reli-giously it meant the adoration of the absurd. That was what the notion of 'verities without substance' would lead to–an extreme of blasphemy.

Wyclif's philosophic arguments against both the Thomists and the Scotists take up many pages of the *De Eucharistia* and the *De Apostasia*, his two last Oxford works, and of the *Trialogus*, the best of his Lutter-worth writings. His objections to both were essentially the same, that if the consecrated host had accidents which had no substance, then it was nothing; and the central Christian sacrament was nothing; men venerated a nothing in the elevated host, and so blasphemed. These objections are clearly based in the system of metaphysics that he had elaborated as an artist, and which he had set out as a system in the *Summa de Ente*. For this reason, it has been usual to accept that Wyclif's reasons for attacking the doctrine of transubstantiation were intellectual; that his essentially academic speculation carried him

[24] Ockham, *Summa Totius Logicae*, i. 15; quoted by W. and M. Kneale, *The Development of Logic* (Oxford, 1962), 265.

'ineluctably' into his central heresy, rather than the evangelical zeal which gives its ring of strong personal conviction to the *De Veritate Sacre Scripture* and that inspired his vision of Biblical communism in the *De Civili Dominio*. 'His final position grew directly out of his metaphysics', writes G. Leff; 'it could have been reached at any time within the previous fifteen or more years.'[25] 'He approached the eucharist from the point of view not of abuses, but of a metaphysical system,' says Workman.[26] Robson is clear that the decisive moment in the development of Wyclif's Eucharistic thought must have been quite early, in the years 1370-2, when he was first applying his metaphysic to theological issues, quoting on this behalf the friar William Woodford, who was long a close friend, and later, like so many other friars, a distinguished opponent. 'When the said Master John was first lecturing on the *Sentences* [that would be in 1371 or 2]', so Woodford says 'he asserted that though the sacramental accidents had a subject, yet the bread ceased to exist at consecration. And being much pressed as to what the subject of those accidents was, he replied that it was a mathematical body. Afterwards, when this position had been much argued against, he answered that he did not know what the subject of the accidents was, yet he asserted clearly that they had a subject. Now [Woodford was writing in 1381] he lays down expressly that the bread remains after consecration and is the subject of the accidents.'[27] Here we seem to have a clear history of the evolution of Wyclif's view, through puzzlement *via* Thomism to his own individual standpoint, which was reached through the course of parry and thrust in pure academic argument.

Nevertheless, and in spite of Woodford, I must say that I am not happy with this account as the whole story of Wyclif's developing thought on the Eucharist. First, it seems to me to impose an uncomfortably long gap between Wyclif's first attempt to grapple with the question and what Leff has called the ineluctable conclusion.[28] Here in parenthesis it is perhaps worth noting that though Wyclif's Eucharistic teaching was condemned at Oxford in 1381 and by the Canterbury convocation in 1382, his philosophical teaching, which supposedly gave rise to that ineluctable conclusion, was not: his metaphysics continued to stir interest in Oxford through the 1380s and 90s,

---

[25] Leff (above, n. 7), ii. 499, 550.

[26] Workman (above, n. 4), ii. 30.

[27] *FZ*, xv n. 4: and see Robson (above, n. 1), 192-3.

[28] Woodford says that Wyclif first considered the matter when he was a 'responding bachelor', i.e. before 1373.

which was why they influenced Czech realist thought at an early stage, when Czech scholars were as yet ignorant of his teaching on the Eucharist. Apparently his contemporaries did not see his metaphysics as being quite so perilous as their 'ineluctable conclusion' ought to have made them. But there is a more important point than this. Though Wyclif denied transubstantiation, he was never entirely clear as to what he wished to put in its place. If he was still uncertain in 1379 of what the true explanation was, why did he not continue to confess his ignorance, as on Woodford's evidence he had done for some time past: 'afterwards ... he answered that he did not know what the subject of the accidents was, yet he asserted clearly that they had a subject.'[29] And lastly, if all that was in issue was a point in metaphysics, why is it that in all Wyclif's works on the subject–even in the first, the *De Eucharistia*–his attack on transubstantiation appears to be linked in his mind with the abuses in the Church that he had been concentrating on in earlier but more recent works, in the *De Ecclesia* and the *De Potestate Pape*, for example? This makes me very unhappy about Workman's statement in particular, that Wyclif attacked the current Eucharistic teaching 'not from the point of view of abuses, but of a metaphysical system'.

The true story of the development of his thought is, I believe, somewhat different from that usually accepted explanation. What has given that explanation its currency, I think, is the fact (which is undoubted) that Wyclif concentrated so much on the negative side of the argument; whence the natural conclusion, that that was what was really important to him. But I do not believe that is really why he did concentrate on it; this was rather because he believed that on this one point of accidents without substance he could make those whom he regarded as the pillars of abuse, the followers of Antichrist or 'western Mahomets' as he made them out to be,[30] look ridiculous and fraudulent (as he believed they really were). In other words, I believe almost the opposite of Workman's view, that Wyclif attacked transubstantiation rather from the point of view of abuse than of a metaphysical system, and further, that the positive side of his discussion of the mass–which is often somewhat neglected–supports this interpretation.

The central positive point in Wyclif's conclusions on the Eucharist was that bread and wine remained after consecration. To prove this

<hr />

[29] Above, n. 27.
[30] *Polemical Works*, i. 30, 80; ii. 597-8.

affirmatively, he did not rely on metaphysic. What he relied on was
Scripture and the teaching of the early Church, and to this end in the
De Apostasia he attempted a remarkable and impressive survey of the
history of the doctrine of the mass, in which he paid particular attention to the wording of the Bible and the Fathers.[31] When they spoke of
the mass, he pointed out, they invariably mentioned bread. When
Christ said 'This is my body' (*hoc est corpus meum*) he did not mean *hoc
corpus est corpus meum*–an absurd tautology–but *hic panis est corpus meum*:
and as he then stood bodily before his disciples, he can only have been
speaking 'in a figure',[32] just as he was when he said 'upon this rock will
I build my church'. Turning to Augustine, he found that he supported
his reading. 'What we see', says the great Father 'is the bread and the
chalice that the eyes announce: and faith receives that the bread is the
body and that in the chalice is the blood of our Lord. These are sacraments, since one thing is seen, another understood.'[33] Faith, not the
senses, touched the body of Christ, according to Wyclif's gloss on the
African. The belief of the Church was still true to Christ and Scripture
in the eleventh century, Wyclif thought, quoting Berengar's confession: 'I believe that the bread and wine which are placed upon the altar
after consecration are not only a sacrament but the true body and
blood of Jesus Christ'–but still bread and wine too according to the
letter, Wyclif points out.[34] Actually, I think that he was at this point
misreading the decretal of Nicholas II that embodies Berengar's confession, and giving the opposite of its intended sense–but that is not
germane: he believed he had got it right, and in any case, Scripture
and the teaching of the early Church was the real basis of his authority.

This seems to me to tell its own story. Wyclif put forward his teaching on the Eucharist in the year 1379, the year after he had completed
the *De Veritate Sacre Scripture* and probably not more than eighteen
months after concluding the monumental task that he had set himself
back in 1371 (or thereabout), of making a commentary on the whole of
Scripture–what is now called his *Postilla Super Totam Bibliam*.[35] What
settled his conviction about the remanence of the bread was not realist
metaphysic, at least not directly, but what he called the logic of Holy

[31] *De Apostasia*, chapters 15 and 16.
[32] *De Eucharistia*, 34, 37, 38.
[33] Ibid., 125; quoting from *Decret.* iii, 'De Consacr.', Dist. II, ch. 108.
[34] *De Eucharistia*, 25-7; *De Apostasia*, 68, 79, and Dziewicki's introduction to *De Apostasia*, xxxv.
[35] B. Smalley, '*John Wyclif's Postilla super totam Bibliam*', *Bodleian Library Quarterly*, 4
(1953), 186-205.

Scripture. It was that same logic–and the history of the early Church–that had already convinced him that the pope's powers had no sacred foundation, and that his decretals were for the most part an imperfect addition to the all-sufficient teaching of Scripture; and that pope and decretals alike were leading the Church out of the evangelical way. Now he had found a still more startling way in which what he called the carnal as opposed to the true Church was leading Christians astray to damnation. It had made its own fresh account of the central sacrament, a fudged teaching of its own that it had tacked on to what Christ enjoined upon his faithful for all time. The carnal Church was claiming that its priests–many of them men of unholy life, preknown to hell–could make Christ's own body, the Truth itself: and was enjoining silence upon all questioning, knowing that the detection of its fraud could knock the keystone out of the arch of priestly power.

Let me be clear about what I am suggesting. It is that Wyclif had long been worried by contemporary teaching on the Eucharist, but that what finally convinced him that it was wrong were his scriptural studies of the year 1372-9. Once he had come to the conclusion that this doctrine of transubstantiation was unsupported by Scripture and fraudulent, he had no option but to speak out, and speak out he did. If this is the right account of the way in which Wyclif's Eucharistic thought developed, there are consequences for a view of his personality. He appears as something more than a don in a difficulty, rather as one moved at the crucial crossroad of his life not by the rigidity of his own intellectual system, as Workman would have it, but by evangelical religious conviction. It is the passion of that conviction, I believe, that makes his late writing often seem so wrathful, not disappointed ambition, as McFarlane suspected.[36] He really was angry. When, in the first two chapters of his *De Apostasia*, he opened his great attack on the friars, he had three main charges against them. One was that they followed what he called 'private religions', in other words that the rules of the mendicant orders were a superfluous addition to the fully sufficient rule of Scripture and of necessity, as human additions to it, less perfect than the original. The second was that they were the chief agents in purveying the merely human means and instruments through which the clergy–and the pope above all–sought to raise money on the basis of their claim to *cause* God's acts, through absolutions (which only God can give) and indulgences. Thirdly and above all, they were the chief preachers among the people of the

[36] McFarlane (above, n. 5), 66-8, 85.

modern heresy concerning the miracle of the mass. In this he suspected them of deliberate fraud. 'They say among themselves, truths on such matters are not for preaching among the people, lest their devotion be shaken; and thus they consent to idolatry',[37] says Wyclif, taking up the same point in the *De Blasphemia*–so they preach lies instead.

There is a common thread running through all these charges, which illuminates, I think, the real basis of Wyclif's passionate anger. The friars live by a rule which is a human addition to Scripture: they sell absolutions and indulgences which are given by man, not by the Truth which speaks through Scripture: and they preach a doctrine of the mass which claims that man can make the body of God and which has no foundation in Scripture. The matter is always connected with putting the human above the divine, the cardinal sin and the error that is carnal by definition. What horrified Wyclif most of all about the doctrine of transubstantiation was just this, its carnality. The priests who followed that teaching sold the host, which the eye can perceive is bread, as the corporeal body of God: they taught men to bow before what was material and corruptible, the very essence of idolatry; and they taught men to believe that they bit the body of Christ and were nourished bodily thereby, which was blasphemy. A shoddy claim for physical, sacerdotal magic, that was what Wyclif thought of transubstantiation; and a claim moreover that would not and could not stand the test of scriptural authority through which alone God's scheme of salvation for man could be understood, a claim therefore that fell into the same category as Mahomet's twisting of the Holy Book to his own fell purposes.

Wyclif did not deny the importance of the mass, or the real presence of Christ at his Eucharist. The sacrament was founded solidly in Christ's scriptural injunction–'do this'–and nothing could have persuaded him to challenge that. Reality he could admit too, because his definition of reality was not that of the Ockhamites: according to his metaphysical system it did not have to be corporeal. Christ's presence was sacramental and spiritual;[38] none the less real, but real in the same sense as when he said 'I am with you always', not in the sense as when he hung upon the Cross bodily. Hence for Wyclif the significance of the mass was different from what it was to most of his contemporaries. The words of the priest were not what mattered: as he pointed out, in

[37] *De Blasphemia*, 21: compare *Trialogus*, 260, 263.
[38] *FZ*, 115-17.

Scripture the words of consecration were given differently in different places,[39] so it was not the words that counted but the Word, Christ himself. The miracle of the mass was the repetition of the miracle of the Incarnation, two substances present in the same moment,[40] the spiritual body of Christ and the physical substance of bread, and it was God who brought this to pass in accordance with his promise, not the priest by his liturgy. He saw no reason why the mass of a devout layman should not be as effective as that of a priest;[41] and he was certain that the foreknown—the damned— could not partake of spiritual sustenance at it, for God does not know them and they cannot be nourished by him in their hearts. What mattered to him about the mass was not what he called the false miracle following on consecration, but Christ's spiritual presence and the communion of the faithful in Christ: 'they ought rather to procure that all Christians and secular men, being one bread, may all eat of one bread, as members of one and the same Church, so that they may despise worldly honours and thus come to the supper of the Lord. When they have perfectly learned this doctrine of the sacrament of the altar, then they will begin to approach the end for which it was instituted, and will as sons of peace celebrate the mass in truth.'[42] The significance of the mass for Wyclif is the spritual union of the faithful in Christ's real and sacramental presence, with all human distinctions as of priest and layman and all thoughts of earthly honour laid aside. This is an attitude with strongly protestant overtones, with the priest cast in the role of the minister of the tight little group of God's elect, as he was one day to be in the high days of presbytery.

Wyclif's own views on the Eucharist were, I believe, incomplete and still developing when he died. There was no room for development, it is true, in his negative denial of transubstantiation, but its only importance, for him, was to highlight the mendacity and carnality of his opponents. But the further implications of his repeated calls for a doctrine based on the authority of Scripture were wide indeed. One begins to see a glimpse of the shape of these implications in the four articles of Prague, with their demand for no law that is not based in Scripture and for communion in both kinds for both laity and priesthood, a claim that the Hussites, following Wyclif in spirit, based on

[39] *De Eucharistia*, 90-1.
[40] *FZ* 122.
[41] *Trialogus*, 280; *De Eucharistia*, 99, 101, and see Loserth's introduction, xxi.
[42] *De Eucharistia*, 325.

Scripture and the practice of the early Church; one sees their shape more clearly in the astonishment of the fathers of Basle when they witnessed in the mass of the Taborites a rite which they could barely recognize, but which a seventeenth century Protestant would have recognized at once as 'coming to the Lord's table'.[43]

Incomplete as they were, however, Wyclif's views on the mass were central to his later thinking, and help us to identify that for what it was. It was something genuinely new and radical. Wyclif lived in an age when the call for reform of the Church was sounding all around Christendom and that is why his denunciation of abuses in the contemporary Church long seemed no more remarkable than the denunciations of other radicals, as Marsilius, Ockham, and Dietrich of Niem. But with these authors the overriding concern was with the Church polity and especially with papal power and the abuse of endowments by means of provision; and the tide of criticism of papal monarchy in which they were carried along reached its flood level in the great conciliar experiment of the early fifteenth century. Their teaching was often, like Wyclif's, Erastian in tendency, because, like him, they saw in secular authority a bastion against ecclesiastical tyranny. But Wyclif, in contrast, was in the long run concerned not so much with the government of the Church as with evangelical religious revival. The long term implication of his teaching on lordship was not Erastian but scriptural and communistic. The long term implications of his teaching on the Eucharist were scriptural and–if one may so put it–puritan and socialistic, the union of the faithful in Christ without distinction of persons. The true preparation for that union was the evangelical life, open to all. His mass was for the saints, nourished in biblical teaching and conscious of a union with one another more important and more real than any human association. That is why the publication, by Wyclif, of his views upon the mass was a crucial turning-point (and not for him only but for any who cared to follow him), one that anticipated the rise of a sect.

---

[43] E. F. Jacob, 'The Bohemians at the Council of Basel', *Prague Essays*, ed. R. Seton Watson (London, 1949), 87. Dr Jacob evoked this point much more vividly in an Oxford lecture, but I have been unable to recover the reference to the authority that he quoted, which I failed to note.

2

The Realism of the
De Universalibus

ANTHONY KENNY

WYCLIF has long been famous as a realist, but the precise content of his philosophical realism has never been exactly determined. The publication by Ivan Mueller of an edition of the *De Universalibus* (Oxford, 1985) gives the general reader, for the first time, an opportunity to take the measure of Wyclif's theory. The present article aims to single out some of the main themes of Wyclif's realism and to make them intelligible to those more familiar with contemporary than with scholastic philosophy. Passages from the *De Universalibus* will be identified by the abbreviation '*U*' followed by chapter and line number. (The numbering is common both to Mueller's edition and to the simultaneously published translation by myself.)

Realism, for Wyclif, is above all a theory about the nature of universals; and the key to the understanding of universals is a grasp of the nature of predication. Everyone is familiar with the division of sentences into subject and predicate: in the sentence 'Banquo lives', 'Banquo' is the subject and 'lives' is the predicate; so too 'dogs' is the subject and 'bark' the predicate in 'dogs bark', or so at least a medieval grammarian would have been likely to say. This distinction is a distinction between bits of language: we are talking about terms and sentences, not about anything which terms or sentences might mean or represent or stand for. The word 'Banquo' is the subject of the sentence 'Banquo lives': it is a particular part of that sentence. But what about the man Banquo? Is he the subject of the sentence too? Well, if he is—and there are a number of idioms which make it natural to say so—he is not any part of the sentence in the way that the word 'Banquo' is. Banquo is the extralinguistic item for which the word 'Banquo' stands; he is what the sentence 'Banquo lives' is about, but he is not anything which that sentence contains (as it contains the word 'Banquo').

Wyclif, like everybody else, recognizes as the most obvious form of predication that in which subject and predicate are linguistic items, parts of sentences. The first philosophical sense which he attributes to the verb '*predicare*' or 'predicate' is 'the predication of one term of another'. 'This', he says 'is the sense much talked about by modern writers, who think that there is no other.' (*U* i.33.) But in fact, he says, this kind of predication is modelled on a different kind of predication, real predication, which is 'being shared by or said of many things in common' (*U* i. 35).

Real predication, then, is not a relationship between two terms, two bits of language. It is a relationship between the things in the world to which the linguistic items correspond. It is not the relationship between the subject-term 'Banquo' and the predicate-term 'lives', but the relationship between what the term 'Banquo' stands for, namely Banquo, and what it is in the world which corresponds to the term 'lives'. But what *is* the extramental entity which corresponds to 'lives'? Indeed *is* there anything in the world which corresponds to predicates? Wyclif's answer to the second question is that if not, then there is no difference between true and false sentences. His answer to the first question is his theory of universals.

Life is the universal which corresponds to the predicate 'lives'. It is life which is shared by or said of many things in common. (The use of 'said of' should not mislead one into thinking that life is a linguistic entity, like the word 'life'. That is not so, any more than the fact that Caesar is much spoken of means that Caesar is a piece of speech.) 'It is in this manner', Wyclif says, 'that every actual universal is predicated of its inferiors in nature.' (*U* i. 35.) Plants live and stones do not; plants are inferiors, and stones are not, of life, in the sense that plants *come under* life in a pyramid of classification of the things there are in the world, whereas stones do not come under that heading.

Wyclif's adversaries, the nominalists, deny that there is any such thing as real predication, anything in the world corresponding to the predicate of a true proposition. They object as follows: 'Nothing is a subject or a predicate unless it is a part of a proposition. But things in the external world are not parts of propositions; therefore they are not predicates or subjects. Consequently no real universal is predicated.' (*U* i. 80.)[1] But this objection, Wyclif retorts, depends on a

---

[1] Sed obicitur contra illud per hoc quod nihil est praedicatum vel subiectum, nisi pars propositionis. Sed res extra non sunt partes propositionis. Igitur non sunt praedicata vel subiecta. Et per consequens nullum universale ex parte rei praedicatur.

misunderstanding of the nature of a proposition. Besides the written or spoken propositions, sentences which are linguistic entities, there are real propositions in the extralinguistic world. A real proposition is what a true sentence corresponds to, just as real predication corresponds to the predication of terms. Walter Burley is cited as authority for the thesis that 'the truth on the side of reality, which God puts together from subject and predicate, is the real proposition' (*U* i. 91).[2] Human beings put sentences together from verbal subjects and verbal predicates; it is God who puts together, from non-linguistic entities, the real proposition which makes the verbal sentence true.

If we look in modern philosophy for a terminology to correspond to the 'real proposition' of Burley and Wyclif, we find it in the *sachverhalt* of Husserl and the early Wittgenstein. The problems which arise from Wyclif's account of the real proposition are the same as those which arise from the theory of *sachverhalt* in the modern philosophers: what makes negative propositions true? What makes false propositions false? What makes the truth of true future and past-tensed propositions?

Wyclif adopts a number of traditional Aristotelian distinctions between types of predication. There is *per se* predication, as in 'Socrates is human', and *per accidens* predication as in 'Socrates is white'. Subdivisions of *per se* predication are quidditative predication (as 'Socrates is human' or 'Socrates is animal') and qualitative predication (as 'Socrates is rational'). *Per accidens* predication comes in nine types corresponding to the last nine of Aristotle's ten categories (*U* i. 40-74). For Wyclif, in all cases of real predication a subject *says* its predicate (thus 'each man *per se* says the specific human nature which is the quiddity of each man', *U* i. 44) and a predicate is *said of* its subject (thus 'white is said of man', *U* i. 67).

It is thus that Wyclif interprets familiar passages of Aristotle.

Thus, in the Categories, in the chapter on substance, he maintains that primary substance is not said or predicated of anything. But secondary substance, such as genera and species, is said or predicated of a subject, as will become clear. This is more easily understood about things signified than about their signs, and it is a sense of predication which must be carefully noted.[3] (*U* i. 150-5.)

---

[2] Veritas ex parte rei, quam Deus componit ex subiecto et praedicato, (est) realis propositio, ut ponit Magister Walterus Burleigh.

[3] Ut in Praedicamentis, capitulo de substantia, ponit primam substantiam de nullo dici vel praedicari. Secundam vero substantiam, ut genera et species, dici vel praedicari

All this, while controversial, covers familiar ground. Less common-place is Wyclif's threefold classification of real predication. (*U* i. 157-69.)

We must note carefully the three different kinds of predication, namely formal predication, essential predication and habitual predication. All such predication is principally in the real world. And this is why philosophers do not speak of false predication of signs, nor of negative predication, nor of predication about the past or the future, because that is not in the real world; only true predication is in the real world, though truly in the real world one thing is denied or removed from another, as man from donkey and similarly with other negative truths. But only that which is form is really predicated of a subject.[4]

Wyclif's definition of formal predication is not altogether easy to understand, but the examples he gives to illustrate this kind of predication—such as 'man is an animal' and 'Peter is musical'—suggest that what he has in mind is the case where a predication is made true by the inherence of an appropriate form (whether substantial, as in the case of animality or accidental, as in the case of musicality) in a subject. Habitudinal predication, on the other hand, is not made true by the inherence of a form. The accidental form of size inhering in Socrates does not vary while, owing to the growth of Simmias, Socrates changes from being taller than to being smaller than Simmias. Similarly if Socrates is thought of by Wyclif, this does not, as such, involve any change taking place in Socrates. Habitudinal predication, Wyclif says, is 'where a relationship of a kind attaches to a subject without making it as such strictly speaking changeable. Thus a thing can be thought of or loved, can cause various effects, can acquire place and location in time and many kinds of notional relations without as such being changed or changeable.' (*U* i. 235-46.)[5]

But it is essential predication which is the hardest to understand,

de subiecto, ut patebit. Hoc melius intelligitur de signatis quam suis signis et iste sensus praedicationis cum diligentia est notandus. Cf. Aristotle, *Categories*, 5, 2ª 13.

[4] Diligenter est notandum de triplici praedicandi manerie, scilicet de praedicatione formali, de praedicatione secundum esentiam et de praedicatione secundum habitudinem. Talis autem praedicatio principaliter est ex parte rei. Et hinc philosophi non loquuntur de falsa praedicatione signorum nec de praedicatione negativa, nec de praedicatione de praeterito vel de futuro, quia talis non est ex parte rei, sed solum vera praedicatio, licet vere ex parte rei una res negatur vel removeatur a reliqua, ut homo ab asino et sic de aliis veritatibus negativis. Solum autem illud quod est forma praedicatur realiter de subiecto.

[5] Tertia est praedicatio secundum habitudinem ex qua secundum genus adveniente subiecto non oportet ipsum ut sic esse proprie mobile, ut contingit rem intelligi, amari, varie causare et acquirere sibi ubicationem, quandalitatem et quotlibet relationes rationis, sine hoc quod ipsum ut sic moveatur vel sit mobile.

and the matter remains dark when Wyclif gives us the examples that are meant to illustrate what kind of thing he has in mind: 'God is man', 'Fire is water', 'The universal is particular'. It is clear from the context that, in terms of Wyclif's theology, physics, and logic, each of these propositions is meant to be in some sense true.

Given the doctrine of the Incarnation, the theological example appears easier to understand than the others. Its truth clearly depends in some way on there being one person, Jesus, who is both God and man. But in fact Wyclif does not say this: he says that in essential predication the same *essence* is the subject and the predicate. And in the case of the physical example he explains that 'the same essence which is at one time fire is at another time water'. And to explain the logical example he says, 'in the same essence there inheres both being a man and being this man. And being a man is common to every man, and this is formally universal, while being this man is restricted individually to this essence'.[6] (*U* i. 195-217.) The notion of 'essence' involved here is obscure, and clearly different from the standard medieval scholastic one. Anyone who could clarify it would do a great service to Wyclif scholars.

For Wyclif believes that the correct understanding of predication as he explains it will enable us to accept the realist definition of universals rather than the nominalist one. The realist definition of 'genus' is brief and clear: 'Genus is what is predicated quidditatively of many things which differ in species'. The genus of animal is not a word, or symbol, but a reality: it is what is common to each animal, and is what is predicated—really predicated—of each animal quidditatively. (Quidditative predication, as contrasted with qualitative predication, tells you what kind of thing something is, as opposed to what properties or qualities it has.) 'Not all modern logicians gathered together', says Wyclif, 'could improve a single word of the definition.' (*U* i. 350.)

The modern logicians, or nominalists, since they do not accept real predication but only the predication of terms, are forced into terrible mazes when they try to define genus. They offer something like the following: a genus is a term or concept which is predicable (or whose counterpart is predicable) *per se* in the nominative quidditatively of many terms which signify things specifically distinct (*U* i. 857-60).[7]

[6] Eidem essentiae inest esse hominem et esse istum hominem. Et esse hominem est commune omni homini et sic universale formaliter, sed isse istum hominem est individualiter appropriatum isti essentiae. ,

[7] Genus est terminus vel conceptus qui–vel secum convertibilis–est per se praedicabilis in recto et in quid de multis terminis significantibus res distinctas specifice.

For the realist, genus is an extra-linguistic reality; for the nominalist it is a term, an element of language, or a concept, an element of thought. The realist can say that genus is predicated, whereas the nominalist can only say it is predicable. Dogs are always animals, whether or not anyone is thinking or talking of animals; but it is only when someone is thinking or talking of animals that the *term* 'animal' is predicated. Moreover, if you take a single term such as the sound 'animal' produced by me at this moment–and if you are a nominalist keen to keep your ontology down to empirical particulars this is the only kind of thing you have a right to be talking about–then it is not true that it is even predicable of all animals. The sound would not last long enough to form part of all the different true sentences which would attribute animality to the various kinds of animal. That is why the nominalists have to add the rider 'or whose counterpart is predicable'. Now it is essential to genus that it should be related to different species; it is essential to a nominalist definition of genus that this relationship should be a relationship to different terms, not different extramental realities. But the nominalist cannot say that the term is predicated of terms differing in species; the word 'dog' does not differ in species from the word 'cat'. So the nominalist has to say that the terms signify things that are specifically distinct. But in doing so he checkmates himself: he is making specific difference something on the side of the things signified, not something belonging purely to the signs. But that is realism, not nominalism (*U* i. 355, 371).

For a consistent nominalist, Wyclif insists, substances do not resemble or differ in species, nor do they belong to any species; there cannot be any such thing as a species except as the product of a mind. But signs and thoughts are human creations; words and terms can change their meaning at their users' whim. If species therefore were signs or thoughts, we could change the species of anything simply by taking thought. 'Thus any thing could belong to the species of anything; a man could belong to the species of donkey, simply through a change in the signification of terms.' (*U* i. 389-91.)

Nominalism, according to Wyclif, is a ridiculous attempt to put the cart before the horse.

Neither the possibility nor the fact of assigning a term can cause extramental things to resemble each other more or less. The specific resemblance or difference between things is not the reason for the resemblance of extramental things; it is the other way round–in the first and principal place you have to look in the things themselves for the specific resemblances and differences, and only subsequently in the signs.[8] (*U* i. 425-30.)

The nominalist's attempt to give an account of meaning without universals collapses under its own weight, containing its own refutation. The existence of universals is established by the refutation of the opposing view. But if there are universals, what kind of thing are they? Can the realist be sure that his own position, like that of the nominalist, will not turn out to be internally incoherent? It is to these questions that Wyclif devotes the major part of his treatise.

Drawing on Grosseste's commentary on the *Posterior Analytics*,[9] Wyclif explains that there are five types of universal.

The first and foremost kind is the eternal notion or exemplar idea in God. The second kind is the common created notion in the superior causes, like the intelligences and the heavenly spheres. The third kind of universal is the common form rooted in its individuals. This, says Grosseteste, is what Aristotle's genera and species are. Fourthly, there is the universal which is the common form in its accidents, apprehended by the lowest form of intellect. There is a fifth kind of universal–signs and mental acts–which Grosseteste sets aside as irrelevant to his concerns.[10] (*U* ii. 165-77.)

We may note in this fivefold scheme two points of agreement between Wyclif and his adversaries. The fifth kind of universal is one which nominalists and conceptualists accept: it is the only created kind of universal they are prepared to admit. The acceptance by Wyclif that the first and foremost kind of universal is a notion in the mind of God goes some way to meeting the conceptualists' claim that it is in the mind that universals have their home: but of course these universals of the first kind are prior to any human mind. From all eternity, in God's mind there is the thought of all he will or can make:

[8] Cum nec impositio nec imponibilitas termini sit causa quare res extra magis aut minus conveniant–quod convenientia et differentia rerum fundantur essentialiter in rerum principiis et non in signis, ut praedicatio signorum vel eorum praedicabilitas non est causa convenientiae rerum exterarum sed econtra–oportet igitur scrutari in rebus ipsis convenientias et differentias specificas primo et principaliter, et consequenter in eorum signis.

[9] Robertus Grosseteste, *In Aristotelis Posteriorum Analyticorum Libros* (Venice 1514; repr. Minerva GmbH, Frankfurt, 1966), i. 7, f. 8ᵛ.

[10] Primum et supremum genus est ratio vel idea exemplaris aeterna in Deo. Secundum genus est ratio communis creata in causis superioribus ut intelligentiis et orbibus caelestibus. Tertium genus universalium est forma communis fundata in suis individuis. Et illa, inquit Lincolniensis, sunt genera et species de quibus loquitur Aristoteles. Quarto forma communis in suis accidentibus, apprehensa ab intellectu infimo, est universale. Sed quintum modum universalium–pro signis vel actibus intelligendi–dimittit Lincolniensis ut sibi impertinens.

these are the patterns and paradigms by which he creates, referred to by Wyclif, as by other Latin theologians, under the Greek word 'Idea'.

The second kind of universal we may leave aside as being of interest only within the context of medieval Aristotelian cosmology. It is the third kind of universal over which the battle between realists and nominalists principally rages.

Unlike the divine Ideas, which exist eternally whether or not there is a created universe, the universals of this third kind are brought into existence by creation. These universals are the forms which are shared in common by all the individuals of a kind. This, Wyclif maintains, is what Aristotle meant by genera and species. Elsewhere he calls them metaphysical universals (U ii. 245).

Metaphysical universals are all universals: they are themselves instances of the universal 'universal'. But this is something which it takes an abstractive intellect to grasp: a dog may perhaps have a grasp of caninity (in that it recognizes other dogs as beings of the same kind as itself) but it certainly cannot grasp that caninity is a universal. Hence, universals, considered as universals in relation to their contingent instantiations, have a universality which is introduced by the intellect. This appears to be what Wyclif means when he talks about the fourth kind of universal ('the common form in its accidents, apprehended by the lowest form of intellect'), which he elsewhere calls logical universals (U ii. 245).

The fifth kind of universal, the kind accepted even by nominalists, might be called 'grammatical universals', though Wyclif does not seem to use exactly this expression. Logic, he says, is midway between grammar and metaphysics. Logic shares in the conditions of each, treating primarily of realities, since it is the route to metaphysics, and secondarily of signs, since it is the terminus of grammar (U ii. 108-11). Thus the logical universals come between metaphysical universals and grammatical universals. To grasp the logical universal is to realize the link between the metaphysical, extralinguistic universal, and its conceptualization in language. Logical universals, unlike metaphysical universals, presuppose created minds (U ii. 240-50).

In propounding this fivefold scheme Wyclif reveals himself as being a realist but not a Platonist. He is not a Platonist because he does not accept that there are any universals outside the divine mind which are independent both of the existence of individuals and of the existence of created minds. Metaphysical universals are independent of created minds, but they are not independent of the existence of individuals of particular kinds. Logical universals may be independent of the existence of individuals (such at least seems to be the case with the universal 'chimaera') but they are not independent of the existence of created minds. Because of these qualifications to his realism, Wyclif is able to present himself as being an orthodox Aristotelian.

It is true that there are many passages in Aristotle where universals are criticized, most famously the dictum of chapter fifteen of the first book of the *Posterior Analytics*, which read, in the version known to Wyclif, 'goodbye to the universals, for they are monsters'.[11] But, Wyclif maintains, when Aristotle is attacking universals his target is never the metaphysical universals which are the third kind in the Grosseteste scheme. It is the ideal universals of the first class. Wyclif agrees that if such Ideas are regarded as self-subsistent substances, separate from God and from individuals, then they are superfluous monstrosities (*U* ii. 197). But none of Aristotle's arguments, he claims, are successful against ideal universals considered as notions in the mind of God. Wyclif is not quite sure whether Plato's own theory involved the superfluous monstrosities Aristotle attacked, or whether Aristotle had got his master's doctrine wrong. Wyclif himself, of course, did not know Plato at first hand. 'But it seems to me more probable', he said, 'that Plato's view of ideas was sound and in accordance with our own sacred Scripture as Augustine testifies.' (*U* ii. 200-3.)

On the positive side, Wyclif can point to many passages in Aristotle which favour realism about metaphysical universals. One of the clearest occurs in the chapter on substance in the *Categories*, where the Philosopher says that primary substance is not said or predicated of anything, but that secondary substance, such as genera and species, is predicated.[12] This, Wyclif argues, must be understood as meaning real predication; and the substance which is thus predicated is universal, the common natures which make individuals the kinds of things they are.

Now are these metaphysical universals prior or posterior to the relevant individuals ('supposits')? Wyclif's answer contains a distinction that is not at first sight obvious.

The universal of which Aristotle is speaking is the common nature rooted in its supposits. In this way, in the order of generation in which they cause the

---

[11] *Analytica Posteriora*, I. 15, 83ᵃ 34-5.
[12] *Categories*, 5, 2ᵃ 13.

universals, the subjects come first. Universals, on the other hand, take precedence in the order of origin, in which, both formally and finally, they cause their supposits.[13] (*U* ii. 235-40.)

What this seems to mean is this. There is no such thing as human nature until there are individual human beings: there is no Platonic Ideal Man outside the divine mind. In this sense the existence of human beings brings into existence the universal humanity. But when there are human beings it is their humanity which makes them human (causes them formally) and the point of the succession of human beings is the perpetuation of the human species (which therefore causes them finally).[14]

Such then, in broad outline, is Wyclif's theory of universals. How does he argue for its correctness? How does he argue for the existence of universals other than by criticizing nominalism?

The argument is essentially simple: Wyclif maintains that anyone who believes in objective truth is thereby already committed, whether they know it or not, to belief in real universals. The two beliefs are in fact two forms of the same belief: one a complex form and the other a non-complex form. If the only truths we knew were protocols of immediate experience, perhaps it would not be obvious that there must be universals; but for most of Wyclif's adversaries it is common ground that the mind knows at least some universal, abstract truths.

Since, therefore, we have to grant that there is a universal abstract truth of this kind, beyond the scope of a material sense-faculty to know, it must be concluded that there is a supra-sensible faculty, a kind of intellect, to consider it. And this is what philosophers call the agent intellect. To conceive the universal intention by abstracting from the phantasm, as the intellect does, is to perceive that every man resembles every other in being a man. And once the intellect has abstracted an everlasting eternal truth of this kind from perishable particulars, it sets itself the task of conceiving, in a non-complex manner, the name of the universal, whether specific or generic.[15] (*U.* iii. 37-46.)

---

[13] Universale de quo loquitur Aristoteles, est natura communis fundata in suis suppositis. Et sic praecedunt subiecta in via generationis, qua causant universalia. Econtra autem universalia praecedunt in via originis, qua formaliter et finaliter causant sua supposita.

[14] This account seems to apply only to those universals which are natures, where we have a species propagated by natural generation.

[15] Cum igitur sit dare talem veritatem universalem abstractam quam non est sensus materialis cognoscere, relinquitur quod sit dare virtutem supra sensum, ut puta intellectum, qui illam consideret. Et hoc est quod philosophi dicunt intellectuma gentem. A phantasmatibus abstrahendo concipere intentionem universalem ut intellectus est percipere quod omnis homo convenit cum quolibet in esse hominem. Et postquam

The point can be generalized. If the mind is aware that an individual A resembles an individual B, there must be some respect C in which A resembles B. But in seeing that A resembles B in respect C, the intellect is *eo ipso* seeing the C-ness of A and B; that is to say, it is conceiving C-ness, a universal common to A and B. Seeing that A is like B in respect of C is the very same thing as seeing the common C-ness; so what is indicated by the complex clause in the first expression must be the same as what is indicated by the abstract noun in the second. Universals, then, are just universal truths grasped in a non-complex manner, and anyone who can make judgements of likeness automatically knows what a universal is.

So someone who wants to be made acquainted with the quiddity of universals has to think confusedly and abstractly, by genus and species, of the same thing as he first thought of by means of a complex whose subject is the specific or generic term; thus the species of man is the same thing as there being a man, and the genus of animal is the same thing as being an animal. And each of these is common to its supposits.[16] (*U* iii. 90-5.)

For Wyclif it is not enough to criticize nominalists or to offer this proof of the reality of universals. It is necessary also to provide answers to the conundrums by which nominalists seek to impugn the coherence of real universals. If we postulate a common humanity, must we also postulate a common personality, since every man is a person; and if so, does that mean that the whole human race is one person? (*U* viii. 8.) If you postulate something common to two human beings, are you set off on an infinite regress, like the one sketched by Plato's Third Man argument? (*U* ix. 9 ff.) Can a universal be created or changed or brought into being in any way? (*U* xii. 145 ff.) Can universals be annihilated? (*U* xiii. 3 ff.)

Typical of the nominalist cavils which Wyclif has to answer is the following passage from the eleventh chapter of the treatise:

The human species is the subject of its own species and of other accidents. So too, then, it is characterised by them, e.g. it is created, it moves from place to place, it is multiplied in quantity, and so on with each of the accidental

abstraxerit a singularibus corruptibilibus huiusmodi perpetuam veritatem, imponit sibi ut incomplexe concipitur nomen universalis vel speciei vel generis.

[16] Volens igitur manuduci in notitiam de quidditate universalium debet intelligere confuse et abstracte idem per genus et speciem quod intelligit primo per complexum, cuius subiectum est terminus specificus vel terminus generis, ut idem est species hominis et hominem esse, idem genus animalis et esse animal. Et utrumque illorum est commune suis suppositis.

predicates. But if you grant this, many absurdities follow, as that the same thing is black and white, hot and cold. And, briefly, whatever predicate inheres in any man, inheres in the species of man, so that in one place it is most virtuous and most beautiful, in another most vicious and monstrous; it had more heads than Argus, eats more than Milo, is more procreative than Priapus, and so on.[17] (*U* xi. 27-38.)

'Many people', Wyclif comments, 'bring up ridiculous points when they are short of arguments'. But he makes a patient attempt to answer the difficulties, and to show how non-absurd and non-arbitrary answers can be given to these and similar trick questions. In dealing with the paradoxes he makes great use of the notion of essential predication.

Wyclif's realism is not a mere logical thesis and his devotion to universals sometimes takes on an almost mystical tone. Thus in answer to the objection that universals are superfluous unless they do something in the world, he replies, 'It is clear, since universals regularly do what they ought to, that they do great service to their God, since he is Lord of them before he is Lord of individuals.'[18] (*U* xi. 230-2.) Moreover, Wyclif believes that error about the nature of universals leads to all kinds of moral error. Here he enlists the support of Augustine's *De Vera Religione*, chapter nine.[19]

What everyone must principally love in his neighbour is that he is a human being, and not that he is his own son, or someone useful; for according to Augustine it is being a man which is what is common and is in an especial manner the work of God, since it precedes every particular human being, while being your son, or your mistress, is something you have brought about yourself.[20] (*U* iii. 115-20.)

Augustine may well be right that every Christian ought, as Wyclif says, to love his neighbour in his common nature and not primarily with an

[17] Sicut igitur species humana subicitur proprio speciei et aliis accidentibus, sic denominatur eisdem, sicut creatur, movetur localiter, multiplicatur in quantitate et sic de quolibet praedicatis accidentibus. Sed, hoc dato, multiplicantur quotlibet inconvenientia, ut quod eadem res sit alba et nigra, calida et frigida. Et, breviter, quaecumque praedicatio inest alicui homini, inest speciei hominis, ut hic esset virtuosissima, pulcherrima, ibi viciosissima et monstrusissima, cum habet plura capita quam Argus, magis edula quam Milo, plus procretiva quam Priapus, et sic de multis ridiculose adductis a pluribus quando eis deficiunt argumenta.

[18] Cum universalia regulariter faciunt quod debent, patet quod multum deserviunt Deo suo, cum prius sit dominus eorum quam individuorum.

[19] *Patrologia Latina*, 34. 161.

[20] Ut quilibet debet principaliter amare in proximo quod est homo et non quod est filius suus vel sibi utilis, quia esse hominem, secundum Augustinum, est commune et praecipue opus Dei, cum praecedit quemlibet hominem singularem. Sed esse filium tuum vel amicam tuam, hoc est opus tuum.

eye to private utility, kinship, or pleasure. But the argument that one should love the more universal rather than the more particular would lead to odd conclusions which Wyclif would surely not have accepted: for instance, that one should love one's fellows as fellow animals rather than as fellow men.

Wyclif is prepared to go so far as to say that all actual sin is caused by the lack of an ordered love of universals: because sin consists in preferring lesser good to greater good and in general the more universal good is the greater good.

Thus if proprietors who are devoted to particulars were more concerned that a well-ordered commonwealth should thrive, than that their kinsfolk should prosper, or their relations or the people linked to them by locality or some other individuating condition, then beyond doubt they would not press, in the disordered way they do, for their own people to be raised to wealth, office, prelacy and other dignities.[21] (*U* iii. 152-8.)

In this passage we can see, in the young Wyclif, the logician linking hands with the reformer. Nominalism leads to selfishness, charity demands realism. 'Intellectual and emotional error about universals is the cause of all the sin that reigns in the world.' (*U* iii. 162-5.) In the whole history of philosophy has realism ever had a more enthusiastic champion than Wyclif?

---

[21] Ut si proprietarii singularibus dediti plus appretiarentur quod res plublica vigeat ordinata, quam quod cognati vel affines sui vel quomodocumque ex loco vel alia conditione individuante confoederati promoveantur, tunc indubie non inordinate sic instarent ut sui sint exaltati ad divitas, officia, praelatias vel alias dignitates.

3

Continua, Indivisibles, and Change in Wyclif's Logic of Scripture*

1. *Continuism and indivisibilism*

AT the heart of John Wyclif's theory of the nature of fundamental physical reality is a view of time and space, of motion and other change, that is radically different from the view shared by all but a handful of other fourteenth-century thinkers, by the vast majority of philosophers and scientists before and after Wyclif, and by almost all educated people of the twentieth century.[1]

To provide a setting for the issues on which Wyclif's view is opposed to ours, we can consider some ordinary phenomena about which we and Wyclif are in basic theoretical agreement. Think of a wooden bowl of apples and a measure of music in which a violin holds a single note over four drumbeats. The violin's note sounds the way the wood looks–continuous, without gaps or discrete constituents– while the drum's part in the measure is like the contents of the fruit bowl–obviously dicontinuous, with constituents that are not only

---

* I am grateful to the University of Oxford's Sub-Faculty of Philosophy and Balliol College for having provided the occasion for this paper. In preparing it I was helped in various ways by several people: Christine Brousseau, Georgette Sinkler, Edith Sylla, John Murdoch (who lent me an indispensable microfilm and gave generously of his time and learning), Rega Wood (who wrote a careful, learned set of comments on an earlier draft), Paul Spade (who offered some crucial corrections), and Eleonore Stump (whose objections to my first interpretation of Wyclif on beginning and ceasing enabled me to improve the paper substantially). I am very grateful to all of them and, in particular, to Anthony Kenny, the Master of Balliol.

[1] Wyclif was born probably between 1325 and 1330; he died on 31 December 1384. He was a probationary Fellow of Merton in 1356 and Master of Balliol in 1360. For details of his life and career see H. B. Workman, *John Wyclif: A Study of the English Medieval Church*, 2 vols. (Oxford, 1926). The best study of his career as a scholastic philosopher is J. A. Robson's *Wyclif and the Oxford Schools* (Cambridge, 1961). No full study of Wyclif's philosophy has yet been published, but Anthony Kenny's brief, lucid, and insightful *Wyclif* (Oxford, 1985) makes an excellent beginning. W. R. Thomson has recently published an admirably well-informed, thorough bibliographical study, *The Latin Writings of John Wyclyf* (Toronto, 1983).

discrete but even separated by gaps. This distinction between the continuous and the discontinuous (a distinction we can so readily draw in our experience of such ordinary physical things and processes) sometimes applies only superficially. Much of what appears to be continuous we know to be really discontinuous, and so did Wyclif. We learn that in the reality beneath appearance the wood constituting the bowl, like the contents of the bowl, has discrete constituents—the cells of the wood; and we learn that what produces the sensation of the violin's sustained single note is a series of waves in the air, so that in its underlying reality the violin's part in the measure is a sequence of discrete constituents, as the drum's part is to the ear.[2]

A thing or a process that is not really a continuum, whether or not it appears to be so, is something that admits of a last division, something that has ultimate discrete constituents, whether they are contiguous or separated by gaps—as water has molecules and oxygen has atoms. The dividing of a fundamentally discontinuous thing of that sort comes to an end when its ultimate constituents have been isolated or at least identified. The last division of water yields H_2O molecules; if those molecules themselves are then divided, the results of the further division are no longer water. But, of course, the ultimacy of H_2O molecules as constituents is not absolute, but only relative to water, just as the ultimacy of oxygen atoms as constituents is relative to oxygen. My paradigms of such specifically ultimate constituents are drawn from the atomic theory familiar to us, but Wyclif and other medievals already recognized specifically ultimate constituents under the concept of *minima naturalia*,[3] and they would readily have acknowledged H_2O molecules and oxygen atoms as the *minima naturalia* of water and of oxygen respectively if they had known about them. Wyclif expressly maintains that most apparent continua are fundamentally aggregates of appropriate *minima naturalia*,[4] and this

---

[2] For Wyclif's recognition of the merely apparent continuity of sound and particularly of the sound of stringed instruments see iii. 40. 38-41; cf. iii. 193. 30-40. (In this paper references to Wyclif's writings are, unless otherwise identified, to M. H. Dziewicki's edition of the *Tractatus de Logica* in three volumes of the Wyclif Society's edition of Wyclif's Latin Works (London, 1893, 1896, and 1899).)

[3] The concept of *minima naturalia* appears to have originated in Aristotle's discussion of Anaxagoras in *Physics* I. 4, 187^b 18-34, and to have been formulated first by Averroes. As far as I know, the best discussion of the development and use of the concept in the Middle Ages is Anneliese Maier's in her book *Die Vorläufer Galileis im 14. Jahrhundert: Studien zur Naturphilosophie der Spätscholastik* (Rome, 1949), 179-96.

[4] For Wyclif's use of the concept of *minima naturalia* see e.g., ii. 162. 6-13; ii. 163. 13-166. 19.

part of his theory of fundamental physical reality strikes me as differing only in philosophically discountable details from most such theories in any historical period, including our own.

But most people, past and present, have been convinced that besides natural substances consisting of discrete *minima naturalia* there are other features of our experience that not only appear to be but really are continua; and of course those are things of which there can be no last division, things that have no ultimate constituents–time, for instance, or space. A century or a second can indeed be considered a constituent of time, but no such constituent can be even specifically ultimate because each of them is itself infinitely divisible into its proportional parts (its halves, quarters, eighths, and so on) and every proportional part of time is itself a time, no matter how short. We divide time into times by designating instants, as the instant of midnight divides Monday from Tuesday and the instant of noon divides a.m. from p.m. But the instants themselves are not times any more than the cuts made in slicing a salami are themselves slices of salami, and time is not made up of instants any more than the salami could be reconstructed out of the cuts rather than the slices. So a second cannot be an ultimate constituent of time because it cannot be ultimate, and an instant cannot be an ultimate constituent of time because it cannot be a constituent. An instant cannot be a constituent just because there is nothing to it, it is a non-quantum; and for that same reason it is absolutely, mathematically indivisible. And analogous remarks are true of space–about points relative to lines, lines relative to surfaces, or surfaces relative to volumes. So, unlike natural substances, whether solids, liquids, or gases, time and space are continua, just as they seem to be, devoid of gaps and of ultimate constituents.

The continuism I have just sketched, the view that there are real as well as apparent continua, was given its first systematic formulation by Aristotle; and in physics as well as in metaphysics some version of continuism, at least as regards time and space, has almost always been held by almost everyone[5]–but not by Wyclif, who rejects it thoroughly and fervently. The central thesis of Wyclif's anti-continuist position on continuity in nature, a thesis he repeats again and again,[6] is a claim

---

[5] On pre-medieval indivisibilism and continuism see, e.g., D. J. Furley, 'The Greek Commentators' Treatment of Aristotle's Theory of the Continuous', in Norman Kretzmann, ed., *Infinity and Continuity in Ancient and Medieval Thought* [*ICAMT*] (Ithaca, NY, 1982), 17-36; R. Sorabji, 'Atoms and Time Atoms', *ICAMT*, 37-86; F. D. Miller, Jr., 'Aristotle Against the Atomists', *ICAMT*, 87-111; and esp. R. Sorabji's book *Time, Creation and the Continuum: Theories in Antiquity and the Early Middle Ages* (London, 1983).

(*See p. 34 for n. 6*)

about ultimate constituents. Continua, he maintains, are composed of indivisibles, or non-quanta[7]–that is, time is composed of instants, a line of points, a surface of lines, and so on–the very sort of composition continuism denies the possibility of. Moreover, on Wyclif's view instants and points, in virtue of being the specifically ultimate constituents of time and space, are the absolutely ultimate constituents of all spatio-temporal phenomena.

It is this indivisibilism of Wyclif's that I mean to focus on, particularly as it is manifested in his analysis of change. I will present and discuss what I believe to be some crucial developments in his indivisibilism, but I want also to show how (and try to explain why) Wyclif was estranged from the dominant continuism and committed to the view that time, space, and all spatio-temporal phenomena have as their ultimate constituents non-quanta, indivisibles. Historically and philosophically it seems to be a very unlikely view for a philosopher to have adopted in the latter half of the fourteenth century.

2. *Wyclif among the indivisibilists*

In maintaining an anti-continuist indivisibilism Wyclif belongs to a tiny, embattled minority up against formidable opponents. I know of only eight medieval philosophers before Wyclif who have been identified as indivisibilists.[8] Five of them had exclusively Parisian academic careers and are probably irrelevant to Wyclif's adoption of indivisibilism.[9] Of the three earlier indivisibilists at Oxford, where medieval indivisibilism seems to have arisen, only Henry of Harclay and Walter Chatton seem to have been widely recognized (and criticized) for their positions on the composition of continua.[10] Wyclif is likely to have

---

[6] See, e.g., i. 195. 8-11; i. 197. 3-4; i. 216. 6-12; i. 220. 20-1; i. 223. 23-5; ii. 140. 18-19; iii. 30. 1-2; iii. 104. 20-2; iii. 162. 15-16. For related passages see, e.g., i. 13. 9-20; i. 198. 25-6; ii. 81. 16-32; ii. 166. 41-167. 4; iii. 19. 39-40; iii. 70. 12; iii. 175. 29-30; iii. 184. 33-4; iii. 197. 32-5.

[7] Wyclif uses both these terms–'*indivisibilia*' and '*non quanta*'–apparently indifferently, possibly with some preference for the latter.

[8] On the medieval indivisibilists see, e.g., Maier (above, n. 3), 155-79; J. E. Murdoch, 'Infinity and Continuity', ch. 28 in *The Cambridge History of Later Medieval Philosophy* [*CHLMP*], ed. N. Kretzmann, A. Kenny, and J. Pinborg (Cambridge, 1982), 564-91; J. E. Murdoch, 'Naissance et développement de l'atomisme au bas moyen âge latin', in *La Science de la nature: théories et pratiques* (Cahiers d'Études Médiévales, 2; Montreal, 1974); J. E. Murdoch and E. Synan, 'Two Questions on the Continuum: Walter Chatton (?), O.F.M. and Adam Wodeham, O.F.M.', *Franciscan Studies* 26 (1966), 212-88; R. Wood, 'Introduction' to her edition and translation of Adam Wodeham's *Tractatus de Indivisibilibus*, Dordrecht and Boston, forthcoming.

[9] Gerard of Odo (*fl.* 1325), Nicholas Bonet (d. 1343), Nicholas of Autrecourt (*c.*1300-after 1350), and Marcus Trevisano Veneti and John Gedo, followers of Gerard.

[*See opposite page for n. 10*]

learned a good deal of his indivisibilism from reading them,[11] but not from attending their lectures. Harclay died in 1317 and Chatton was most active in Oxford around 1330 or earlier, when Wyclif is likely to have been only a couple of years old at most. The flurry of indivisibilism in the first three decades of the century is a little easier to understand (even if its origins are still obscure[12]) in view of Harclay's prominence as Chancellor of Oxford and the fact that several of the authors on both sides of the controversy were linked by membership in the Franciscan order.[13] But the work of all these authors is separated from Wyclif's work by thirty years or so, during which indivisibilism must have seemed dead and buried, particularly because it had been so thoroughly criticized—most of us would say refuted—under the onslaught of such defenders of continuism as John Duns Scotus, William Alnwick, Walter Burley, William Ockham, Thomas Bradwardine, Adam Wodeham, and John the Canon.[14] And although the

---

[10] Henry of Harclay (1270-1317), Walter Chatton (1285-1344), and William Crathorn (*fl.* 1330).

[11] I have not found Wyclif citing any of these medieval indivisibilists by name; Democritus, Plato, Augustine, and Grosseteste are the intellectual ancestors he acknowledges (see p. 48 below). A comparison of Wyclif's arguments for indivisibilism and replies to well-known objections (to be found esp. in Tr. iii, ch. 9 of the *Logicae continuatio*) with Harclay's and Chatton's similar attempts would teach us a good deal about Wyclif's dependence on them, but as far as I know such a comparison has yet to be made.

[12] See, e.g., Murdoch (above, n. 8), *CHLMP* esp. 576-7, and N. Kretzmann, 'Adam Wodeham's Anti-Aristotelian Anti-Atomism', *History of Philosophy Quarterly* 1 (1984), 381-98, n. 46.

[13] Harclay studied at Paris (while Scotus was there) and became Chancellor of Oxford in 1312 (see Biographies in *CHLMP*). Rega Wood has pointed out to me that Harclay was by far the most influential of the indivisibilists; 'Chatton', she says, 'seems to have been known [as an indivisibilist] only to Ockham and Wodeham' among opponents of indivisibilism in the first half of the fourteenth century (private correspondence of October 1984). 'Harclay', she goes on, 'influenced Franciscans through the writings of William of Alnwick, Scotus' socius, on the Continent and in England. As we have discovered in editing Ockham's works, he gives great weight to the opinion of even minor Franciscan authors. ... In England, where he was Chancellor of Oxford, Harclay's influence was not confined to Franciscans, as witness Bradwardine's critique. Also Chatton says of Alnwick's argument . . . against Harclay's "God can see any point on a line" that it is *"commune in villa"* (*Oxoniae*). See *Rep.* II, d. 2, q. 3; Paris MS 18887, fol. 93va.' (ibid.)

[14] Scotus (*c.*1265-1308), Alnwick (*fl.* 1315), Burley (*c.*1275-1344/5), Ockham (*c.*1285-1347/9), Bradwardine (*c.*1295-1349), Wodeham (*c.*1298-1358), John the Canon (*fl.* 1340). On these anti-indivisibilists in general see the sources listed in n. 8 above. On Ockham in this connection see J. E. Murdoch, 'William of Ockham and the Logic of Infinity and Continuity', *ICAMT*, 165-206; and Eleonore Stump, 'Theology and Physics in *De Sacramento altaris*: Ockham's Theory of Indivisibles', *ICAMT*, 207-30. On Bradwardine in this connection see J. E. Murdoch, 'Geometry and the Continuum in the Fourteenth Century: A Philosophical Analysis of Thomas Bradwardine's *Tractatus de continuo*'

continuist-indivisibilist controversy would certainly have been recognized as relevant to many philosophical and theological issues prominent in Oxford in the first half of the fourteenth century, most continuists writing in Oxford then simply ignored indivisibilism,[15] presumably because they considered its untenability to have been demonstrated, most pointedly in Bradwardine's *Tractatus de Continuo*.[16]

So Wyclif's indivisibilism is not merely an unpopular view; it is his resuscitation of an unpopular view in the face of general disregard preceded by devastating criticism, delivered most effectively by Bradwardine, whom Wyclif reveres as *Doctor Profundus* and on whom he often relies in theology.[17] Furthermore, the concerns that may have motivated the adoption of indivisibilism by Harclay or Chatton—disproving the possibility of a beginningless universe, avoiding the admission of unequal infinities, or proving the possibility of angelic motion[18]–play no part, as far as I have seen, in Wyclif's adoption of it. Placing Wyclif against the background of his indivisibilist predecessors explains his indivisibilism not at all but rather makes it look even more unlikely.

And yet, though Wyclif clearly recognized the size and respectability of the anti-indivisibilist forces ranged against him, at least once referring to them as 'the general run of logicians',[19] he forthrightly says of their continuist views regarding time, for instance, that 'it is *certain* that such things are *impossible*'.[20] Despite his beleaguered position, Wyclif considered himself especially favoured by God in having been released from the all-but-universal error of continuism with its attendant logical subtleties (some of which we will be considering): 'Then blessed be the Lord of time, who enlightens my mind above

(unpublished PhD dissertation, University of Wisconsin, 1957). On Wodeham in this connection see Kretzmann (above, n. 12) and esp. Wood forthcoming (above, n. 8).

[15] Except for Bradwardine, the Oxford Calculators generally seem to fit this description. For example, Richard Kilvington in his *Sophismata* deals with many of the issues that exercised the indivisibilists and their opponents without ever indicating that he knows anything of the quarrel going on around him in Oxford. See, e.g., N. Kretzmann, 'Continuity, Contrariety, Contradiction, and Change', *ICAMT*, 270-96.

[16] For a summary of the contents of Bradwardine's treatise see Murdoch (above, n. 8), *CHLMP*, 578-80; for the text and a full discussion see Murdoch 1957 (above, n. 14).

[17] See Workman (above, n. 1), i. 125; also Robson (above, n. 1), 31, 39, 178-82, 184, 198-202, 207-8, 210-11, 214-15.

[18] Murdoch (above, n. 8), *CHLMP*, 576-7.

[19] iii. 185. 21-2.

[20] iii. 185. 27.

time, enabling me to break free of these linguistic constraints on spirit!'[21]

Having stressed the historical improbability of Wyclif's indivisibilism, I want now to indicate its philosophical unattractiveness by providing just two representative samples of the formidable logical and mathematical obstacles facing any would-be indivisibilist in the fourteenth century.

3. Indivisibles and theoretical obstacles to indivisibilism

Medieval philosophers, whether they were continuists or indivisibilists, typically recognized four sorts of indivisibles. The indivisibles of time are *instants*; the three varieties of the indivisibles of space are *points* (absolutely indivisible), *lines* (indivisible in the second and third dimensions), and *surfaces* (indivisible in the third dimension); the indivisibles of quality (broadly conceived) are *degrees* (precise limits of amounts of colour, heat, weight, speed, etc.); and the indivisibles of change are *mutata esse* (instantaneous acquisitions of changed states). Degrees and *mutata esse*, for all their theoretical importance,[22] can be conveniently left to one side while we consider the more familiar indivisibles; in fact, the problems associated with the spatial indivisibles alone are representative of the problems associated with any indivisibles.

The important problems, the theoretical issues that give rise to continuism and indivisibilism as well as to almost all the philosophical and scientific interest in indivisibles, can be brought back to these two questions:

> Are indivisibles real entities outside the mind and not just theoretical objects?
>
> If they are real, are space and time and all spatio-temporal things and processes composed of them?

(I will call the first of these the reality question and the second the composition question.) The composition question divides continuists from indivisibilists, who, as we have seen, answer it affirmatively. As its wording indicates, the composition question arises only for people

---

[21] iii. 194. 27-9; cf. iii. 142. 39-143. 1.

[22] In, e.g., medieval theories of the intension and remission of forms (on which see Edith Sylla, 'Medieval Quantifications of Qualities: The "Merton School"', *Archive for History of Exact Sciences* 8 (1971), 9-39; 'Medieval Concepts of the Latitude of Forms: The Oxford Calculators', *Archives d'Histoire doctrinale et littéraire du moyen âge* 40 (1973), 223-83) and medieval analyses of beginning and ceasing, which we will be considering below.

who answer the reality question affirmatively. Some continuists–Ockham and Wodeham, for instance, or Albert of Saxony[23]–answer the reality question negatively (not because they think indivisibles are not real, but because they think indivisibles are not entities) and are thus in a position simply to dismiss the composition question. Aristotle himself is hard to pin down on the reality question,[24] but is of course the acknowledged leader of those who say no to the composition question. Many medieval continuists, especially before the surprising appearance of the early fourteenth-century indivisibilism, would have readily said yes to the reality question while offering the standard Aristotelian negative answer to the composition question. Their realism regarding indivisibles was moderate, however; it permitted them to recognize that the limit of a real body is a real surface, but it certainly did not countenance independently existing surfaces (or lines, or points).[25] So, at least until the eruption of indivisibilism sharpened the issue, continuists believed they had license to be realists regarding indivisibles, perhaps partly because it would have struck them as incredible that anyone could seriously consider answering the composition question affirmatively in the face of Aristotle's evidently insurmountable objections to such an answer.

At the beginning of *Physics* VI. 1, 231ᵃ 21-ᵇ 6), for instance, Aristotle argues that the constituents of a continuous line must be continuous with each other in the sense that the extremity of one constituent would have to coincide (be one) with, and not merely touch, the extremity of the next–an arrangement impossible for points, which, as non-quanta, cannot have extremities. Aristotle presses this objection further with his contiguity argument: two points cannot even touch each other without totally coinciding. Since an indivisible is unextended, indivisibles must touch each other, if at all, as wholes; consequently, points could not even be contiguous (much less continuous) constituents of lines because they cannot be accumulated

---

[23] See, e.g., Ockham, *Expositio Physicorum* vi, t. 3, quoted in Murdoch (above, n. 14), *ICAMT*, 178 n. 35; for Wodeham, see Wood (above, n. 8), Introduction; for Albert of Saxony (d. 1390), see C. G. Normore, 'Walter Burley on Continuity', *ICAMT*, 258-69; 260 n. 5.

[24] Maier (above, n. 3), 157-8: 'Der Punkt, das schlechthin Ausdehnungslose oder das simpliciter indivisibile, wird von Aristoteles nicht als Grösse angesehen, so wenig wie die Null als Zahl betrachtet wird: er ist für ihn weder endlich noch unendlich, sondern fällt überhaupt nicht unter den Massbegriff. Seine Realität ist von Aristoteles nirgends ausdrücklich bestritten und oft implicite anerkannt worden. Aber jedenfalls bedeutet er für ihn kein aktuell unendlich Kleines.'

[25] See Maier (above, n. 3), 158.

to produce any extension at all.[26] In terms of my sliced salami example, there cannot be two cuts adjacent to each other; if there is no salami between them, they coalesce into a single cut.

Aristotle's logical objections were supplemented in the eleventh century with al-Ghāzalī's geometrical arguments, which were promulgated in the West most effectively by Duns Scotus,[27] and which greatly lengthened the odds against anyone's taking indivisibilism seriously. The incommensurability argument can serve to represent these post-Aristotelian obstacles to indivisibilism. If lines were composed of points, then a greatest possible number of parallel transverse lines could be drawn perpendicularly from each point in one side of a square to each point in its opposite side, and those lines would intersect the square's diagonal at each of its points, which would therefore be the same in number as the points in a side; but the diagonal is visibly longer than the side of the square. And even if the number of points composing the diagonal is said to be greater than the number of points composing the side, those two numbers will be integers and therefore commensurable; but the diagonal of a square is provably incommensurable with the side. The force of the incommensurability argument might be brought out by saying that in order to be an indivisibilist one would have to reject either the Pythagorean theorem or the demonstration that the square root of two is an irrational number.[28]

How did Wyclif try to meet these objections, and what led him to make the attempt?

4. *The place of indivisibilism in Wyclif's logic*

Almost everything I have to say in reply to those questions comes from Wyclif's general logical treatises.[29] Before I try to expound and explain

[26] Cf. the discussion in Murdoch (above, n. 8), *CHLMP*, 577.

[27] See Maier (above, n. 3), 164, and Murdoch (above, n. 8), *CHLMP*, 579. The references provided are *Algazel, Metaphysics: A Medieval Translation*, ed. J. T. Muckle, CSB (Toronto, 1933); and Duns Scotus, *Opus Oxoniense* ii, d. 2, q. 9. See esp. Wyclif's version, iii. 53. 41-54. 12; 54. 23-37.

[28] Cf. Murdoch (above, n. 8), *CHLMP*, 579.

[29] i.e., those included in Dziewicki's edition of *Tractatus de Logica* and not the specialized treatise *Summa Insolubilium* (recently edited by Paul Vincent Spade and Gordon Wilson and soon to be published by The Center for Medieval and Early Renaissance Studies at the State University of New York at Binghamton). I have taken account of the relevant chapter in Wyclif's *Trialogus* (ii. 3), but in order to keep this project manageable I have deliberately avoided looking at other treatises of Wyclif's that are likely to be relevant, especially his *De Tempore* (part of *De Ente*), which is being edited by Allen W. Breck. I cannot even claim to have studied all of Wyclif's *Tractatus de Logica*, although

his indivisibilism, I must briefly characterize its perhaps unexpected literary setting. The treatises edited together under the general title *Tractatus de Logica* by Michael Henry Dziewicki at the end of the nineteenth century[30] consist of *De Logica* (an elementary textbook of twenty-two short chapters, with some unusual features and doctrines[31]), and *Logicae Continuatio* (in three treatises comprising twenty-eight chapters[32] in which the topics and the discussions become progressively broader and more philosophical). Almost certainly the brief *De Logica* was written near the beginning of Wyclif's career as a philosopher, around 1360, when he was the Master of Balliol.[33] There are indications that he began the *Logicae Continuatio*

I did go through the three volumes of the edition in a search for relevant material. (Dziewicki cannot be blamed for the fact that his marginal summaries are often unhelpful or misleading; he wrote them at a time when medieval logic was almost entirely unappreciated and misunderstood. But nothing in the circumstances of the edition excuses the superficiality of the indexes.)

[30] Dziewicki's edition of *De Logica* is based on one of the two manuscripts now known to have survived (see Thomson (above, n. 1) for all details regarding manuscripts). His edition of *Logicae continuatio* Trs. i and ii is based on two manuscripts, only one of which also contains Tr. iii. Of the edition of Trs. i and ii Thomson says, 'The two MSS from which Dziewicki prepared his text are far from satisfactory. A new edition, deploying the four other copies listed above, would eliminate several of the egregious misreadings of which he properly complained' (p. 5). I did not have access to the MSS Dziewicki used, and so I have no basis for assessing his readings; but I found so many passages that seemed garbled or otherwise unlikely that I could not have continued with this project if John Murdoch had not lent me his microfilm of Assisi Biblioteca Communale MS 662. This manuscript contains all three treatises of *Logicae Continuatio* (fols. 1ra-109va) and is apparently the earliest surviving copy (1385). In many passages its readings were all that enabled me to make sense of Wyclif's text. In what follows I supply the Latin for all quotations from *Logicae continuatio*; variant readings derived from Assisi MS 662 are indicated, all spelling is classicized, and Dziewicki's punctuation is sometimes altered.

[31] e.g., the doctrine of the principles of the categories in ch. 4 (i. 13; see p. 46 below), the expressed intention to have it culminate in a treatment of the verb 'know' (i. 1. 15-16), which seems never to have been written (but cf. *Logicae Continuatio* Tr. ii, ch. 13, on the verbs 'know' and 'doubt'), and especially its announced purpose of presenting 'the logic of Holy Scripture' (i. 1. 3).

[32] The numbering of the chapters is confusing in that the chapters of Tr. ii are numbered consecutively with those of Tr. i, although the numbering of the chapters of Tr. iii begins again with 1. (Perhaps this is another slight consideration, besides the manuscript tradition cited by Thomson (above, n. 1), 6–in favour of considering Trs. i and ii as constituting *Logicae Continuatio* and Tr. iii as 'De logica tractatus tertius'.) There are seven chapters in Tr. i, eleven in Tr. ii, and ten in Tr. iii. Thus Tr. ii, ch. 13, is actually the sixth chapter of Tr. ii. The chapters are untitled in the edition; for a table of contents with my supplied titles, see the Appendix below.

[33] See Dziewicki's Introduction to vol. i of his edition, pp. vi-viii; also Thomson, 4-8. For an argument in support of a later date (between 1368 and 1372 for the *De Logica*) see Workman (above, n. 1), i. 333.

soon afterwards[34] and some less reliable indications that he may have been working on its final chapters, the ones that contain the fullest presentation of his indivisibilism, near the end of his life.[35]

By the time Wyclif began writing his logic, the consideration of certain problems concerning time and change had become part of the standard subject matter of logic, especially in connection with the analysis of propositions involving the verbs 'begin' and 'cease'.[36] Wyclif's *Logicae Continuatio* contains a chapter on beginning and ceasing,[37] as is only to be expected, a chapter which, as I will try to show, is essential for understanding his adoption of indivisibilism. But although such a chapter inevitably involves a consideration of the logic of change (and therefore some attention to time and space, to quality and quantity), and although Wyclif's indivisibilism is explicit in that chapter, he does not develop it until much later in his logical treatises. The development takes place under the guise of considerations of hypothetical propositions involving locational or temporal connectives such as 'where' or 'when', considerations which would ordinarily occupy at most a few paragraphs of a medieval logic book.

[34] Dziewicki's marginal note to the Proemium (i. 75) draws a probably mistaken inference regarding the relationship between *De Logica* and *Logicae Continuatio* (cf. Thomson, 5), but the first sentence of the latter's ch. 1 may offer better evidence for the connection Dziewicki thought he saw. Further evidence of the writing of *Logicae Continuatio* early in Wyclif's career can be found in an example in Tr. ii which depends on the author's being then not yet forty years old (i. 169. 6-7). Workman's later dating would make Wyclif much closer to forty at the time of its writing, which may make the example even more apt (and Workman's dating consequently more plausible).

[35] The references to Wyclif's students (*iuvenes*) are more frequent in *De Logica* and the first two Trs. of the *Logicae Continuatio*. In Tr. iii, esp. in chs. 9 and 10, the content and tone are less and less appropriate for a logic treatise and more and more what one would expect of a general philosophical treatise, with fewer (if any) references to *iuvenes* and more references to himself as an old man (*senex*)–e.g. iii. 144. 20-1. But the single most interesting passage in this regard is in the last chapter of the work (iii. 183. 39), which identifies the then current year as 1383. Dziewicki says, 'It is indeed possible that this great treatise was let unfinished until the last years of Wyclif's life; which would account both for the expression, "*senex*" and the date; so we must not necessarily conclude that the number given is wrong. But it is much more likely that it may have been changed from 1361(?) by the ignorant correction of a scribe writing in 1383.' (Introduction, i. vii.) But, as Thomson observes (p. 7), the same date is unmistakably spelled out in Latin words in Assisi MS 662, the oldest surviving manuscript. On the basis of this passage Workman says that the *Tractatus de Logica* 'was touched up and edited in 1383 (ib. iii. 183), though the alterations were slight, as we see from the absence of all eucharistic comment' (above, n. 1, i. 333).

[36] For some general information on medieval logicians' treatment of these verbs see n. 89 below.

[37] Tr. ii, ch. 14 (i.e., the seventh chapter of the second treatise; see n. 32 above), i. 191-202. Also, the first paragraph of *De Logica*, ch. 20 (i. 65. 1-16) contains a brief but interesting treatment of 'begin' and 'cease'.

But the two chapters Wyclif devotes to those considerations, the last two of the fifty chapters of his combined *Tractatus de Logica*, take up a full third of its almost seven hundred printed pages. It is primarily to those two final chapters, the ninth and tenth of the third treatise of the *Logicae continuatio*, that we have to look for Wyclif's rejoinders to the logical and geometrical objections to indivisibilism.

Because those rejoinders often involve theological considerations, it may be worth noting one more peculiarity of the literary setting of Wyclif's indivisibilism: he claims to have undertaken to write on logic as a kind of religious obligation. In the opening words of the first of his logical treatises he announces an aim that I believe to be unique among medieval logicians:

Certain people who love God's law have persuaded me to compose a reliable treatise aimed at making plain the logic of Holy Scripture. For in view of the fact that many people go into logic having imagined they would thereby come to know God's law better, and then, because of the tasteless concoction of pagan terms in every analysis or proof of propositions, because of the emptiness of the enterprise, abandon it, I propose to sharpen the minds of the faithful by introducing analyses and proofs of propositions that are to be drawn from the Scriptures.[38]

Wyclif only rarely manages (or, perhaps, remembers) to choose his logical examples from Scripture,[39] and it is possible that he intended only the *De Logica* as an exposition of the logic of Scripture.[40] But in a broad sense that aim characterizes all of his logic, in which the evidence of the author's religious motivation and theological commitments is much more interesting and important than even a regular employment of biblical examples would have been, and much more pervasive

[38] i. 1. 2-10. I have translated *probatio propositionum* as 'analysis or proof of propositions' because the fourteenth-century techniques of *probatio propositionum* involve what we would recognize as the analysis of propositions more obviously than anything we would recognize as proof, although often enough the analysis provides clarification of a sort that might aid proof. See A. Maierù, *Terminologia logica della tarda scolastica* (Rome, 1972), ch. 6, '*Probatio propositionis*', 393-498; Jan Pinborg, *Logik und Semantik im Mittelalter: Ein Ueberblick* (Stuttgart-Bad Canstatt, 1972), 103-11.

[39] There is a little cluster of biblical examples in *De Logica*, chs. 7 and 8, and at least two such examples in ch. 16. No doubt there are others, but I have not seen enough of them to warrant Dziewicki's claim that 'There are plenty of them throughout the book' (i. 22 n. 29). Wyclif does, however, often use 'Petrus' and 'Paulus' instead of the more traditional 'Socrates' and 'Plato', and his examples often have theological roots.

[40] Concern with the concept of the logic of Scripture evidently lasted all his life, however. See, e.g., his last philosophical work, *Trialogus* (ed. G. Lechler, *Joannis Wiclif: Trialogus, cum supplemento Trialogi* (Oxford, 1869), Bk. i, ch. 8, 64; ch. 9, 65; and Bk. iii, ch. 31, 241-3.

than the occasional theological concerns that show up haphazardly in other fourteenth-century logic books.

5. *Some relevant characteristics of Wyclif's indivisibilism*

As an indivisibilist, Wyclif is of course a realist regarding indivisibles. Bodies, he would say, are undoubtedly real, and therefore so are their surfaces; real surfaces, furthermore, involve real lines, and real lines involve real points.[41] For those continuists who are also realists regarding indivisibles Wyclif has several embarrassing observations. For instance, since they maintain that points, although real, are not *parts* of lines, they must be committed to the view that any number of points can be removed from a line without shortening the line—indeed, that *all* those real points can be removed while the line retains its original length—which is absurd.[42] Again, since they maintain that any line can be divided into two precisely equal halves Wyclif invites them to say what happens to the line's midpoint when the line is bisected. If it survives as the endpoint of one of the two sections, the sections are not equal. If it is destroyed, the two equal sections are not the halves of the original line.[43] Continuists who *deny* the reality of indivisibles, considering them to be only theoretical objects, or real only as limits of real continua, are dealt with more briefly and less effectively by Wyclif. He would simply like to know how they dare to use geometrical arguments against indivisibilism if they maintain that such geometrical entities as points and lines cannot exist in reality.[44]

Any continuist would interpret the central thesis of Wyclif's indivisibilism—continua are composed of indivisibles—as a rejection of the reality of continua. But Wyclif plainly believes himself entitled to go on speaking of continua, no doubt just because his indivisibilism is intended to offer the explantion of the *appearance* of continuity. And so

[41] I have not yet found Wyclif arguing plainly in just this way, but this line of thought evidently lies behind his realism regarding indivisibles. See, e.g., ii. 49. 21-8; iii. 2. 3-7, 46. 2-7.

[42] iii. 30. 21-36. There is more to Wyclif's argument than I am using here.

[43] iii. 53. 7-12. Wyclif's stated conclusions are more elaborate than those I am drawing here. In order to retain the Aristotelian doctrine that any continuum can be divided in half, Wyclif is forced to adopt an extended notion of a half: *either* 'a part that is simply in a ratio of one to two relative to its whole' *or* 'a part that is simply in a ratio of one to two relative to what is indivisibly more or less than its whole' (medietatem quae est pars simpliciter subdupla *ad suum totum, et medietatem quae est simpliciter subdupla* ad indivisibiliter plus vel minus suo toto*) (iii. 36. 4-5). (See n. 30 above; italicized words or passages are added from Assisi MS 662 and asterisked words are variant forms found in Assisi MS 662.)

[44] iii. 45. 37-46. 7.

Wyclif's use of 'continua' must be understood as short for 'apparent continua', like our use of the term 'sunset'. The appearance of continuity in the spatio-temporal phenomenon of local motion, for instance, is, he says, somewhat like the appearance of a fiery circle against the darkness when someone whirls a torch around at night, 'because the greatest deception occurs in the senses in connection with signifying the continuity of motion'.[45] And he attributes much of the disrepute of indivisibilism in general to that limitation of the senses: 'The most important reason why this way [of viewing fundamental physical reality] is abhorrent to so many is that the composition of a continuum out of non-quanta is not something they perceive by sense.'[46] The detailed composition of the world out of non-quanta is, he acknowledges, 'known to God alone'.[47]

In retaining the term 'continuum' Wyclif tried to maintain as much of the Aristotelian concept as he could. Accordingly, he is prepared to go on describing a continuum as infinitely divisible, but only in a certain respect: 'It is not the case that every continuum is infinitely divisible, since (as will be said later) there is an end [to the division] at the number of the indivisibles [composing it]. Nevertheless, everything of that sort is divisible beyond what we are capable of knowing.'[48] And so Wyclif's customary use of the term 'infinity' must also be understood as short for 'apparent infinity': 'if there are any things the number of which is not precisely knowable by us, then those things are naturally infinitely many. For example, if some [points] are all the points of this line, it is not ours to know precisely how many they are, or what ratio they have to the number 4, or to any number that is finite to us.'[49] '... such things as are immeasurable by human beings I call infinite in a certain respect, or as far as mankind is concerned; and that is what I mean whenever I posit an infinite number.'[50] Given what

---

[45] iii. 40. 6-8: 'quod maxima deceptio contingit in sensibus in sentiendo* continuitatem motus.' Cf. iii. 40. 1-34; also iii. 193. 35-40.

[46] iii. 85. 17-20: 'Causa praecipua quare illa via abhorretur a pluribus est quod non per sensum percipiunt ad* compositionem* continui ex non quantis.'

[47] iii. 104. 20-22: 'situs mundi, cum componitur ex non quantis, habeat eorum compositionem soli Deo notam ...'

[48] ii. 166. 41-167. 4: 'Nec est omne continuum divisibile in infinitum, cum sit status ad numerum indivisibilium, ut postea dicetur. Verumtamen ultra hoc quod nos sufficimus cognoscere est quodlibet tale divisibile; ...'

[49] ii. 81. 18-23: 'si sunt aliqua quorum numerus non sit distincte a nobis noscibilis, tunc illa sunt naturaliter infinita. Ut si aliqua sunt omnia puncta illius lineae non est nostrum distincte scire quot sunt, nec in qua proportione se habent ad 4rium, vel ad quemcumque numerum nobis finitum.'

[50] iii. 37. 12-15: 'talia quae sunt hominibus immensurabilia et illa voco infinita

Wyclif believes about the imperceptibility of indivisibles, it follows that every perceptible continuum is composed of a Wycliffian infinity of indivisibles: 'bodily vision cannot see a non-quantum or anything completely composed of non-quanta that are finitely many to us.'[51] And so, on this understanding of infinity, Aristotle is easily accommodated: 'for what the Philosopher has in mind, it is enough that every continuum be infinitely divisible in a certain respect, beyond every finite number that is precisely knowable by someone in this life. Thus no one who wants to argue for an *absolute* infinity [of divisibility] by means of the ordinary exponents will ever make good on that monstrous leap: "and so on, *ad infinitum*".'[52]

In reality, then, Wyclif is a finitist; and his primary motivation for finitism is clearly theological. God alone knows the detailed composition of things out of indivisibles, but in Wyclif's view that sort of knowledge necessarily includes knowing the precise number of the indivisible constituents of the world and of each thing in it.[53] If there are literally infinitely many points in a line, then, it is logically impossible that anyone, even omniscient God himself, can know the number of its points. And the principal reason why it will not do to say simply that God knows there are infinitely many of them is, I think, that since they are real and natural, God made them; and omniscient God must know each of his creatures individually. As Wyclif puts it more than once, quoting or paraphrasing Genesis 1: 31, 'God sees all the things that he has made'.[54]

On the basis of these sketches of the literary setting and some relevant characteristics of Wyclif's indivisibilism, I want to return to the first of the questions I asked earlier about the logical and mathematical objections to indivisibilism: how did Wyclif try to meet those objections?

secundum quid, vel quoad hominem; et ita intelligo quandocumque pono numerum infinitum.'

[51] ii. 176. 8-9: 'visus corporalis non potest videre non quantum nec compositum adaequate ex non quantis nobis finitis; . . .'

[52] iii. 38. 5-10: 'Unde satis est pro sensu Philosophi quod omne continuum sit secundum quid divisibile in infinitum, et ultra omnem numerum finitum a viatore distincte noscibilem. Unde volens argumentare infinitatem simpliciter per communes exponentes numquam probabit illum saltum monstruosum: et sic in infinitum.'

[53] iii. 35. 19-21: 'Verumtamen apud Deum est notum ex quot non quantis mundus componitur et quaecumque pars eius corporea; . . .'

[54] e.g., ii. 82. 10 (and see the surrounding material, ii. 81. 16-82. 28) and *Trialogus*, Bk. ii, ch. 3, 83. I have not found Wyclif citing Heb. 4: 13 (a passage that is, if anything, even more apt for his purposes), but Rega Wood tells me that Harclay does cite that verse in support of his indivisibilism.

6. Wyclif's rejoinders to the contiguity and incommensurability arguments

From an indivisibilist's standpoint, Aristotle's contiguity argument is a challenge to explain how unextended things, non-quanta—no matter how many of them—can add up to an extended thing. The only sort of explanation that seems available had been attempted long before Wyclif was born, by Henry of Harclay. Since points would indeed simply coincide if they were contiguous 'in one and the same location', they must, Harclay thought, be contiguous 'in respect of distinct locations'.[55] On this view, then, Aristotle is right about the impossiblity of an extended thing's being composed of contiguous unextended things, and Harclay's way around the contiguity argument is to introduce the point-location, not the point itself, as the real constituent of a line. Each real point seems to be pictured as occurring in an irreducible envelope of space, a minimal quantum with a real non-quantum at its centre.

I have prefaced my discussion of Wyclif's rejoinder to the contiguity argument with some observations about Harclay's because Harclay's is clearer and because what I have been able to identify as Wyclif's rejoinder leads me to think he must have intended something very close to Harclay's line. The evidence begins to accumulate with Wyclif's presentation of his doctrine of the first principles of the categories, very early in his *De Logica*, where some of the categories themselves are said to be based upon appropriate indivisibles[56]—quality, for instance, upon degrees, 'because every latitude [or range] of quality is composed of degrees',[57] and time upon instants.[58] It is Wyclif's first principle of the category of place that is most relevant to his rejoinder to the contiguity argument, however: 'the first principle of the category *where* is the location of a point'—not the *point*, notice, but its *location*—'because the entire location of the world is composed of punctal locations',[59] and, just a few lines further down, 'the world is composed of punctals'.[60] As far as I can tell, Wyclif's punctals cannot

---

[55] See Murdoch (above, n. 8), *CHLMP*, 577, esp. n. 39.

[56] Cf. the radically different set of principles of these categories put forward by Wyclif in his *De Universalibus*, ch. 10. (Ivan Mueller's edition of *De Universalibus* was published in 1985 by Oxford with a translation by Anthony Kenny and an introduction by Paul Vincent Spade. I am grateful to Professor Spade for making the typescript available to me in advance of publication.)

[57] i. 13. 8-10.   [58] i. 13. 17-20.   [59] i. 13. 15-17.

[60] i. 13. 19; cf. ii. 2. 16-18. Most dictionaries of classical or medieval Latin have no entry for Wyclif's adjective 'punctalis' or substantive 'punctale', but Paul Spade has pointed out to me that the *Revised Medieval Latin Word List* has an entry for this word dated 1250 (besides its entry for Wyclif's use of it) and I suppose that Grosseteste is the

be anything other than the locations of points, and they play a large part in his exposition of indivisibilism. Although he sometimes shows no hesitation in describing points as touching one another,[61] when he is arguing for or defending his position he seems more cautious, shifting from points to punctals or locations of points, or from touching to being immediate to one another.[62] And when he faces up to Aristotle's argument explicitly, caution seems to overwhelm him, vitiating his rejoinder: 'One indivisible can, nevertheless, touch another indivisible *broadly speaking*, because [it can] be placed at (or up against) (*ad*) the same indivisible location together with another indivisible; and in that way it can be made continuous with the other *broadly speaking*, because [it can] make a single continuum with the other.'[63]

If Wyclif had simply explained the composition of a line in terms of punctals, he would at least have had a coherent, Harclayan position on the issue. Of course, that position amounts to abandoning the central thesis that a continuum is composed of non-quanta, since the punctals appear to be minimal *quanta* of space, each inhabited by a solitary non-quantum; and that position is in no respect a rejoinder to the Aristotelian contiguity argument. But even that position is preferable to what Wyclif actually offers here, which is at best too avowedly imprecise to settle anything and which may (if '*ad*' is read, quite naturally, as no more than 'at') gratuitously be making the very mistake Harclay took special pains to avoid. If Wyclif were ordinarily or even often as inept as he appears to be in this rejoinder, he would not be worth serious philosophical consideration. But this fumbling and perhaps incoherent attempt at a rejoinder is indeed uncharacteristic of him and only deepens the mystery of his adoption of indivisibilism.

Before turning from the Aristotelian contiguity argument, it may be worth noting that in Wyclif's logical treatises he tries to show that his indivisibilism is compatible with, even entailed by, Aristotle's continuism properly understood.[64] But in the *Trialogus*, Wyclif's last philosophical work, written in 1382 or 1383,[65] he disdainfully dismisses

author who ought to be checked first in that connection. (In the *OED* entry for 'punctal' the only recorded occurrence of the word in its appropriate sense is in Dziewicki's introduction to his edition of Wyclif's logic.)

[61] See, e.g., ii. 21. 32-7.   [62] See, e.g., iii. 30. 37-31. 13.

[63] iii. 35. 33-7: 'Verumtamen unum indivisibile potest tangere aliud* large loquendo, quia esse ad eundem situm indivisibilem positum cum alio; et sic potest continuari cum alio large loquendo, quia facere unum continuum cum alio.'

[64] See, e.g., iii. 35. 5-29, 85. 13-17.

[65] Thomson (above, n. 1), 79.

the Aristotelian objections to indivisibilism: 'As for the text of Aristotle and his followers, it obviously is not conducive to belief; for he frequently went wrong. But Democritus, Plato, Augustine, and Grosseteste, who thought along these [indivisibilist] lines, are more illustrious philosophers by far and more brilliant in many of the metaphysical sciences.'[66]

Wyclif develops the incommensurability argument and his reply to it at considerable length.[67] The argument's first, less important objection–that the geometrical construction of the transverse lines proves that if indivisibilism is true the square's diagonal is equal to its side–he tries to counter by treating the oblique intersection of mathematical lines as if it were an oblique crossing of two sticks, covering more of each other than they would if crossed perpendicularly.[68] There is something to be said for such an account only if it is applied not to the mathematical entities but to their physical representations in quasi-lines of ink or chalk, and Wyclif sometimes writes as if his subject matter is not the same as the geometer's,[69] perhaps most suggestively in his stipulations that the figures he is discussing are 'perceptible'.[70] But, of course, particles of ink or chalk are not points, and strings of such particles are not lines. If Wyclif really meant to talk only about such things he should have simply dismissed all the logical and mathematical objections as irrelevant; but he would then also have had to revise his central thesis radically, to something like 'Perceptible quasi-continua are composed of imperceptible quanta', which would have been neither indivisibilism nor interesting. The truth of the matter seems to be that in replying to the geometrical arguments he did mean to be talking about the mathematical entities, but he was thinking about them in terms of their misleading physical representations.

The physical-mathematical confusion that afflicts Wyclif's reply to

[66] *Trialogus*, Bk. ii, ch. 3, 83-4. Two of Loserth's four sources have 'mathematicis scientiis' rather than 'metaphisicis scientiis'.

[67] iii. 53. 27-58. 31, including some digressions the relevance of which is not clear to me.

[68] iii. 53. 27-40, and at many other places in the passage cited in n. 67 above. See Murdoch (above, n. 8), *CHLMP*, 579 and esp. n. 46, for an appraisal of this sort of tactic among indivisibilists generally. Ockham points out that the indivisibilists argue against the incommensurability objection as if lines were sticks (*Quodlibeta septem*, ed. J. C. Wey; St Bonaventure, NY, 1980; i. q. 9, 52-3).

[69] e.g., iii. 55. 5-9, 57. 25-40, 58. 13-21.

[70] e.g., iii. 55. 2, 56. 36, 58. 18, 23; see also n. 72 below, the first passage cited in n. 75, and the passage cited in n. 77.

the incommensurability argument's first objection is not the main issue in his reply to the second objection–the charge that if indivisibilism is true, the square's diagonal must, *per impossibile*, be commensurable with its side. His rejoinder to this more important objection is reminiscent, both in its form and in its theological motivation, of his treatment of infinity. To begin with, Wyclif observes, it is simply false to say that *in general* the diagonal is incommensurable with the side, 'for in the minimal square [a side of which consists of just two points] . . ., the diagonal is *equal* to the side'.[71] In the case of any perceptible square, however–i.e. one whose sides are composed of a Wycliffian infinity of points–Wycliffian incommensurability does obtain: 'It is obvious that *to any person in this life* it is *uncertain* what the ratio of a perceptible diagonal to the side of its square may be'.[72] But incommensurability relative to us is definitely not to be confused with incommensurability *simpliciter*, which is indeed ruled out by indivisibilism: 'whatever is demonstrated of any continuum you choose is demonstrated of the number of the indivisibles that constitute it'.[73] And, as we have seen, 'as far as *God* is concerned it is *known* how many non-quanta the world and each corporeal part of it is composed of';[74] therefore, '*God* knows adequately how every square that is perceptible in itself is integrated out of [imperceptible] minimal squares and their cumulated indivisible principles. . . . He also knows the ratio in which each number of points stands to another–[ratios] regarding which *we* have *irremovable ignorance*'.[75] Wyclif's last formulation of this rejoinder, in his *Trialogus*, brings out its theological component even more plainly:

And so *sensible* philosophers[76] say that of such continua [whose ultimate constituents are non-quanta] one [sort of] part is aliquot as far as God is

---

[71] iii. 55. 2-4: 'Nam in minimo quadrato . . . diameter est aequalis suo lateri; . . .'

[72] iii. 56. 35-7: 'patet quod incertum est cuilibet hic vianti de proportione diametri sensibilis ad costam sui quadrati . . .' It is worth noting that in an altogether different context where he is simply providing examples of absolutely necessary truths his mathematical examples are 'that 3 and 2 are 5, [and] that the diagonal of a *perceptible* square is not commensurable with its side' (iii. 179. 21-2: 'tria et duo esse quinque, diametrum quadrati sensibilis non esse commetram suae costae').

[73] iii. 58. 11-13: 'Quicquid ergo demonstratur de quovis continuo demonstratur de numero indivisibilium qui ipsum constituunt.'

[74] iii. 35. 19-21; see n. 53 above.

[75] iii. 36. 31-4; 36-8: 'Immo Deus satis noscit quomodo omne quadratum per se sensibile integratur ex quadratis* minimis et principiis eorum indivisibilibus cumulatis. . . . Novit etiam in qua proportione quicumque numerus punctorum se habet ad alium; et de istis habemus nos inseparabilem ignorantiam.'

[76] In the context 'sensibiles philosophi' are clearly indivisibilists; and since

concerned but not aliquot for us, while another [sort of] part is *perceptibly* aliquot; and it is in that way that they distinguish commensurable and incommensurable parts. The indivisibles, however, are not aliquot, commensurable parts as far as *we* are concerned; as far as *God* is concerned, however, they *are* aliquot, commensurable parts.[77]

Wyclif embraced what must have been a notoriously anachronistic indivisibilism to which he had no philosophical right if he could not satisfactorily overcome the well-known logical and mathematical objections to it. I think we are now in a position to see that his rejoinders to the contiguity and incommensurability arguments are clearly unsatisfactory. The failure of the early indivisibilists' attempts to refute the classic objections is excusable; but Wyclif cannot have been ignorant of those failures and his own are not novel in any interesting respect. Why, then, was Wyclif an indivisibilist? Since he clearly was not stupid, he must have believed he was committed to it in spite of its unhappy intellectual consequences.[78] All that we have seen that might have prompted such a belief on his part is certain theological considerations, especially concerning the requirements of omniscience, and I think there can be no doubt that they are indeed the bedrock of his indivisibilism. In his final defence of the position, at the beginning of the relevant chapter of the *Trialogus*, he offers four arguments in support of indivisibilism,[79] only the third of which–a version of the

'sensibilis' is the word that must be translated elsewhere in Wyclif's exposition and defence of indivisibilism, even in this same passage, as 'perceptible', I suppose it is possible that the *sensibiles philosophi* are so called in virtue of their empiricist approach to problems of continuity and infinity–not sensible philosophers so much as philosophers of the sensible.

[77] *Trialogus*, Bk. ii, ch. 3, 84. Aliquot parts are parts contained a whole number of times in the whole. Five is an aliquot part of twenty, but not of twenty-four.

[78] A passage particularly intriguing in this connection occurs at iii. 57. 39-40, in the midst of Wyclif's attempt to deal with the incommensurability objection: 'Nec scio adhuc aliquam istarum trium responsionum efficaciter improbare', the most natural reading of which is 'And I do not yet know how to disprove any of these three replies effectively'. In his marginal notes Dziewicki paraphrases it as 'I have not as yet been able to refute these two [*sic*] last opinions'. If Wyclif is indeed saying what he seems to be saying, he is here confessing that in spite of all his apparent effort to overcome the incommensurability objection he does not have a really satisfactory reply. But it seems barely possible to read the passage as his announcement that he has not yet found any flaws in his own three replies (to three phases of the objection). If he did mean what he seems to mean, his adherence to indivisibilism is still harder to account for. Perhaps the scribe of Assisi MS 662 also had a hard time squaring this passage with the rest of Wyclif's position; in any case he writes 'nunc', not 'nec', which fits the context better but is less well suited to the grammar of the sentence.

[79] Wyclif provides seven arguments in support of indivisibilism in Tr. iii, ch. 9 (iii. 30. 7-35.4), and all of them are more sophisticated than those found in *Trialogus*. But the

atomists' argument discussed by Aristotle[80]–is the sort of thing one might expect in such a context. The least that must be said against the first and second is that they could not conceivably be taken as even relevant to the central thesis of his indivisibilism.[81] But the fourth and last, offered as the presupposition of the first three, reveals, I think, his one permanent motivation for trying to hold this position: 'Now in this reply [to the interlocutor's challenge[82]] I am assuming, in keeping with Augustine and the faith of Scripture, that just as God saw all the things that he had made, so with perfect distinctness he understands all the parts of any continuum whatever, so that no further or different components of that continuum can be given [i.e. no components more fundamental than or different from indivisibles[83]] And on that basis the reasoning [of my position] seems plainly to succeed.'[84]

What first interested me in the topics of this paper, however, was neither the contents of Wyclif's indivisibilism nor his theological motivation for adopting it but rather a development in his analysis of change that struck me as quite possibly having provided the single most important philosophical impetus to Wyclif's rejection of continuism. Whether or not I am right about the role this development played in Wyclif's intellectual life, it is, I believe, historically unusual if not unique, and philosophically interesting in its own right.

7. The Calculators' continuist analysis of change

The analysis of change assumed a new importance in logic and attained an unprecedented level of sophistication as a result of the work of a group of philosophers, theologians, and mathematicians at

most promising line of thought represented in them will be considered in the next section of this paper, and the *Trialogus* arguments are, after all, apparently the ones he was content with as part of his final discussion of indivisibilism.

[80] *De Generatione et Corruptione* I. 2, 316ᵃ 14 ff. On the atomists' argument in Aristotle and the ancient commentators, see Furley (above, n. 5), *ICAMT*, 31-4; on the argument in connection with medieval indivisibilism, see Kretzmann (above, n. 12).

[81] The point of the first argument is that spirit, a non-quantum, is a component of a human being, a quantum; the point of the second is that every perceptible substance, a quantum, is composed of its genus and its differentia, which are non-quanta–'indivisible in respect of extension' (ii, ch. 3, 83).

[82] 'You [Phronesis, Wyclif's spokesman] often assume what is impossible–that a continuum is composed of non-quanta–something Aristotle often condemns in opposing Plato and Democritus. In any case, powerful reasoning and mathematical demonstration prove its impossibility.' (ii. 3. 83.)

[83] The immediately preceding argument makes it clear that only indivisibles can fill the bill in this context.

[84] *Trialogus*, ii. 3. 83.

Oxford in the generations just before Wyclif's—the Oxford Calculators (or 'Mertonians'), including, for instance, Thomas Bradwardine, Richard Kilvington, William Heytesbury, John Dumbleton, and Richard Swineshead.[85] Wyclif's teachers at Oxford must have included some of these Calculators, as formidable and original a school of interdisciplinary thinkers as has ever been associated with Oxford. One of the reasons Wyclif's views on time and change take their unusual indivisibilist direction and one of the reasons they particularly interest me is that they are formed in conscious, sometimes angry, opposition to the Calculators' techniques of logical analysis and the continuism on which they are based.[86] I admire the work of the Calculators, but Wyclif's criticisms, both explicit and implicit, strike me as immeasurably more challenging philosophically than all the humanists' fulminations against the Calculators' subtleties.[87] And the significant development in Wyclif's analysis of change is associated with his discovery of an apparent paradox in the standard continuist analysis on which the Calculators based some of their most ingenious sophismata.

Their analysis of change is founded on the Aristotle continuist doctrine of instantaneous transition.[88] It is clear that many, if not all

---

[85] Bradwardine (c.1295-1349); Kilvington (c.1300-1361); Heytesbury (before 1313-72/3); Dumbleton (fl. 1350); Swineshead (fl. 1340-55). For basic literature on these men, see the Biographies in CHLMP. For an introduction to their work, see Edith Sylla's chapter 27, 'The Oxford Calculators', 540-63 in CHLMP.

[86] Wyclif was a probationary fellow of Merton in 1356, when Richard Billingham was Third Bursar of the college (Robson (above, n. 1), 10-11), and Billingham wrote on Kilvington's Sophismata, which contain a great deal of material directly relevant to this discussion. (For Billingham's work on Kilvington, see S. Knuuttila and A. I. Lehtinen, 'Plato in infinitum remisse incipit esse albus: New Texts on the Late Medieval Discussion on the Concept of Infinity in Sophismata Literature', in E. Saarinen et al., eds., Essays in Honour of Jaakko Hintikka (Dordrecht, 1979)). Wyclif shows signs of direct acquaintance with Kilvington's work in Tr. ii, ch. 17 (see esp. ii. 225. 24-226. 9), but as far as I know he does not cite him by name. For Wyclif's connection with Bradwardine, see n. 17 above. Wyclif certainly knows how to use the Calculators' techniques on examples of the sort they were particularly fond of, as we shall see, but he had turned against them before he wrote Logicae continuatio, as can be seen in such passages as iii. 70. 11-17 and 132. 25-36.

[87] If Wyclif's criticisms of the Calculators' analysis of change had been understood and taken seriously, they would have provoked a serious response from what remained of the Calculatorial tradition in Oxford after 1360. I have not tried to find evidence for or against the existence of such a response, but the fact that it is hard to identify important English scholastic logicians after Wyclif (Iohannes Venator Anglicus may be his only important successor) might be construed as evidence that his work did have some inhibiting effect.

[88] For an excellent discussion of this doctrine in Aristotle himself, see R. Sorabji, 'Aristotle on the Instant of Change', Aristotelian Society Supplementary Volume 50 (1976),

changes can be considered as situations in which it is first not the case that some object, a, has some characteristic, F, and then, later, a does have F. Those two states of affairs must be temporally exclusive (in accordance with the law of non-contradiction) and temporally immediate to each other (in accordance with the law of the excluded middle). Therefore the change from a's not having F to a's having F must be instantaneous. For example, the change in the level of the mercury in a thermometer from not being at 100° to being at 100°, or the change of a man from not being married to being married, or the change of a ball from not being in motion to being in motion—each takes place at an instant. Every change, furthermore, involves a beginning and a ceasing: the ceasing of one state and the beginning of another. And in the light of the doctrine of instantaneous transition those beginnings and ceasings must take place at instants—instants which serve to limit the temporal intervals in which the different states obtain. A limiting instant may be either intrinsic or extrinsic to the interval it limits. The instant at which a begins to have F, for example, may be either the first instant of a's having F (intrinsic) or the last instant of a's not having F (extrinsic). And since in accordance with Aristotelian continuism instants cannot be immediate to each other, the designation of either of those limits rules out the possibility of designating the other of them.

Medieval logicians, including Wyclif and the Calculators, carry out their analysis of change in terms of analyses (or 'expositions') of sentences involving the verbs 'begin' and 'cease'.[89] Thus if at the instant when Princess Elizabeth's father dies one says (a little stiltedly) 'Elizabeth begins to reign,' the sentence gets expounded into an affirmative present-tense exponent—'Now Elizabeth is reigning'—and a negative past-tense exponent: 'Immediately before now Elizabeth was not reigning.' On the other hand, the standard exposition of 'Elizabeth begins to move' yields a negative present-tense exponent and an affirmative future-tense exponent: 'Now Elizabeth is not moving, and immediately after now she will be moving.' The reigning example requires an intrinsic-limit exposition while the moving

69-89. (The remainder of this paragraph of the paper is a paraphrase of material from my article 'Socrates is Whiter Than Plato Begins To Be White', *Nous* 11 (1977), 3-15.)

[89] On the development and the nature of this literature, see N. Kretzmann, 'Incipit/ Desinit' in P. Machamer and R. Turnbull, eds., *Motion and Time, Space and Matter: Interrelations in the History of Science and Philosophy* (Columbus, Ohio, 1976), 101-36; also L. O. Nielsen, 'Thomas Bradwardine's Treatise on "*incipit*" and "*desinit*"', *Cahiers de l'Institut du Moyen-Âge Grec et Latin* 47 (1983), Introduction (2-46).

example requires an extrinsic-limit exposition because, on the standard account, reigning is a 'permanent' state while moving is a 'successive' state. States whose essential parts all occur at one and the same time are called permanent: a queen's reign may be long or short, but she is fully reigning at any given instant of it, including its first instant. States whose essential parts cannot all occur simultaneously are called successive. Since any motion takes some time, no motion, however brief, can go on at an instant: reigning-at-an-instant is a characteristic of Elizabeth's, but moving-at-an-instant cannot be characteristic of anything. Of course, at any given instant of an interval during which Elizabeth is moving she may be said to be moving, but only in virtue of her being in motion just before and just after that instant. It is for that reason that 'Elizabeth begins to move' requires an extrinsic-limit exposition: since there cannot be a first instant of being in motion, the instant of transition from not moving to moving must be the last instant before the interval during which the motion goes on.

Although the Calculators raised many difficulties for this standard account, they typically did so with a view to refining its details.[90] In any event, they seem never to have encountered a difficulty that called into question the continuist presuppositions of the account. But that is precisely the intended effect of some of the difficulties Wyclif raises in his chapter on the verbs 'begin' and 'cease'.

8. *A problem for continuists: the vacillating man*

Near the beginning of the chapter[91] Wyclif introduces the standard intrinsic-limit and extrinsic-limit expositions as the ones that were 'ordinarily' used 'in the old days'.[92] After digressing to consider special difficulties associated with claims of beginning and ceasing as

[90] See, e.g., Kilvington's revised interpretation of 'immediately', based on considerations of an apparent paradox generated in one of his *sophismata* (expounded and discussed in Kretzmann (above, n. 15), *ICAMT*, 291-4, and applied to a problem of Wyclif's on pp. 58-9 below).

[91] *Logicae continuatio* Tr. ii, ch. 14 (see n. 37 above); i. 191-202. The chapter is dense and difficult. I do not claim to have mastered all of it or even to have extracted from it everything that might be pertinent to my purposes here.

[92] i. 191. 15 and 25. Wyclif presents the standard expositions in a disjunctive format which discounts the importance of the distinction between intrinsic-limit and extrinsic-limit expositions(and between 'permanent' and 'successive' states) if it does not disown it altogether. Some precedent for such a format can be found in Burley's *Tractatus longior* (ed. P. Boehner; St. Bonaventure, NY, 1955), 192, and it became important after Wyclif in the treatments of 'begin' and 'cease' by Iohannes Venator Anglicus (d. 1427?) and others (see Kretzmann, above, n. 89, 118 and nn. 52 and 53).

applied to God and to the creation, especially in connection with the very first instant of time[93]–a digression in the course of which he introduces and sets aside some alternative expositions[94]–he returns to the standard expositions for a closer look. At first he seems concerned with only minor technical details: 'As long as we are staying with that first exposition, we have to arrange the terms in accordance with what the earlier logicians taught.'[95] But in examining one of those details of word order, a reported disagreement among logicians over the relative locations of 'immediately' and 'not' in exponents involving both of them, Wyclif introduces a *sophisma* in which serious difficulties for the standard exposition begin to emerge. The *sophisma* is complicated and subtle, but in just the respects in which the Calculators' *sophismata* were complicated and subtle,[96] and Wyclif classifies it among 'familiar imaginary examples'.[97] In using it to make trouble for the standard exposition (and everything it represents), he is turning the Calculators' weapons against them. The case at issue in the *sophisma* involves an instant of transition in the progress of a moving sphere.[98] Wyclif believes that the details of the case justify his concluding that at the instant in question it must be said that the sphere *begins to cease* to be in contact with a designated point on the line it is traversing. 'At any rate,' he says, 'a man who correspondingly was alive and was destroyed would [at the corresponding instant] begin to die'[99]–i.e. would begin to cease to exist. And Wyclif generalizes this claim: if

[93] i. 192. 1-193. 9.

[94] The most interesting of the alternatives is the one introduced at i. 193. 3-9: 'si quicquam incipit esse, tunc nunc primo est vel nunc ultimo non est, et econtra; similiter, si desinit esse, tunc nunc ultimo est vel nunc primo non est' ('if anything begins to be, then now it initially is, or now it terminally is not (and vice versa); similarly, if it ceases to be, then now it terminally is, or now it initially is not'). Wyclif is disparaging of it here and points out a respect in which it is obviously unsatisfactory. But after developing his criticism of the standard exposition, he offers a carefully modified version of this exposition (i. 197. 8-25), concluding with the observation that 'once the foundation has been laid, this seems to me shorter and easier than to expound by means of those long exponents' ('illud videtur mihi brevius et facilius, supposito fundamento, quam exponere per istas* longas exponentes', i. 197. 25-7). For an even briefer and more obviously indivisibilist exposition offered by Wyclif after he has raised difficulties for the standard exposition, see n. 108 below.

[95] i. 193. 10-11: 'Tenendo ergo istam primam expositionem, ordinandi sunt termini secundum quod priores logici docuerunt.'

[96] This *sophisma* of Wyclif's should be compared with, e.g., Kilvington's Sophisma 16 (ed. and tr. in *ICAMT*, Appendix F, 333-40), to which it bears a strong family resemblance, at least as regards the case at issue.

[97] i. 193. 32-3: 'in imaginationibus communibus'.   [98] i. 193. 31-194. 22.

[99] i. 194. 19-20: 'Immo unus *homo* qui correspondenter viveret et corrumperetur inciperet mori.'

there are cases in which the standard exposition requires beginning to cease, there will also be cases in which it requires beginning to begin, and so on.[100] If he is right about the import of such cases, they have a devastating effect either on the doctrine of instantaneous transition, which seems guaranteed by logical considerations alone, or on the continuism underlying the standard exposition of beginning and ceasing. But I will not try to examine these issues on the basis of the problem of the moving sphere, because he introduces them more generally and more effectively in another *sophisma* immediately after-wards–the problem of the vacillating man.

Imagine that the present instant is the middle instant of this hour, both parts of which are divided into their proportional parts, with the smaller parts toward the instant that is present; and that (in keeping with some causal account [that might be] given) in each even-numbered part belonging to them Socrates is at rest, while in each odd-numbered part he moves with an oppo-site motion (as may be imagined).[101]

It will help to have a clearer picture of the situation before trying to understand the problem Wyclif means to extract from it (Fig. 1). M is 'the present instant, . . . the middle instant of this hour'. Both halves of the hour are 'divided into their proportional parts', the first propor-tional part of each half-hour being $\frac{1}{2}$ of it, the second $\frac{1}{4}$, and so on *ad infinitum* (the nth proportional part being $1/2^n$ of the interval divided into its proportional parts), 'with the smaller [proportional] parts to-ward the instant that is present'. In the parenthetical bits of this hypo-thesis Wyclif seems to be saying that one could tell a story that would explain what he wants to stipulate about Socrates, the vacillating man, but it would obviously have to be a very imaginative (and physically impossible) story.[102] So during the first quarter-hour, the first propor-tional part on the left of the time line, Socrates moves east at a rate, shall

[100] i. 194. 23-30. I do not understand everything in this passage. The word 'temporalis' in line 28 is particularly perplexing here; the scribe of Assisi MS 662 seems to have corrected it only partially or inexpertly into something that might be 'operalis'(?!).

[101] i. 194. 30-6: 'Unde imaginato quod instans praesens sit medium instans huius horae, cuius utraque pars dividatur in suas *partes* proportionales, minores versus hoc instans quod est praesens; et quod Sor in qualibet parte pari illarum–secundum datam causationem*–quiescat, et in qualibet parte impari moveatur motu opposito–secun-dum imaginationem.'

[102] On the use of imaginable though physically impossible cases in fourteenth-century natural philosophy, see, e.g., E. Grant's chapter 26, 'The Effect of the Con-demnation of 1277', 537-9 in *CHLMP*, and E. Sylla's chapter 27, 'The Oxford Calculators', esp. 557-63.

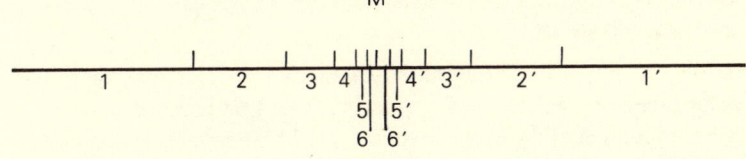

Figure 1

we say, of four miles per hour; during the second proportional part he is at rest; during the third he moves west at the same rate; during the fourth he is at rest, and so on. He covers one mile during the first, $\frac{1}{4}$ mile during the third, $\frac{1}{16}$ mile during the fifth, and so on. (For any odd-numbered proportional part n the mileage traversed during n will be $1/2^{n-1}$.) I think the stipulation that the motion in each odd-numbered interval is opposite to that in the preceding interval of motion is intended to make the infinitely many beginnings and ceasings around instant M more readily distinguishable in thought. And because around instant M there are shorter and shorter rests between shorter and shorter intervals of motion, in the specious present around M, the present instant, Socrates is in a state of vacillation so rapid as to look like a static blur. But the condition of instant M itself is as important to the problem as is Socrates's state at and around M. At first glance, M seems to have the same sort of limiting, dividing role as does the middle instant of the first half-hour, which divides the first proportional part from the second. *That* instant would ordinarily be understood as intrinsic either to the first (as its last instant) or to the second (as its first instant). But, as for M, since there cannot be a latest proportional part in the first half-hour or an earliest proportional part in the second half-hour, there cannot be any designatable proportional part to which M could be intrinsic; nor can there be any designatable pair of proportional parts that M could divide from each other. So M is forced into the status of a neutral instant, intrinsic to *neither* half-hour, extrinsic to *every* proportional part.

That is Wyclif's setting for the problem of the vacillating man, and here is the problem as he poses it:

Then at this instant [M] Socrates begins to move, and at this instant he begins to be at rest. And yet immediately after this [instant] he will begin to move, and the same holds regarding rest. Indeed, now he is not moving, and immediately after this he will not be moving, and immediately before this he was not moving; and yet he begins to move, and he ceases not moving—just as immediately before this he ceased not moving, and immediately after this he will cease not moving.[103]

So Wyclif poses the problem by extracting at least two paradoxes regarding Socrates's state at instant M. The first paradox consists in the conjunction of these two claims: (1) at M S begins to move, and (2) at M S begins to be at rest. The paradoxical character of this conjunction becomes clearer if we replace (1) and (2) with their standard expositions, as Wyclif could count on any fourteenth-century philosopher to do:

(1E) (a) At M S is not in motion, and (b) immediately after M S will be in motion.

(2E) (a) At M S is not at rest, and (b) immediately after M S will be at rest.

The opposition between (1Ea) and (2Ea), the first exponents, is merely apparent if motion and rest are not contradictory opposites for S and if M's status as a neutral instant is acceptable. Each of those conditions is problematic, but because the difficulties they involve are not especially relevant to Wyclif's purposes here, I will ignore them now.[104] The opposition between the second exponents, (1Eb) and (2Eb), is more to the point.

Whatever could be said in support of the possibility of S's being neither in motion nor at rest at a given time would do nothing to mitigate the absurdity of S's being both in motion and at rest at the same time, and so the opposition between (1Eb) and (2Eb) looks even sharper. But just that sort of difficulty had been resolved by the Oxford Calculator Richard Kilvington, whose *Sophismata* Wyclif seems to have known.[105] In his Sophisma 15 Kilvington rejects as invalid the form of argument that would be used to infer from (1Eb) and (2Eb) that at one and the same time S will be in motion and at rest. The ultimate basis of Kilvington's rejection of such inferences is the continuist view of time, which entails the impossibility of there being any instant immediately after another instant, so that 'immediately

[103] i. 194. 36-195. 2: 'Tunc* in hoc instanti incipit Sor moveri, et in hoc instanti incipit quiescere. Et tamen immediate post hoc incipiet moveri, et sic de quiescere. Immo nunc* non movetur, et immediate post hoc *non* movebitur, et immediate ante hoc non movebatur; et tamen incipit moveri, et desinit non moveri–sicut immediate ante hoc desiit non moveri, et immediate post *hoc* desinet non moveri.'

[104] On the neutral-instant analysis and some of its problems, see, e.g., Kretzmann (above, n. 89), esp. 114-16.

[105] See n. 86 above. My exposition of Kilvington here is derived more or less directly from my treatment of this material in Kretzmann (above, n. 15), *ICAMT*.

after M' can be correctly prefixed to two contrary descriptions of the same individual without entailing that there is some single instant at which both descriptions apply. On the continuist view of time, then, 'immediately after M' must be understood as picking out not an instant but an interval; but, as Kilvington shows in his Sophisma 16, the way that interval is picked out makes a difference to cases like that of the vacillating man. Kilvington's two analyses of temporal immediacy can be adapted to the problem of the vacillating man in this way: immediately after M S will be in motion (at rest) if and only if

> [*strong form*] there is a future interval extrinsically limited by M such that S will be in motion (at rest) at every instant of that interval

or

> [*weak form*] every future interval extrinsically limited by M is such that there is an instant of that interval at which S will be in motion (at rest).

The strong form of analysis may seem more natural as an interpretation of immediacy, but the weak form can accommodate all ordinary cases as well as such bizarre cases as the vacillating man, which cannot be accommodated by the strong form. Since every future interval extrinsically limted by M, no matter how brief it may be, includes infinitely many odd-numbered and even-numbered proportional parts, every future interval extrinsically limited by M is such that there is an instant of that interval at which S will be in motion *and* there is an instant of that interval at which S will be at rest. Therefore, the appearance of opposition between (1Eb) and (2Eb) can be dispelled on the basis of continuism employing Calculatorial techniques.

I am convinced, on textual and historical grounds, that moves of the sort I have just been making in order to resolve the first paradox in the problem of the vacillating man would have been entirely familiar to Wyclif and would have disconcerted him not at all. On the contrary, they strike me as moves he would have anticipated with relish, since they establish a context in which the second paradox can make its anti-continuist point more effectively. The second paradox arises because any interval immediately after M is characterized not only by S's being in motion and being at rest, but also by S's ceasing to rest and beginning to move, ceasing to move and beginning to rest. For Wyclif's purposes a single aspect of one of these transitions is enough, and we can concentrate on beginning to move.

The devastating effect Wyclif intends these circumstances to have on the standard exposition can be seen more plainly if his claim is expressed as (3) immediately after M S will begin to move. The paradox at issue in these circumstances emerges clearly only when (3) is expounded in the way I think Wyclif intended:

(3E) (a) Immediately after M S will be in motion, and
(b) Immediately after immediately after M S will be in motion.

(3Eb), the affirmative exponent that may seem to be required by the standard exposition, is incoherent. The phrase 'immediately after M' designates an open-ended interval, one that has a *terminus a quo* but no *terminus ad quem*. It is not hard to construct contexts that do provide a *terminus ad quem* for intervals immediately after some instant; for example, the *terminus ad quem* of the half-hour immediately after M is obviously the instant at which that half-hour ends, and there is nothing problematic about the designation 'immediately after the half-hour immediately after M'. But the interval at issue in the problem of the vacillating man is an interval that must be extrinsically limited by the open end of an open-ended interval immediately after M, and it is the unfulfillability of that requirement that guarantees the incoherence of (3Eb).

I think Wyclif displays dialectical skill as well as subtlety in not spelling out the expositions on which his argument depends, but as a consequence of that technique of his I cannot be sure I have provided the exposition he intended. One reason for thinking I have it right is that the incoherence Wyclif does expressly point to in this paradox might be recognized as the metaphysical side of the incoherence this exposition presents, and the way in which he points to it seems designed to bring out its embarrassing consequence for the continuists' treatment of instantaneous transition:

But neither beginning nor ceasing is continuous. Continuity of that sort would require that during a time immediately before the instant that is present and during a time immediately after the instant that is present there was and there will be part of a beginning or ceasing that occurs *now*.[106]

Wyclif thinks that the circumstances of the vacillating man–just the sort of circumstances the Calculators were particularly fond of–

[106] i. 195. 3-7: 'Et tamen nec est inceptio nec desitio continua, quia *oportet* ad talem continuationem quod per tempus immediatum ante instans quod est praesens et per tempus immediatum post instans quod est praesens fuit et erit pars* talis inceptionis vel desitionis quae sit modo.

require conceiving of beginning not as an instantaneous transition but as a successive state, and that is the absurdity to which he thinks he has reduced Calculatorial continuism. Before considering the use Wyclif makes of that result, I have to say that for all its ingenuity his attempted *reductio* fails. The exposition of (3) generates an incoherent exponent and thereby appears to embarrass continuism only because it treats the temporal designation 'immediately after M' in 'immediately after M S will begin to move' as if it corresponded precisely to the temporal designation 'now' in the present-tense paradigm 'now S begins to move'. But since for the continuist Calculators 'immediately after M' always designates an interval rather than an instant, it corresponds more nearly to some such expression as 'in the next half-hour'. And 'in the next half-hour S will begin to move' would be expounded as '*At some instant* in the next half-hour S will not be moving, and immediately after *that instant* S will be moving.' Now it might be thought, especially by Wyclif, that such a correction plays into the indivisibilist's hands another way, requiring the recognition of an instant immediately after another instant (which is surely a major aim of Wyclif's here[107]), but the Kilvingtonian weak analysis of 'immediately' evades that difficulty as well. So I think the Calculatorial version of the exposition of (3) would have to look like this:

(3E) (*a'*) Every future interval extrinsically limited by M is such that there is an instant of that interval at which S will not be in motion, and

(*b'*) immediately after at least one such instant S will be in motion.

When it is expounded in keeping with the Calculators' technical advances in the understanding of continuism, not even the second paradox of the vacillating man is an embarrassment to continuism or to the Calculators.

But that is certainly not the way Wyclif saw it, and so he might be excused for triumphantly introducing indivisibilism as the antidote to the problem of the vacillating man—not so much its solution as its prevention. In the passage immediately following the one last quoted he comes very close to doing so, but the note of triumph is oddly muted:

But those who claim that a continuum is composed of indivisibles—e.g., time composed of instants, a line composed of points, a surface composed of lines, a body composed of surfaces, a motion composed of *mutata esse*, and so on as

[107] See, e.g., i. 195. 8-29 (n. 109 below).

regards infinitely many other things under consideration–feel one way, while other people, who deny it, feel otherwise. For the members of the first group say that it is impossible that any entity begin or cease to be except in virtue of the introduction of the present [i.e. all sentences involving 'begin' or 'cease' are to be given uniform intrinsic-limit expositions].[108] And on this view two instants will be immediate to each other . . . And I am an adherent of this view. . . . Nevertheless, in connection with this subject matter I leave it to my students to support the side that seems more agreeable to them . . .[109]

9. *Wyclif's courage*

Some of the details of the explanation of Wyclif's guarded attitude toward the apparently vanquished continuism are to be found in the rest of this very interesting and difficult chapter, only a bit of which has been taken into account here. But I am convinced that the root of the explanation lies in his awareness that he does not have satisfactory solutions for all the difficulties besetting indivisibilism. And the reason he tells his students that they are free to choose between continuism and indivisibilism is, I think, that he knows he cannot give them a convincing, purely philosophical argument for and defence of indivisibilism. He is himself 'an adherent of this view', I think, because revealed truths (of which Genesis 1: 31 is the appropriate paradigm) when combined with his anti-continuist arguments tip the scales decisively on the indivisibilist side. But it is the logic of Scripture and not unaided reason that provides the decisive argument for Wyclif's indivisibilism.

[108] See, e.g., i. 197. 3-8: 'Unde ponendo continuum componi ex non quantis exponerem* ista verba altero istorum modorum. Si ens incipit ((incipit)) esse, tunc est effectus, et in instanti proximo praeterito non fuit, et econtra. Si vero desinit esse, tunc est effectus et in instanti proximo futuro non erit, et econtra.' (Double parentheses indicate a word omitted from the text on the basis of its omission from Assisi MS 662.) ('Thus in virtue of claiming that a continuum is composed of non-quanta I would expound these verbs in one or the other of the following ways. If an entity begins to be, then it has been caused, and at the last past instant it did not exist (and vice versa). On the other hand, if it ceases to be, then it has been caused and at the next future instant it will not exist (and vice versa).') Cf. iii. 38. 11-12: 'Sed do ultimum cuiuscumque corporis, superficiei, lineae, vel finiti, termino intrinseco.' ('But I offer a last element of any and every body, surface, line, or of anything finite, on the basis of an intrinsic limit.')

[109] i. 195. 8-15, 17, 28-29: 'Aliter tamen sentiunt qui ponunt continuum componi ex indivisibilibus–ut tempus ex instantibus, lineam ex punctis, superficiem ex lineis, ((et)) corpus ex superficiebus, motus ex mutatis* *esse*, et sic de aliis infinitis* sumptis–et aliter *alii* hoc negantes. Primi* enim dicunt* quod impossibile est aliquod ens incipere vel desinere esse nisi per positionem de praesenti. Et sic duo instantia erunt immediata; . . . Et isti opinioni* ego adhaereo. . . . In ista materia* tamen* relinquo iuvenibus partem suae apparentiae plus consonam sustinendam . . .'

Nevertheless, against all the odds, and very likely convinced from the outset that he would not succeed, he tried in the last two chapters of his *Tractatus de Logica* to establish indivisibilism on philosophical grounds. We have already seen some indications that he knew he was not succeeding,[110] and those acknowledgements of the weak spots in his position are among the most surprising and appealing features of his writings. He thought he saw that certain revealed truths entailed an unpopular, vulnerable philosophical position and he thought he saw through some of the glamour of the apparently victorious opposing position, and he resolutely took on the task of redressing the philosophical balance between the established continuism and the discredited indivisibilism. His efforts deserve sympathy as well as criticism, but they ought to earn him some honour as well–not so much for his displays of considerable subtlety and ingenuity along the way as for the philosophical spirit that drove him even when he was working in the service of a revealed truth, the spirit that animates the concluding paragraph of his most sustained attempt to establish indivisibilism:

Leaving the deeper investigation of all these matters to the subtle logicians and natural philosophers, I ask those who read through this chapter not to condemn or deride the things that have been said here in the manner of things that have been worked out as plausible–for I know that these things are rejected by many authorities, and that they demolish the Calculators' arguments [along with] many doctrines and many fanciful examples put forward by the moderns. But in any examination of truth it is reason that takes the lead, since authorities are drawn to agreement by reason, and not the other way around. And there is no doubt that it is reason that taught Aristotle, Plato, Parmenides, Democritus, or any other human being any bit of truth he may have discovered.[111]

---

[110] See, e.g., n. 78 above.

[111] iii. 132. 25-36: 'Sed de omnibus istis relinquens subtilibus logicis et naturalibus profundum scrutinium, rogo perlegentes illud capitulum non condemnare vel deridere haec dicta tamquam probabiliter opiniata. Scio enim quod multis auctoribus discreparant, et argumenta calculantium interimunt, multas opiniones et multas imaginationes modernorum. In omni namque veritatis examine praecellit ratio, cum auctores trahendi sunt ad concordantiam rationis iuvamine, non econtra. Nam non dubium quin ratio docuit Aristotelem, Platonem, Parmenidem et Democritum, vel quemcumque alium hominem quidquid invenerit veritatis.'

APPENDIX

Table of Contents of *Tractatus de Logica*

4

Wycliffism in Oxford 1381-1411

ANNE HUDSON

AT some point in the spring of 1381 John Wyclif was teaching his views on the Eucharist in the schools of the Austin friars, on the site in Oxford where now is situated the King's Arms public house. He was interrupted by a messenger who came to promulgate against him the conclusions of a committee of twelve under the chancellor William Barton, which had condemned the views on the Eucharist he was then propounding, and had forbidden the holding, teaching, or defending of such views in the schools or outside them in public. Wyclif later claimed that the vote on that committee had been divided against him by only seven to five. Characteristically at the time Wyclif, though confused, did not abandon his lecture and said that the condemnation would not change his mind.[1] Shortly afterwards he appealed against the sentence to the king. John of Gaunt apparently came to Oxford to try to persuade Wyclif that silence on the subject of the Eucharist would be prudent. His efforts were in vain, and by 10 May 1381 Wyclif had issued a formal statement of his views, not shifting his position at all.[2] Despite this, Wyclif withdrew from Oxford in the course of the second half of 1381.[3] Fortunately, however, enough material concerning the following year's events survive to enable us to see how major a scandal ensued upon this condemnation.

[1] For the narrative of this, as in disordered fashion of much of the ensuing events in Oxford, see *Fasciculi Zizaniorum* (henceforward *FZ*), ed. W. W. Shirley (Rolls Series, London, 1858), 104-14, 272-333, here 110-13. The material has been surveyed, though with different emphasis from mine here, by J. H. Dahmus, *The Prosecution of John Wyclyf* (New Haven, 1952), 89-128.

[2] *FZ*, 114, confirmed by Archbishop Sudbury's register, fo. 76ᵛ printed in D. Wilkins, *Concilia Magnae Britanniae et Hiberniae*, 4 vols. (London, 1737), iii. 171; Wyclif mentions Gaunt's visit obscurely in *Trialogus*, ed. G. Lechler (Oxford, 1869), 375; the formal statement is found in *FZ*, 115-32, and other manuscripts are listed by W. R. Thomson, *The Latin Writings of John Wyclyf* (Toronto, 1983), no. 39.

[3] The precise date is uncertain, but Wyclif is not recorded as having rented a room at Queen's College, as he had done in several previous years, for the academic year 1381-2. The latest evidence for Wyclif's presence in Oxford is the pledge note in which he, with four other masters, deposited a copy of the *Decretum*, now British Library MS Royal 10 E. ii, in an Oxford loan chest on 23 October 1381.

The chancellor William Barton was succeeded the following academic year by Robert Rygge of Exeter College. Rygge had been a member of Barton's committee, but from his subsequent actions must be assumed to have been one of those who had voted in favour of Wyclif.[4] During Lent 1382 Wyclif's chief disciple, Nicholas Hereford, preached in St Mary's church in Latin before all the clergy: he urged that men of private religion, by which he meant the monastic and fraternal orders, should not take a degree in the university on pain of apostasy, and that any member of these orders who had done so in the past should be considered an apostate.[5] Hereford's sermon apparently only publicized a view he had been known to hold for some time: a week before Lent that year the four orders of friars had written to Gaunt asking his protection against Hereford and others who had been slandering them in public.[6] Rygge the chancellor was apparently not present at Hereford's sermon, but the proctors who were, far from protesting at his outrageous statement, applauded.[7] News of Hereford's opinions was conveyed to Rygge by the Benedictine John Wells, another former member of Barton's committee, and by the Carmelite Peter Stokes. Rygge took no action against Hereford.[8] Stokes is an important figure in the ensuing events of 1382 in Oxford: at a later stage he was evidently under the instructions of Archbishop Courtenay of Canterbury to watch and record events in Oxford and to retail his information back to the archbishop in London. At what point contact between Stokes and Courtenay began is unclear, nor is it certain at whose initiative the surveillance began. What is clear is that Stokes, from Hereford's Lenten sermon onwards, was making a record of the events.[9]

---

[4] *FZ*, 113. For all the Oxford men mentioned here see A. B. Emden, *A Biographical Register of the University of Oxford to A.D. 1500*, 3 vols. (Oxford, 1957-9); Rygge is pp. 1616-17.

[5] *FZ*, 305.

[6] *FZ*, 292-5; note particularly 294, 'in illius vulgi publicis auribus incessanter proclamat et asserit'.

[7] *FZ*, 305, 'Et ipsi procuratores tunc praesentes erant, quando Nicolaus sic praedicavit, et ei applaudebant, nec contra eum processerunt modo caritativo nec juridico; non obstante quod tam plane praedicavit contra universitatis consuetudines et statuta et privilegia.'

[8] *FZ*, 305 and 113. For Wells see Emden, *Oxford*, 2008; he seems to have been the *canis niger de ordine Benedicti*, against whom Wyclif wrote in two sermons (Thomson (above, n. 2) nos. 205-6), and to which Wells replied, as recorded by *FZ*, 239-41.

[9] For Stokes see Emden, *Oxford*, 1783-4; he may be the *canis albus* mentioned by Wyclif (see Thomson nos. 205, 209, 216, though the case may be supported by the poem on the Council of London mentioned by Emden, but ignored by Thomson). It seems

Rygge showed his colours very plainly only a few weeks later by inviting Nicholas Hereford to give the Ascension Day sermon in St Frideswide's churchyard in Oxford, and by asking the younger disciple of Wyclif, Philip Repingdon, an Augustinian canon from St Mary's Leicester studying in Oxford, to give the Corpus Christi Day sermon in the same place. The invitation to Repingdon was particularly pointed, since the sermon was a prestigious event but at that time Repingdon had still not quite completed the exercises for his doctorate.[10] Ascension Day 1382 fell on 15 May. Peter Stokes commissioned a notary, one John Fykyes from the Rochester diocese, to authenticate an account of Hereford's sermon, and this account survives though in Latin.[11] The account confirms the evidence of the *Fasciculi Zizaniorum* that the sermon was delivered in English,[12] and explains that the congregation included Rygge and a considerable crowd of clerics, regular and secular, and of the laity. Hereford began by observing that, just as Christ's actions had effected more after his death than they had during his lifetime, so FitzRalph's attack against the friars was succeeding now more than in his own lifetime; Fitz-Ralph provocatively he called 'St Richard'.[13] In his ensuing prayer Hereford asked for supplications for the king, the queen, the queen mother, the duke of Lancaster and for all the temporal rulers of the realm, for spiritual leaders, for the chancellor, university, mayor, and city of Oxford–but pointedly not for the pope.[14] He then proceeded to his main argument, that all men seek temporal rather than spiritual goods, the laity notably through gluttony and lechery, the clergy preeminently through avarice and especially through the sale of spiritual benefits. He denounced first the corruptions of the canons and monks, who falsely acquire wealth and appropriate benefices, divert the intentions of the founders of their houses, proudly engage in secular business, turn to the law to increase their endowments, give none of their excessive wealth to the poor but, on the rare occasions when they dispense money, hand it to rich men and to lawyers. He then turned

likely that Stokes's record formed the basis for the documents concerning 1381-2 in *FZ*: *FZ* is certainly a Carmelite compilation. See J. Crompton, '*Fasciculi Zizaniorum*', *Journal of Ecclesiastical History* 12 (1961), 35-45, 155-66, especially here 156.

[10] *FZ*, 306 'etiam antequam fuit doctor'; Emden, *Oxford*, 913-15, 1565-7.

[11] Oxford MS Bodley 240, pp. 848-50.

[12] MS p. 848 *in vulgari*; *FZ*, 306.

[13] MS p. 848; cf. K. Walsh, *A Fourteenth-Century Scholar and Primate: Richard FitzRalph in Oxford, Avignon and Armagh* (Oxford, 1981), esp. 452-68.

[14] MS p. 848, 'Et in tota recomendacione non fecit mencionem de summo pontifice specialem.'

to the friars: they, he urged, also seek wealth only, begging from poor and rich alike for themselves and for their communities; but in truth to give money to a friar is to put an enemy between yourself and God.[15] Friars who are graduates claim to need even more money–but such are not masters of theology but masters of vanity, seeking honours in a secular university.[16] No good will come in England whilst such men are tolerated; the possessioners should be disinherited and the friars not allowed to beg. All present, clergy and laity, should work to this end. The possessioners own large hoards of money in secret; if the king seized their superfluous wealth, he would not need to tax the poor in the present fashion.[17] He ended with a rousing peroration:

But alas, and woe, that the king does not have any justiciars in his kingdom to carry out this task. Since, however, there are no officers specially appointed to this duty, it is necessary for you, faithful christian people, to take up the task and carry it through to its right conclusion. And I firmly believe that such an effort will succeed, because I know most certainly that the omnipotent God wishes it to do so.[18]

This open incitement to action came, it should be recalled, less than a year after the Peasants' Revolt. Two days later than Hereford's sermon, on 17 May, the Blackfriars Council assembled in London; four days later it condemned a list of twenty-four propositions taken from Wyclif's writings though at no point mentioning Wyclif by name.[19] Whether by then Courtenay had received Stokes's account of

[15] MS p. 849 'Nam tu, inquit, es fatuus qui das fratri vnum annuale stipendium ad orandum pro te apud Deum, quia tu facis inimicum Dei mediatorem inter te et illum; et ex hoc Deus aduersum te magis irascitur quam placatur.'

[16] MS pp. 849-50, '. . . ideo non sunt magistri theologie, set magistri vanitatis, falsi, praui, lurdici et loselli.'

[17] MS p. 850, 'Vnde, si rex et regnum vellet eis auferre possessiones et thesauros eorum superfluos ut deberet, tunc non operteret regem spoliare pauperem communitatem regni per talagia sicut solet.' The later Lollard views concerning the disendowment of the Church are discussed by M. Aston, '"Caim's Castles": Poverty, Politics and Disendowment', in *The Church, Politics and Patronage in the Fifteenth Century*, ed. R. B. Dobson (Gloucester, 1984), 45-81.

[18] MS p. 850, 'Sed heu! inquit, heu et ve! quod rex non habet aliquos iusticiarios in regno suo ad hanc iusticiam exequendam. Et ex quo non sunt alii iusticiarii ad hoc specialiter ex officio deputati, ideo oportet vos, o fideles christiani, manum apponere vt vos saltum hoc negocium ad finem debitum perducatis. Et tunc firmiter spero quod bene procedet, quia scio certissime quod ipse Deus omnipotens uult quod fiat.'

[19] *FZ*, 275-82, though the frame there given to the propositions is a letter of a week later; text also from Lambeth reg. Courtenay fos. 25^{r-v} in Wilkins (above, n. 2), 157-8, and in Henry Knighton, *Chronicon*, ed. J. R. Lumby, 2 vols. (Rolls Series, London, 1889-95), ii. 158-60, and Thomas Walsingham *Chronicon Angliae*, ed. E. M. Thompson (Rolls Series, London, 1874), 343-4 and *Historia Anglicana*, ed. H. T. Riley, 2 vols. (Rolls Series,

Ascension day events in Oxford is uncertain. But a week later he evidently had and was more accutely conscious of the troubles there; this is seen in a letter of 28 May which he sent to Peter Stokes in Oxford, recording the decisions of the Council and forbidding the teaching of the errors 'in the schools or outside them, publicly or secretly'.[20] Two days after this the archbishop sent a second letter, this time to Rygge, deploring the chancellor's favour towards Hereford, and requiring him to publish the condemnation of the twenty-four errors and to assist Stokes in all his efforts.[21] On the eve of Corpus Christi Day Stokes gave his letter to Rygge; evidently he learnt then to his surprise that Repingdon's sermon the following day was still to go ahead, and Stokes became the more anxious for the publication of the condemnation to forestall this.[22] But Rygge, far from assisting the course of archiepiscopal justice, accused Stokes of infringing the liberties and privileges of the university and apparently gathered a hundred armed men to prevent Stokes from publishing the condemnation, and informed the mayor of the city that he had done so.[23]

Repingdon's sermon on Corpus Christi Day, 5 June, appears to have repeated some of the provocative statements of Hereford's in urging the congregation to insurrection and to despoil churches. Unlike Hereford, he apparently mentioned Wyclif by name and asserted his own agreement with all of Wyclif's ideas; he then went on to speak of the Eucharist, though whether for an understanding of that sacrament in unequivocal Wycliffite terms is not entirely clear.[24] But,

London, 1863-4), ii. 58-9. The propositions are translated and examined by Dahmus (above, n. 2), 93-8; the precise date of the condemnation varies in the authorities, but seems likely to have been 21 May as the Courtenay register states.

[20] *FZ*, 275-82, note 277 'ne quis de cetero, cujuscunque status aut conditionis existat, haereses seu errores praedictos vel eorum aliquem teneat, doceat, praedicet, seu defendat in universitate Oxoniensi, in scholis vel extra, publice vel occulte . . .'

[21] *FZ*, 298-9.

[22] *FZ*, 300-1, a letter written by Stokes to Courtenay after the Corpus Christi Day sermon, explaining the actions he had taken.

[23] *FZ*, 299; Rygge allegedly dissimulated to Stokes 'dixit palam et publice quod voluit Petro [Stokes] praedicto assistere; sed quantum potuit sibi restitit, convocando adversus eum plures armatos circa centum, in loricis et gladiis, vel ad interficiendum, vel repellendum Petrum, si causam attentaret: immo et majorem vocavit ad partem suam sibi dicendo quod centum armatos haberet prompte contra Petrum Carmelitam.'

[24] Indications about Repingdon's attitude and sermon appear in *FZ*, 296-7 where Repingdon's agreement with Wyclif is said to have been limited by his observation that 'digitum ori suo imponere donec Deus illustraret corda cleri de sacramento altaris'; 299-300, 'excusans magistrum Johannem Wycclyff in omnibus sibi favens'; 307 where the sermon's theme appears, as would have been expected for the occasion, to have been the Eucharist. Walsingham (*Chron. Angl.* 345 and *Hist. Angl.* ii. 60) repeats the

since Stokes was too frightened to appear at Repingdon's sermon, we lack an account of the detailed kind that survives for Hereford's.[25] After the sermon the preacher, again accompanied by 'scholars and many lay persons', twenty of whom had swords ostentatiously concealed under their garments, went into St Frideswide's church and awaited Rygge in the porch; when Rygge arrived, he and Repingdon departed together laughing.[26]

The following day, 6 June, Stokes again confronted the chancellor. This time Rygge equivocated: if he could obtain the agreement of the university, he would publish the condemnation from the Blackfriars Council as Courtenay was insisting.[27] On 7 June Repingdon again publicly taught unacceptable ideas, *semper litigiose*.[28] On 10 June Stokes found the courage to determine against Repingdon in the schools, arguing that the pope and bishops had pre-eminence over temporal lords; but he observed twelve armed men in the schools, and thought that he would meet his death before he came down from the dais.[29] He was saved from further hazard in Oxford by a summons of recall to London from the archbishop; his relief is perceptible in the laconic account.[30] However, by the time he reached London he found that he had been overtaken by Rygge and Thomas Brightwell, originally like Rygge of Exeter College but by then at Merton.[31] The Blackfriars Council assembled again on 12 June, and at it Rygge and the proctors were charged with favouring Wyclif and his followers;[32] Rygge and Brightwell for their part sought pardon for their contempt in not publishing the letter of condemnation.[33] Courtenay then gave

information that Repingdon said concerning the Eucharist, 'Custodiam ori meo, donec Deus aliter illustraverit, sive instruxerit, corda cleri.' But the case of Courtenay against Rygge (*FZ*, 306-7) claimed that Repingdon had asserted in his sermon 'quod nunquam Wycclyff aliter determinavit vel docuit in materia de sacramento altaris quam tota ecclesia Dei tenet; et quod opinio sua de sacramento altaris est verissima'.

[25] The information about this sermon in *FZ* is, in at least one respect, suspect: in view of later events, it is highly improbable that Repingdon would, as there is asserted, have called Wyclif's followers 'Lollards' (see *FZ*, 300 'inter cetera dixit quod dominus dux Lancastriae multum afficiebatur, et defendere vellet omnes Lollardos').

[26] *FZ*, 300, 306-7.

[27] *FZ*, 301.

[28] *FZ*, 302.

[29] *FZ*, 302.

[30] *FZ*, 302-4; note 304 'excusando se quod non perfecit commissionem suam propter metum mortis. Et alia dixit quae oculariter vidit.'

[31] *FZ*, 304; Brightwell's career is described by Emden, *Oxford*, 266-7.

[32] *FZ*, 304-8 for the case against them, from which some of the preceding details can be gleaned.

[33] *FZ*, 308.

them two further mandates: the first required Rygge not to harm, impede, or molest those acting on Curtenay's behalf, and not to allow Wyclif, Hereford, Repingdon, John Aston, or Laurence Bedeman to teach or preach 'in the schools or outside them' until they had been cleared of error;[34] the second required Rygge to publish the condemned conclusions in St Mary's church in English and in Latin, and to enquire into those favouring such views and to bring the suspects to purgation or to abjuration.[35] Rygge in his own defence asserted that he did not dare to publish the condemnation 'for fear of death', to which Courtenay retorted that 'the university is the nurse of heresies'.[36] The following day a mandate was issued by the royal council insisting upon publication of the condemnation.[37] On Sunday 15 June Rygge eventually made public the views of the Blackfriars Council in Oxford. Reaction was violent: the seculars were angry with the religious, alleging that they wanted to destroy the university, whilst the religious went in fear of their lives. Hostilities continued in the following days, with the Cistercian Henry Crumpe being suspended from academic acts and accused of disturbing the peace by calling his colleagues who favoured the condemned conclusions 'Lollards'.[38]

At this point the centre of action shifted from Oxford to London, and hence strictly outside the scope of this paper. Briefly, the day before Rygge published the condemnations, Hereford and Repingdon appeared before the third session of the Blackfriars Council and refused to sign the required submission; they appeared again on 20 June with a reply in writing on the twenty-four condemned conclusions, a reply that was found insufficient and their answers to further questions evasive; they were condemned but sentence was postponed until 1 July. In the middle of July two letters came from the king to Rygge, the first requiring him to search out favourers of Wyclif, Hereford, Repingdon, or John Aston and to investigate any book or tract, edition, or compilation by Wyclif or Hereford, the second requiring the restoration of Crumpe, and that Crumpe, Stokes, and a second Carmelite Stephen Patrington should not be molested. In

[34] *FZ*, 310, Lambeth reg. Courtenay fos. 26ᵛ-27ʳ printed in Wilkins (above, n. 2), iii. 159-60.

[35] *FZ*, 309-11; Lambeth reg. Courtenay fos. 27ʳ⁻ᵛ in Wilkins iii. 160.

[36] *FZ*, 311, 'dixit quod non fuit ausus metu mortis eas publicare: et tunc inquit archiepiscopus, "Ergo universitas est fautrix haeresum, quae non permittit veritates catholicas publicari."'

[37] *FZ*, 311.

[38] *FZ*, 311-12; Crumpe's insult is the first recorded instance of the use of the word for the followers of Wyclif.

the autumn of 1382 Repingdon renounced his Wycliffism, but
Hereford, refusing this course of action, fled from imprisonment in
England to appeal in person to the pope.[39]

I have spent so long on this story because it does, I think, illustrate a
number of important aspects of early Wycliffism in Oxford. In the first
place, it reveals two strands of significance that preceded Wyclif's own
teaching but became intricately mixed up in the fortunes of that teaching on his original home ground. The first is the tension between the
seculars and the religious, obviously not limited to the university, but
fostered by certain longstanding jealousies there.[40] In his early days
Wyclif had to a large extent avoided this problem: he had from a very
early time castigated the monastic orders, but had remained on good
terms with many of the friars. This was changed by his teaching on
the Eucharist, probably from the end of 1379, so that by 1382 he and his
followers were using all the polemic of the earlier Parisian strife
between seculars and mendicants, and of FitzRalph's revival of that
feud.[41] Wycliffism became largely, though not absolutely exclusively,
the preserve of the seculars. The second and perhaps the more
important strand is the university's concern for its own privileges and
independence. But, though at a later stage it seems fairly plain that
this was a major motive behind actions that appear to indicate sympathy for Wyclif or for Wycliffite notions, it is insufficient to account
for the events of May and June 1382 in Oxford. Leaving aside the pre-
varications of Rygge, it seems fairly plain that the views put forward by
Hereford and Repingdon commanded at that time considerable
support within the university. The story brings out also that their bid
for support was already not limited to that university audience: the fact
that the two sermons were in English, and that both appealed to the
laity to initiate action against the temporalities of the Church, and that
Courtenay insisted that Rygge publish the condemnation in English
as well as Latin, and that he should not allow the teaching of them
'within the schools or outside them' reveals that the Wycliffites were

[39] For these events see *FZ*, 289-90, 315-33; Repingdon's submission is in Courtenay's
register fo. 34ᵛ (Wilkins iii. 172); for Hereford's flight see Emden, *Oxford*, 914. Omitted
here also is the session of convocation in Oxford in November 1382 (Lambeth reg.
Courtenay fos. 33-5, partly printed in Wilkins iii. 172-3).

[40] For the situation in early Oxford see most recently M. Sheehan 'The Religious
Orders', in *The History of the University of Oxford*, i. *The Early Oxford Schools*, ed. J. I. Catto
(Oxford, 1984), 193-221.

[41] A. Gwynn, *The English Austin Friars in the Time of Wyclif* (Oxford, 1940), 211-79; M.-
M. Dufeil, *Guillaume de Saint-Amour et la polémique universitaire Parisienne 1250-1259*
(Paris, 1972), and Walsh, *FitzRalph*, 349-451.

seen as forging an unholy alliance between town and gown.[42] Both Hereford and Repingdon had begun to take Wycliffism beyond Oxford before their exploits on Ascension and Corpus Christi Days. Earlier in the spring of 1382 Hereford with three other Oxford missionaries had been preaching errors about the sacraments and making 'illicit conventicles' in the diocese of Winchester, and particularly in the parish of Odiham; Repingdon, quite apart from his probable responsibility for the hotbed of Wycliffism that existed in Leicester by 1381, had preached Wyclif's views on the Eucharist in Brackley by 1382.[43]

Before returning to this alliance of the academic and the world of the laity, it is worth looking briefly at a few other Oxford Wycliffites and their activities. The first is a man by name William James, fellow of Merton by 1376, and certainly resident there for many academic years between then and 1411.[44] He first revealed his colours in the events of 1382, when he was described as being very intimate with Rygge. One of the accusations by Courtenay in June 1382 was that Rygge had made no move to stop James from arguing the case for Wyclif's view of the Eucharist in the congregation house—Rygge had merely commented to James that ' "Now you are speaking like a philosopher" ', a remark that Courtenay took to indicate sympathy for James's opinions.[45] James does not appear to have been a very important figure in 1382, since nothing more is heard of him then. But he was a most persistent Wycliffite. In December 1394 orders were given for his arrest and for that of his fellow Mertonian John Gamylgay. In the case of Gamylgay the order was renewed in May 1395, when his name was linked with those of Richard Whelpyngton and Thomas Lucas, both also of Merton; these three were imprisoned in Beaumaris Castle on Anglesey that month.[46] Two months later James was pursued and

---

[42] Note particularly Rygge's involvement of the mayor in actions against Stokes prior to Repingdon's sermon (*FZ*, 299). Since this paper was prepared, Margaret Aston has considered the significance of the use of English by the Wycliffites at this early stage; her article 'Wyclif and the Vernacular' will be published in *Studies in Church History, Subsidia* 5 (1986).

[43] For the first see *Wykeham's Register*, ed. T. F. Kirby, 2 vols. (Hampshire Record Society, 1896–9), ii. 337–8; for the second J. Crompton, 'Leicestershire Lollards', *Transactions of the Leicestershire Archaeological and Historical Society*, 44 (1968–9), 11–44, and *FZ*, 296–7.

[44] Emden, *Oxford*, 1012–13.

[45] *FZ*, 307.

[46] *Calendar of Patent Rolls 1391–6* (London, 1905), 586, 591, *Calendar of Close Rolls 1392–6* (London, 1925), 344; for the three see Emden, *Oxford*, 741, 2032, and 1170 respectively.

apparently caught in Bristol.[47] Unfortunately the case against them does not survive, but James was evidently also imprisoned. Gamylgay is not known to have returned to Oxford, but the other three eventually resumed an academic career: Whelpyngton was resident at Merton in 1401-2, Lucas became junior proctor in 1403-4, and James was welcomed back to Merton on Michaelmas term 1399 on release from prison with a party from the subwarden.[48] James and Lucas, at least, were not deterred from Wycliffism by their experiences. Lucas was said in 1416 to have been 'counselling and abetting all the works of Oldcastle both in opinions of Lollardy and all his other evil deeds'. By that time he was probably no longer in Oxford, but he was certainly still present in 1408 when he borrowed twelve volumes from Merton library.[49] James appeared before Archbishop Chichele in March 1420, having been imprisoned for many years on suspicion of heresy; he abjured, but was confined to the manor and college of Maidstone, where he was allowed to practice medicine and see visitors, but not to leave without permission.[50] Netter tells an undated story about James's beliefs: present at a celebration of the Eucharist, James had turned to a beautiful woman standing by him and had observed that he could see God more clearly in her face than in the host.[51]

At about the same time as James and his fellow Mertonians ran into trouble, a fourth Mertonian, Robert Lychlade was expelled from the university at the order of Richard II because of his long teaching there and elsewhere of 'nefarious opinions and conclusions and detestable allegations repugnant to the catholic faith'.[52] Like James and Lucas, Lychlade was also restored, again in 1399 and this time at the order of Henry IV; it was then said that Lychlade's expulsion had been ordered 'without reasonable cause'.[53] But Lychlade's subsequent

---

[47] *CPR 1391-6*, 651.   [48] Merton College Archives no. 3724.

[49] PRO KB 27/624 Rex m. 9r; he was also accused of disseminating the view that Richard II was still alive, and of plotting Henry V's destruction (see M. Aston, 'Lollardy and Sedition, 1381-1431', *Past and Present* 17 (1960), 21). F. M. Powicke, *The Medieval Books of Merton College* (Oxford, 1931), 73, 188.

[50] *The Register of Henry Chichele, Archbishop of Canterbury 1414-1443*, ed. E. F. Jacob, 4 vols. (Oxford, 1938-47), iv. 203-4. James's punishment suggests that he may by that trial have been a relapse but have been spared by the archbishop from execution because of his age; similar leniency was shown by Chichele to other persistent offenders such as Robert Hoke and Thomas Drayton at a slightly later time (*Chichele Reg.* iii. 105-12 of 1425 for both).

[51] Thomas Netter of Walden, *Doctrinale Antiquitatum Fidei Ecclesiae Catholicae : ..*, ed. B. Blanciotti, 3 vols. (Venice, 1757-9, reprinted Farnborough, 1967), ii. 177-8.

[52] *CPR 1392-6*, 434, dated 18 July 1395; Emden, *Oxford*, 1184.

[53] *CPR 1399-1401* (London, 1903), 84; similarly for James p. 75.

activities make him look rather less innocent: in 1401 he became rector of Kemerton, a small village in Gloucestershire, a benefice in the gift of Sir William Beauchamp, a man whom McFarlane associated with the Lollard knights.[54] In 1402 he acted as an executor of the will of Dame Anne Latimer, widow of the most notorious of the Lollard knights, Sir Thomas Latimer; intriguingly, the overseers of that will were Sir Lewis Clifford, a third Lollard knight, Robert Hoke, the longstanding Lollard incumbent of Latimer's home church at Braybrooke, Northamptonshire, and Philip Repingdon, by then the orthodox abbot of Leicester.[55]

If Lychlade provides a link between the first generation of Oxford Wycliffites, represented by Repingdon, he also offers a link with what might be described as the third generation in the figure of Peter Payne. Apart from Lychlade's activity as executor, he also entertained the two Czech visitors, Mikuláš Faulfiš and Jiří Kněhnic, at Kemerton where they copied Wyclif's *De Ecclesia*. The two had also visited Braybrooke, and there transcribed the *De Dominio Divino*. But before their 'Lollard tour', in the course of which they collected a chip from Wyclif's tomb at Lutterworth, they had been in Oxford, probably copying and certainly correcting Wyclif's *De Veritate Sacre Scripture*. Their scribal activity can be traced from the notes in their manuscript, now Vienna Österreichische Nationalbibliothek 1294.[56] It is entirely possible that the relatively long stay that they made in England indicates that they were engaged in procuring more texts by Wyclif and his followers, but these are no longer extant even if their descendants may be. Perhaps their most interesting acquisition, however, was a testimonial concerning Wyclif which they obtained in Oxford through the helpful offices of Peter Payne of St Edmund Hall.[57] On 5 October 1406 was issued under the seal of the Congregation of Regents a letter which praised Wyclif as without equal in logic, philosophy, theology, morals, and speculation in the university, stated that he had written,

---

[54] See K. B. McFarlane, *Lancastrian Kings and Lollard Knights* (Oxford, 1972), 166, 214-15 and further A. Hudson, 'The Debate on Biblical Translation, Oxford 1401', *English Historical Review* 90 (1975), 12-13.

[55] McFarlane, *Lollard Knights*, 214 n. 1; McFarlane, strangely, does not seem to have spotted the identity of Lychlade.

[56] See R. L. Poole's comments in his edition of *De dominio Divino* (London, 1890), ix-xii.

[57] Emden, *Oxford*, 1441-3 and, in more detail, *An Oxford Hall in Medieval Times* (Oxford, rev. edn. 1968), 133-54. Payne's career, with particular reference to its second part in Bohemia, has been studied by W. R. Cook, 'Peter Payne, Theologian and Diplomat of the Hussite Revolution' (Cornell Ph.D. thesis, 1971).

responded, preached, and determined according to the truth of Holy
Scripture and audaciously claimed that he had never been convicted
of heresy. Thomas Gascoigne later alleged that Payne had 'stolen the
common seal of the university' for this testimonial, but his charge
should be regarded with scepticism; Gascoigne's statement that the
letter had said that 'Oxford and all England, save the false mendicant
friars, hold the same beliefs as they do in Prague' is not confirmed by
the surviving copies of the letter.[58]

Though Payne's claims about Wyclif are blatantly mendacious, and
were designed for an audience far away that would be in no position to
ascertain its or his credentials, it would, I think, be rash to dismiss the
episode as simply the exploit of an individual Lollard swashbuckler.
The documents which Salter collected together in his edition of parts
of *Snappe's Formulary* reveal the difficulties that Archbishop Arundel
met in imposing the terms of his Constitutions on the university after
1407, in persuading the university to produce a detailed list of Wyclif's
heresies from the numerous volumes of his works which scholars were
called upon to scrutinize between 1409 and 1411, and in allowing his
visitation in 1411. Salter's assertion that 'Oxford historians seem to
lose their balance when the name of Wickliff is mentioned' is a salu-
tary warning; but it seems questionable whether the evidence he
produces is so clearly innocent of any whiff of Lollardy on the university's side as he would claim. In time Arundel succeeded in ousting
Wycliffism from Oxford, but the battle was not over in 1407.[59]

So far the material has come from sources that deal in specific
evidence, chronicles, documents, notes, or statements in manuscripts;
all of it is fairly familiar, and for the period between 1382 and 1411
could be amplified from similar sources. I want now, however, to
change gear and to consider some rather different evidence, evidence
whose interpretation is much less certain, that of the content, sources,
and methods of various Wycliffite texts. In my paper 'Wyclif and the
English Language' (below) I summarize the processes involved in the
Wycliffite translation of the Bible, and also outline the methods of the

[58] The only surviving medieval copy of the letter is in Prague University Library MS
XI. E. 3, fo. 1^r, but it must have been available in the sixteenth century in England when
it was copied into British Library MS Cotton Faustina C. vii, fo. 125^r from which it was
transcribed by Wilkins iii. 302. Thomas Gascoigne, *Loci e Libro Veritatum*, ed. J. E.
Thorold Rogers (Oxford, 1881), 20.

[59] *Snappe's Formulary and other Records*, ed. H. E. Salter (Oxford Historical Society
80, 1924), 90-215, comment on 98. I hope to examine the evidence here in more detail
in my forthcoming book, *The Premature Reformation: Studies in Wycliffite History and Lollard Texts*.

Glossed Gospels, the exhaustive and entirely derivative commentaries that were made to accompany, in at least three forms, a slightly revised form of the early Gospel translations.[60] It is worth looking here at the range of material used for these latter. All the commentaries except the first seem to have started from Aquinas's *Catena Aurea*, and from it all drew their extracts from the Greek fathers, Basil, Gregory Nazianzen and Gregory Nyssenus, Theophilus, Athanasius, and others. But for the Latin fathers much more work was undertaken, work which expanded Aquinas's efforts in places to three or four times the length of the *Catena Aurea*. For that expansion the minimum texts necessary must have been a complete or almost complete set of Augustine, Gregory, Jerome, Ambrose, Bede, and Bernard plus the whole of pseudo-Chrysostom on Matthew, Peter Comestor's *Historia Scholastica*, the *Glossa Ordinaria*, Grosseteste's sermons, *dicta*, and commentaries on the pseudo-Dionysian canon, FitzRalph's *De Questionibus Armenorum* and *De Pauperie Salvatoris*, and a complete set of canon law. This is the minimum requirement. It is, of course, likely that some secondary means of access, by indexes or concordances, was utilized to facilitate the labour; but even if these provided shortcuts, they cannot have obviated the need for the complete texts to have been accessible to the compilers of the *Glossed Gospels*.[61] Those compilers also noted where, for instance, Bede derived his exegesis from Jerome or Augustine, or where Jerome and Augustine differed in their understanding of a passage; whether these observations derived from existing notes, perhaps in the form of marginal indications, or whether they resulted from the compilers' own labours does not affect the implication that to those compilers such things mattered and were worth recording; just as they thought it useful to indicate the precise location of each extract, and whether it did or did not derive through Aquinas.[62]

On the Wycliffite handbooks, the *Floretum*, and its abbreviated and rearranged relation the *Rosarium Theologie*, more investigation

[60] See pp. 91-4, 98-9 below.

[61] For the debt of medieval writers to such aids see particularly R. H. and M. A. Rouse, *Preachers, Florilegia and Sermons: Studies on the 'Manipulus Florum' of Thomas of Ireland* (Toronto, 1979). Despite the kind help of Richard and Mary Rouse, I have been unable so far to locate any single *accessus* which would have afforded substantial help to the compilers.

[62] See, for instance, the long commentary on Luke in Cambridge University Library MS Kk. 2. 9, fos. 10, 25ᵛ, 148ᵛ, 181ᵛ etc.

has been done.[63] For these almost all the sources of the *Glossed Gospels* were required, plus a comprehensive biblical concordance and a very efficient index to canon law, a fairly complete collection of Anselm, the two Victorines Richard and Hugh, the Lombard, a text of the *Compendium Theologie Veritatis* (cited here as Aquinas), and of Higden's *Polychronicon*. To some of these numerous texts it has been shown that indexes provided the vital key; equally some quotations from even major authors, and more from other authors less frequently cited, came from secondary compilations, notably the *Manipulus Florum*. Again, however, detailed references, in academic form down to the subdividing letters of a chapter or sermon, were thought worth preserving.

This is not the place to continue this enquiry through many more Wycliffite texts, but two are worth adding since authorities are used in them not for their own sake, but to bolster much more contentious positions. The reading matter utilized by the author of the *Thirty-Seven Conclusions of the Lollards* was rather more limited: he apparently was very skilled in and almost certainly had an index to canon law, referred to the commentators Innocent IV and Hostiensis, and seems to have been aware that some passages in Gratian were attributed to the wrong father. But he also used numerous works of Augustine, Gregory, and Jerome, Chrysostom false and genuine, the Lombard's *Sentences*, Peraldus's *Summa de Viciis*, four sermons by Grosseteste, and FitzRalph's Armenian questions. References are given in close detail, down to the *paraf* of long chapters in canon law.[64] A text of later origin is the *Lanterne of Liȝt*, composed between the publication of Arundel's Constitutions in 1407 and 1415 when it was used as evidence in the trial of the London heretic John Claydon.[65] The authorities used are by now familiar, though Odo of Cheriton appears here for the first time; notable also is the range of texts by Bernard that are used. But, since the author of the *Lanterne* seems certainly to have plundered the

---

[63] Especially useful in this regard is the work of Christina von Nolcken, *The Middle English Translation of the 'Rosarium Theologie'* (Heidelberg Middle English Texts x, 1979), esp. 21-9 and 'Some Alphabetical Compendia and how Preachers used them in Fourteenth-Century England', *Viator* 12 (1981), 271-88; see also A. Hudson, 'A Lollard Compilation and the Dissemination of Wycliffite Thought', *Journal of Theological Studies* NS 23 (1972), 65-81 esp. 71-5.

[64] The text was edited under the title *Remonstrance against Romish Corruptions*, by J. Forshall (London, 1851); for the decree *put on Austyn* see p. 21 (cf. *Corpus Iuris Canonici*, ed. E. Friedberg, 2 vols. (Leipzig, 1879-81), i. 1242 where the chapter is said to be a false attribution); some more details are given in the next chapter.

[65] *The Lanterne of Liȝt*, ed. L. M. Swinburn (EETS OS 151, 1917); see further p. 101.

Floretum, if not other secondary sources, his range may not be significant. What is remarkable is that he quoted all his sources, biblical, patristic, canonistic, in full in Latin before he translated them into English.

— The conclusion from this evidence seems inescapable: the most probable place where all of these texts were composed was in Oxford. Only there, it would seem, could there have been the resources of books and the supply of scholars capable of putting these texts together. Certainly, the authorities cited are by no means unusual; it was part of the Lollard propaganda programme that they should not be, since only by means of authorities of unequivocal weight could the enemy be defeated on his own ground. But it should be remembered that from the start the possibility of using monastic libraries was out of the question: Wyclif had been hostile to the monks and to their founding ideals, let alone to their contemporary defects, from the earliest years of his career in theology. After 1382 the friars' libraries must have been out of bounds; fraternal opposition to Wyclif's views on the Eucharist was compouded by their reactions to his ensuing venom against their orders. Though it is true that isolated friars can be found expressing sympathy with some part of the Wycliffite programme after 1382,[66] it must be recalled that almost all of the texts that I have been discussing are the product of collaborative work not of isolated endeavour–a single eccentric friar could not have originated biblical translation, *Glossed Gospels*, *Floretum*, and so on. That it is not a false deduction to argue that monastic and fraternal libraries were resources not open to the Wycliffites is shown by overt statements to this effect in a number of Lollard texts, amongst them the Prologue to the *Floretum*. The authors complain that the religious, and particularly the friars, have shut up all the valuable books in their houses; there they decay unused, beyond the reach of seculars since the religious will neither lend nor even sell them. The tone of these complaints is shrill, even for Lollardy, and perhaps implies that the complete restriction was a new phenomenon, that the formerly open access had within recent memory barred to the writers.[67] But, if monastic and fraternal libraries had been closed, the possible libraries that could have supplied the wealth of books needed were few in

[66] See, for instance, Peter Pateshull OFA or William Russell OFM, on whom see Emden, *Oxford*, 1434, 1611-12.

[67] These complaints, and a Franciscan answer to them, are now studied by R. H. and M. A. Rouse, 'The Franciscans and Books: Lollard Accusations and the Franciscan Response', to appear in *Studies in Church History*, Subsidia 5 (1986).

number; this is especially so when the availability for a number of collaborators is added as a requirement.

Before all the stray Wycliffite sheep are rounded up and herded into a pen marked 'Oxford', it is fair to acknowledge the existence of one recalcitrant animal. This is the *Opus Arduum*, the commentary on the Apocalypse now only surviving in continental manuscripts but certainly written in England between Christmas 1389 and Easter 1390.[68] There is no major discrepancy about the authorities used: the writer seems to have been less familiar with canon law than many Wycliffites, but he knew his fathers as well as any and quotes or refers to a wider range of historians of the early Church than most–Josephus, Eusebius, Orosius, and Peter of Poitiers make frequent appearances. His brand of polemical exegesis makes it reasonable that not all authorities are specified with complete precision, but quotation is frequently too close and reference often too exact for it to be credible that he was working from memory. The *Opus Arduum* is an individual, not a collaborative work; but the individual, judging by his erudition and by his inclusion of material that must have originated as a determination, was evidently of university training. The problem is none of this. It is that the writer states more than once, in comments embedded in the text that are unlikely to have been added after its completion, that he was writing in prison, a penalty imposed by the bishops because of his sympathy for and advocacy of heretical or specifically Lollard views. If, it may be objected, this Lollard, declaredly not in the university, could gain access to such a library, then the argument that acquaintance with a wide range of books in Wycliffite texts must imply an Oxford origin falls to the ground. This is a valid objection, and it is hard to know finally how to answer it. But I think it is not unreasonable to say that the problem is that of the *Opus Arduum*, and not of the rest of these works; on any count, the *Opus Arduum* needs a lot of explanation.[69] Walter Brut in 1391 was required in prison to set down in writing his Lollard views; he did so at great length in Latin, and revealed a daunting familiarity with the Bible–but not with other writers, who are not quoted once.[70] It is reasonable to suppose that he may have been allowed a copy of the Vulgate in

[68] More details about this text appear in my paper 'A Neglected Wycliffite Text', *Journal of Ecclesiastical History* 29 (1978), 257-79.

[69] Not least of the difficulties concerning the text is that of how the text was given circulation; there is no indication within it that its author's imprisonment had come to an end.

[70] See *Registrum Johannis Trefnant*, ed. W. W. Capes (London, 1916), 278-365.

prison, though his ability to make such excellent use of it has unavoidable implications for his education prior to his imprisonment. But under any normal understanding of imprisonment for heresy (a different matter from the comfortable circumstances of men such as Charles of Orleans or Malory), the *Opus Arduum* author's apparent access to a good library is hard to explain. The more so when that author brashly asserts that his enforced leisure has given him the opportunity to study and to write against his episcopal gaolers! It is tempting to wonder whether that incarceration perhaps could have been detention in the Franciscan house at Oxford.

Looking back at the brief review of a few of the pieces of evidence concerning Wycliffites in Oxford between 1382 and 1411, it will be recalled that most of the stories involve more than the individual dissenter. In the spring and early summer of 1382 there is good evidence that Rygge was not wholly evasive when he claimed to Courtenay that there was a high risk of disorder if the mandate against Wyclif and his followers were to be published without the consent of congregation. The Mertonians James, Gamylgay, Whelpyngton, and Lucas in the 1390s were plainly a group, and significantly three of them returned to Oxford after their detention. Peter Payne may have acted illegally to secure the testimonial in favour of Wyclif in 1406, but unless the whole affair was a forgery (which even the hostile Thomas Gascoigne did not claim), he must in the long vacation congregation have had some supporters. The extent of that support is indicated by Arundel's insistence on imposing on Oxford the requirement that each head of house or academical hall should monthly enquire into the theological views of their undergraduates, a blatant infringement of the university's privileges which the events of following years revealed the university to have deeply resented.[71] The irony of the situation, of course, is that it was upon the Lollards William Taylor and later Peter Payne that the duty of investigation fell in St Edmund Hall.

Thus I would suggest that the recent view that Lollardy was a spent force in Oxford by the time Wyclif himself died on 31 December 1384 needs substantial reconsideration.[72] As well as the isolated sympathizer or the marginal note that suggests a continuing interest in the university in issues that Wyclif had raised, as well as the evidence from the opposition side afforded by such things as Woodford's *Quattuor*

---

[71] For the terms of the provision see Wilkins (above, n. 2), 318-19.

[72] For this view see particularly McFarlane, *Wycliffe*, especially 186-8; also G. Leff, *Heresy in the Later Middle Ages*, 2 vols. (Manchester, 1967), ii. 560-70.

Determinationes against Wyclif and his followers and delivered in
Oxford in 1389-90,[73] there were, I would argue, more substantial
groups of men in Oxford who were seriously engaged in the enterprise, often a collaborative one, of producing the basic tools by which
Wyclif's ideas could be propagated. The propagation was to be outside the university, as well as, or indeed rather than, inside it. It was
from Oxford, it appears, that in the 1390s the mayor of Northampton,
John Fox, obtained the preachers of the frequent sermons that were
given in his short-lived Lollard republic.[74] What the citizens made of
the erudition is not revealed, though it is worth remembering that one
of the few cases where both audience and text are known is that of
John Claydon and the *Lanterne of Liȝt*, Claydon illiterate, the *Lanterne*
with extensive quotations as well as detailed argument; but Claydon
paid for the copying of the book, had it read to him repeatedly, and
carried through his conviction of its value to the lengths of dying at the
stake rather than renounce its teaching.[75] But the question of audience
is another problem; here the relevant material concerns authors. That
these authors were incorrigibly academic is, I think, clear. And it is no
accident that one of the most striking proposals of the Lollard Disendowment Bill, presented most probably in 1410, three years after
Arundel's Constitutions, was that the king should use some of the
proceeds confiscated from the established Church to finance the
establishment of fifteen new universities.[76] Far from Wycliffism being
dead in Oxford by 1400, let alone by 1384, university men in the first
decade of the new century aimed to export their unorthodoxy to a new
generation of academic institutions. One of Oxford's earliest lost
causes?

[73] This type of evidence is too bulky to be included here, but equally points to continuing favour in Oxford for the views there refuted. The *Quattuor Determinationes* have
not been printed; they are preserved in various manuscripts, including MS Bodley 703,
fos. 69ʳ-101ᵛ.

[74] See the documents printed by E. Powell and G. M. Trevelyan, *The Peasants' Rising
and the Lollards* (London, 1899), 45-50 at 48.

[75] For the case see p. 101 below.

[76] The text is printed in A. Hudson, *Selections from English Wycliffite Writings* (Cambridge, 1978), no. 27, here lines 66-70. The background to the Bill is described briefly in
the notes, pp. 203-7, and more fully by Aston, '"Caim's Castles"' (above, n. 17), 49-57
and notes; it would not be unfair to describe the eventual brief text as the report of a
lengthy research project, whose interim stages are visible in various other Lollard texts.

5

Wyclif and the English Language

ANNE HUDSON

In the introduction to the first paper in the series of Balliol lectures, the Master spoke of two things concerning Wyclif which were familiar to him as a schoolboy: that Wyclif caused the Peasants' Revolt of 1381 and that Wyclif translated the Bible, both 'facts' that many would now feel to be discredited. It is not within the brief for this paper to re-instate Wyclif as a cause, if not the cause, of the Peasants' Revolt, though I believe that a credible case can be made for this now unfashionable view.[1] The second question is more nearly relevant to the topic in hand. Whether Wyclif himself actually translated a word of the surviving versions of the English Bible made in the late fourteenth century is dubious; but again a credible case can be made to suggest that, if not the immediate cause, Wyclif was the ultimate effective cause of the versions that have come to be known as the Wycliffite Bible.[2] This name is open to two interpretations: translation done by Wyclif, or translation done by Wyclif's followers, the Wycliffites, and under his inspiration. Here it is worth looking again at the nature and origins of that translation and considering the related questions of when and why Wyclif and his disciples turned to the vernacular as their main, if not their only, medium of communication.[3]

Before turning to the main topic of the paper, one piece of terminology should be explained. It has been fashionable to distinguish the

[1] For the basic material on the Revolt see R. B. Dobson, ed., *The Peasants' Revolt of 1381* (London, 2nd edn. 1983), and for modern interpretations of it, with references to the further criticism, R. H. Hilton and T. H. Aston, eds., *The English Rising of 1381* (Cambridge, 1984).

[2] The standard edition of both versions is that edited by J. Forshall and F. Madden, *The Holy Bible . . . made from the Latin Vulgate by John Wycliffe and his Followers*, 4 vols. (Oxford, 1850). For a useful survey of the versions and of the prolific work of various critics see H. Hargreaves, 'The Wycliffite Versions', in *The Cambridge History of the Bible* ii, ed. G. W. H. Lampe (Cambridge, 1969), 387-415.

[3] Six months after this paper was delivered, Margaret Aston gave a paper entitled 'Wyclif and the Vernacular' to a conference in Oxford; her paper will be published in *Studies in Church History*, *Subsidia* 5 (1986). The material in this necessarily overlaps with that here, but as the paper is not yet available in print I have not provided cross references.

names Wycliffite and Lollard, to use the former for the academic
disciples of Wyclif, a group which in the view of those who make the
distinction had largely disappeared by about 1390, and to use Lollard
to name the much larger and much more amorphous group of
religious dissenters persecuted by the episcopal and later the secular
authorities from 1382 until the 1530s. The latter group of heretics was
predominantly artisan, educated if at all in English alone, knowing
little of Wyclif himself and, according to such critics, showing only the
most distant reminiscences of his ideas. According to this view,
Wyclif's influence was short-lived; Lollardy owed much more to
economic forces than to the schoolman, as Wyclif is perceived.[4] There
is not space here to set out all the arguments against this view. Significant evidence that the distinction is inappropriate is provided by the
fact that the first use of the term *Lollardi* to describe the heretics was
by Henry Crumpe in Oxford in 1382; Crumpe used the word to apply
to those of his academic colleagues who favoured Wyclif, and for his
abuse was suspended from academic activities by the chancellor.[5]
Some forty years later the Carmelite Thomas Netter, writing his
enormous *Doctrinale Antiquitatum Fidei Ecclesiae Catholicae*, spoke of
Wyclif as the *inventor* or *patronus prophani ordinis... et tota plenarie religio
Lollardina*, calls him *Wicleffus Lollardus* and uses *Wiclevistae-Lollardi* as
a composite term and the two elements as synonymous alternatives;[6]
the whole argument of his work is based on the supposition that in
confuting Wyclif, Netter was removing the basis of Lollardy. To the
implications of Netter's work I will return later. But these two pieces
of evidence may serve as justification for the use here of the terms
Lollard and Wycliffite as synonyms.

Consideration of the topic of Wyclif and the English language may
conveniently start from the question of the evidence for Wyclif's use
of and interest in, the vernacular. John Bale in the mid-sixteenth century was convinced that Wyclif wrote prolifically in English as well as
Latin; W. W. Shirley in the mid-nineteenth century provided a catalogue of Wyclif's writings, its first half in Latin, its second in English.[7]

---

[4] The most influential proponent of this view was K. B. McFarlane in his book *John
Wycliffe and the Beginnings of English Nonconformity* (London, 1952), though his later, posthumously published book *Lancastrian Kings and Lollard Knights* (Oxford, 1972) suggests
that he might by his death have wished to modify his earlier opinions.

[5] *Fasciculi Zizaniorum*, ed. W. W. Shirley (Rolls Series, London, 1858), 311-12.

[6] Ed. B. Blanciotti, 3 vols. (Venice, 1757-9), i. 801, 72, 11.

[7] John Bale, *Illustrium Maioris Britanniae scriptorum ... summarium* (Ipswich, 1548),
fos. 154ᵛ-158ʳ and *Scriptorum Illustrium maioris Brytannie... Catalogus*, 2 vols. (Basle, 1557-
9), i. 450-6; W. W. Shirley, *A Catalogue of the Original Works of John Wyclif* (Oxford, 1865).

Prominent amongst Bale's account is the translation of the Bible, the first complete rendering of Scripture into English. Bale does not detail the evidence for the assertion of Wyclif's responsibility, but it is not negligible. The first statement is the often quoted lament by the chronicler Henry Knighton.[8] Admitting that Wyclif in philosophy was considered supreme and that he was without peer in the exercises of the schools, Knighton continues,

This master John Wyclif translated the gospel, which Christ had entrusted to clerks and to the doctors of this church so that they might minister it conveniently to the laity and to meaner people according to the needs of the time and the requirement of the listeners in their hunger of mind; he translated it from Latin into the English, not the angelic, idiom [*in Anglicam linguam non angelicam*], so that by this means that which was formerly familiar to learned clerks and to those of good understanding has become common and open to the laity, and even to those women who know how to read. As a result the pearls of the gospel are scattered and spread before swine, and that which had been precious to religious and to lay persons has become a matter of sport to ordinary people of both.

Knighton placed his outraged comment under the year 1382, a dating that is only approximate, where it serves as an introduction to his account of the Lollard movement. Knighton's statements about matters Wycliffite, however, should not lightly be dismissed: Leicester was one of the earliest centres of Lollardy, and a fellow canon at his Augustinian house in Leicester (indeed the abbot by 1394, the approximate date of Knighton's writing) was Philip Repingdon, one of Wyclif's most prominent Oxford disciples up to the autumn of 1382.[9] In many ways Knighton's observations are, despite their exaggerated rhetoric, extraordinarily acute.

Yet this allegation of Wyclif's responsibility for the biblical translation finds strangely few echoes. John Hus in Bohemia in the early years of the fifteenth century knew that *per Anglicos dicitur* that Wyclif had translated the whole Bible into English,[10] but despite Hus's words few of Wyclif's countrymen, friend or foe, repeat Knighton's charge. When the legitimacy of biblical translation was debated in Oxford in

---

[8] *Chronicon*, ed. J. R. Lumby, 2 vols. (Rolls Series, London, 1889-95), ii. 151-2.

[9] For the authorship and date of the *Chronicon* see V. H. Galbraith, 'The Chronicle of Henry Knighton', in *Fritz Saxl . . . A Volume of Memorial Essays*, ed. D. J. Gordon (London, 1957), 136-48; for Repingdon, A. B. Emden, *A Biographical Register of the University of Oxford to A.D. 1500*, 3 vols. (Oxford, 1957-9), 1565-7.

[10] *Contra Iohannem Stokes*, in *Polemica*, ed. J. Ersil (Prague, 1966), 61-2; the text can be dated 1411.

1401, neither side in the argument mentioned Wyclif's name, though it is clear that the issue had arisen in connection with the vernacular versions of Scripture made at the end of the fourteenth century and by then becoming well distributed.[11] Archbishop Arundel's Constitutions of 1407, which were devised specifically to meet the Lollard threat to theological and ecclesiastical order, do not specify any one individual as responsible for the origination of the translations mentioned.[12] The Constitutions forbade the making of new biblical versions, and the ownership or reading of existing versions made in the time of John Wyclif or later; but, though this would seem to have been the easiest way to damn the English translation, neither Wyclif nor his followers are overtly stated to have produced it. After the Constitutions had been issued ownership of vernacular Scriptures became one of the most important ways in which Lollards were detected by the authorities.[13] But despite this, and despite the firm tenacity with which Lollards clung to their right to read the Bible in English, few claims are made about the specific origins of it. There is the isolated reference to 'oure translacioun',[14] but otherwise a dispassionate distance—distance which extends to the virtual absence of quotations from the versions in Lollard writings, whose authors apparently preferred to make their own new renderings.

Before considering the Wycliffite Bible in more detail, it is worth looking at the evidence for Wyclif's own involvement in any other vernacular writing. It is quite clear that Wyclif used the native language to propagate his own views, even if the only certain record of those views surviving now are in Latin. The chroniclers are agreed that Wyclif preached in London, that he gained the enthusiasm of the Londoners at his sermons, and that he did not conceal his unorthodox views when he taught outside the schools.[15] Though this testimony

[11] For this episode see my paper 'The Debate on Bible Translation, Oxford 1401', *English Historical Review* 90 (1975), 1-18.

[12] The Constitutions are printed by D. Wilkins ed., *Concilia Magnae Britanniae et Hiberniae*, 4 vols. (London, 1737), iii. 314-19. Arundel's letter of 1412 to Pope John XXIII (Wilkins iii. 350) does mention that Wyclif had 'novae ad suae malitiae complementum scripturarum in linguam maternam translationis practica adinventa'.

[13] Some details about this are outlined in my paper 'Lollardy: the English Heresy?', *Studies in Church History* 18 (1982), 261-83.

[14] *Remonstrance against Romish Corruptions* (more commonly known as *Thirty-Seven Conclusions of the Lollards*), ed. J. Forshall (London, 1851), 19.

[15] See *Eulogium Historiarum*, ed. F. S. Haydon, 3 vols. (Rolls Series, London, 1858-63), iii. 348; Thomas Walsingham *Historia Anglicana*, ed. H. T. Riley, 2 vols. (Rolls Series, London, 1863-4), i. 363; *Chronicon Angliae*, ed. E. M. Thompson (Rolls Series, London, 1874), 116-17, 189.

may owe something to hindsight, it is unlikely to be entirely un-reliable. Walsingham's account of Wyclif's sermons is dated 1377, and since the chronicler specifies that in them Wyclif condemned the monastic orders but 'supported the mendicant orders, praising their poverty' it is unlikely that his chronology can be badly wrong, because from 1381 Wyclif turned against the friars, calling them, because of their opposition to his Eucharistic views, the limbs and tail of Antichrist.[16] The enthusiasm roused by Wyclif amongst the Londoners must have been engendered by vernacular eloquence, despite the fact that the whole of his surviving output of sermons is in Latin.[17] Very occasionally Wyclif speaks of having set out his views on a topic in Latin and also in English: thus in the *Trialogus*, written during his final years at Lutterworth, he comments in the course of a diatribe against the mendicancy of the friars, 'feci autem contra hoc in vulgari multiplices rationes'.[18] There are also a few manuscript claims for English texts to be by Wyclif. Knighton includes two vernacular confessions on the Eucharist which he states to be Wyclif's; though the second is expressed as a group statement of faith, the first is more difficult to dismiss.[19] One manuscript of the long Wycliffite cycle of English sermons attributes two groups of them to the *Doctor Evangelicus*, Wyclif's Latin byname; one other manuscript has a tract connected with this cycle enigmatically ascribed to *M.J.*, an abbreviation which can be expanded to *Magister Johannes*, with Wyclif suppressed in prudence, but which is capable of many other interpretations.[20] Netter refers several times to Wyclif's statements *in barbarizatione cujusdam Evangelii*, quoting then in Latin extracts from these same vernacular sermons.[21] Equally there are a few shorter Lollard texts which in a single manuscript are ascribed by name to Wyclif; the texts themselves certainly purvey ideas that are characteristic of the heretic.[22]

[16] For Wyclif's relations with the fraternal orders see A. Gwynn, *The English Austin Friars in the Time of Wyclif* (London, 1940), 225-79.

[17] The *Sermones* were edited by J. Loserth, 4 vols. (London, 1887-90). The first three volumes contain sermons that were put together, if not originally composed, after Wyclif retired to Lutterworth late in 1381; in the fourth volume are to be found the *Sermones Quadraginta*, which originated earlier, and some of which are likely to have been preached in London. For these see W. Mallard, 'Dating the *Sermones Quadraginta* of John Wyclif', *Medievalia et Humanistica* 17 (1966), 86-105.

[18] *Trialogus cum Supplemento Trialogi*, ed. G. Lechler (Oxford, 1869), 342/10.

[19] Knighton (above, n. 8), ii. 157-8, 161-2.

[20] *English Wycliffite Sermons* i, ed. A. Hudson (Oxford, 1983), 58, 77.

[21] *Doctrinale* i. 118, 701, 739, 802, 803, 874, ii. 515, iii. 411.

[22] See *English Wycliffite Sermons* i. 76, British Library MS Harley 2385, fos. 3^r, 5^r, 5^v.

It is not clear that any of these attributions has any force. The shorter texts have no more of Wyclif's ideas than other works where no manuscript links with the heresiarch are found, and they survive in other copies which are anonymous. Netter's attribution, like Knighton's of the Bible translation, may well owe its origin not to firm information lost to us but to a desire to discredit the work in question as speedily and unambiguously as possible. More interesting than precise attribution, or than the effort to see Wyclif's individual influence on the vernacular language, is the evidence that Wyclif's ideas inspired others to turn to the medium of English and to use that language to express notions of a complexity unattempted in the vernacular at least since the time of Alfred's translation of Boethius. To some extent, of course, Wycliffite interest in English was shared by other writers of the time, by Gower and the poet of *Sir Gawain and the Green Knight*, not to mention the more dubious ground of Chaucer and Langland where connections with Wycliffite thought are more arguably in question. But, as Wyclif and his followers were well aware, the purposes for which they wished to use the vernacular were more audacious, not to say dangerous: they were attacking the whole edifice of clerical domination in theology, in ecclesiastical theory, indeed in academic speculation generally. Wycliffism in more than one way spelt the end of scholasticism.

Wyclif's own attitude towards the technical problems of this assault was amazingly nonchalant. Language, he asserted, was a *habitus*; whatever the language, whether Hebrew, Greek, Latin, or English, the same gospel message should, and could be delivered.[23] What precisely he meant by *habitus* is not explained, but the context in which the word is applied to language would suggest a sense of 'clothing' as much as 'condition'—almost an 'accident' as opposed to the 'substance' of the gospel message. Wyclif explained, albeit tendentiously, why his opponents did not use English and had no wish to: the four sects of Antichrist, Caesarean clergy including the pope, monks, canons, and friars, did not wish to allow the ordinary people to discern the full gospel message, lest in discerning it they should also perceive the discrepancy between the way of life which Christ and the apostles had taught and the way of life practised by themselves.[24] But, though

[23] *De Contrarietate Duorum Dominorum*, in *Polemical Works*, ed. R. Buddensieg, 2 vols. (London, 1883), ii. 700/29. Note also 'Lingua enim tam in via quam in patria a sentencia et lege Domini est remota, cum in penam peccato superbie edificancium turrim Babel est divisio lingwarum a Deo et per dyabolum introducta.'

[24] For example, *De Nova Prevaricantia Mandatorum*, in *Polemical Works* i. 126/14; *De*

Wyclif in his later writings spoke of the need for disabusing the laity by revealing Christ's gospel directly to them in the vernacular, he seems to have ignored, or been unaware of, the enormous difficulties of the undertaking. To a considerable extent this was due to the insufficiency of his understanding of language, a failure in which during the medieval period he was far from unique. During the Oxford debate on translation in 1401 Richard Ullerston, an orthodox proponent of the notion, showed a more perceptive awareness: he mentioned the fact that whilst interpretation is possible without translation, translation conversely cannot proceed without interpretation.[25] Despite this realization, however, the implications were not fully observed, and Ullerston like Wyclif finally seems to have regarded English as straightforwardly equatable with Latin.

Nevertheless, indirectly Wyclif's desire for the use of the vernacular and his assurance of its complete sufficiency for the gospel message led to the discovery by some of his followers of a much more sophisticated view of language. The fullest evidence for this is to be found in the so-called 'General Prologue', written at the end of the processes of Bible translation and revision probably in the 1390s.[26] The final chapter of the Prologue makes clear the ambitious scope of the enterprise; the writer there speaks of 'diverse fellows and helpers' in the work and distinguishes four stages in it. The first was the effort to establish a reliable Latin text, because, as the author rightly observes, there was wide divergency of readings between different copies of the Vulgate and especially between recent copies of it. This first stage was helped by the second, the examination of the Bible text against the *Glossa Ordinaria* and the commentaries of the fathers and of more recent schoolmen, especially Nicholas of Lyra. This comparison revealed the inadequacy of the contemporary Vulgates, since the comments of writers such as Jerome or Augustine showed them to have had wording in their bibles that do not survive in fourteenth-century copies; it is, the Wycliffite observed, more likely that the wording available to Jerome or Augustine was correct. Equally, the fathers could help the translators to understand the force of obscure passages within Scripture. Lyra's commentaries often explained the

---

Quattuor Sectis Novellis, *Polemical Works* i. 255/19; *Opus Evangelicum*, ed. J. Loserth, 2 vols. (London, 1895-6), ii. 115/4.

[25] Ullerston's text is preserved in Vienna Österreichische Nationalbibliothek 4133, fos. 195^r-207^v; here fos. 196^r-7^v; for the text see the paper cited above n. 11.

[26] Forshall and Madden (above, n. 2), i. 1-60.

implications of Hebrew readings in the Old Testament obscure in the
Vulgate Latin; some of these were noted in marginal comments found
in some copies of the Wycliffite Bible.[27] The General Prologue
remarks upon the particular problems in the Psalter where, as is
correctly observed, the liturgical text used in the contemporary
Church was not the final translation of Jerome, but an earlier, less reliable version. As modern critics have noted, efforts to correct the Latin
by whatever means were inadequate; many places remain where the
translators were using a corrupt version.[28] This should surprise us less
than that the effort was made at all and that some understanding of the
means available for improvement was reached. The third stage in the
work was a further scrutiny of the Latin text, to elucidate textual difficulties, particularly those of syntax and vocabulary. Finally came the
actual translation and its correction.

All of the stages claimed in the General Prologue are traceable to
some extent in surviving versions of the Wycliffite Bible and its
associated texts. The enterprise was enormous; indeed, its very magnitude reveals the futility of attempting to attribute the whole to a
single person, whether Wyclif or another. In the light of later efforts at
translation, one omission is striking: the failure to mention any comparison with earlier vernacular versions. But this was because of the
absence of any useful models for any but a very few of the biblical
books. There exist medieval English versions of the Psalms, of the
gospels, and of parts of the epistles, some of which might have been
available; but many of these were paraphrases rather than strict translations, and for the bulk of the Old Testament no earlier model could
have been found.[29] Apart from the magnitude of the enterprise, the
other thing to emerge from the General Prologue is the scholarship
that went into it, an attitude of academic enquiry that necessitated
access to a multitude of books.

The author of the General Prologue summarized the final stage of
the collaborative enterprise briefly in his review of its progress–
translation and correction. But the reality of both parts must have
been much more arduous, and later in the chapter he describes some
of the individual problems encountered. From this description, and
from the earliest stages traceable in manuscripts such as MS Bodley

[27] For example, the marginal material recorded in Forshall and Madden iii. 1-241.
[28] See Hargreaves (above, n. 2), 412-13 and the same author's paper, 'The Latin Text
of Purvey's Psalter', *Medium Aevum* 24 (1955), 73-90.
[29] Middle English versions are surveyed by L. Muir in *A Manual of the Writings in
Middle English 1050-1500* ii, ed. J. Burke Severs (Hamden, Conn., 1970), 381-409, 534-52.

959, it is clear that the first rendering, one that has come to be known as the Early Version, had aimed to reproduce as exactly as possible Latin idiom and vocabulary in English. So constructions such as various absolute uses of the participles or the resumptive use of the relative pronoun were transferred into English, even though they were alien to that language; many words were crudely anglicized and certain adverbs and connectives frequently used in the Vulgate, such as *autem* or *vero*, were invariably translated in the same fashion every time they occurred. These features, together with an attempt to retain the word order of the Vulgate even when this led to obscurity or even incomprehensibility in the relatively uninflected native language, make the Early Version difficult to follow.[30] The unsatisfactory nature of the version was evidently perceived by the translators, and the General Prologue mentions some of the changes that it was decided should be made: constructions unfamiliar in English were to be replaced by more normal ones, even when this meant considerable expansion in wording; English word order was to be followed, vocabulary was to be that of current contemporary usage as far as possible; recurrent Latin adverbs or connectives were to be replaced by a variety of English substitutes. Again the few sentences of the Prologue disguise an immensely laborious process, a process which must have required a return to the Vulgate text and its commentators since differences of meaning could be made by such substitutions. Because the main alteration was the departure from a rule-of-thumb set of equivalences to variable renderings, the overall sense of the passage was vital to any change. Yet these changes that produced the so-called Later Version were carried through with remarkable regularity: it is hard to discern any discrepancy between one part of the Bible and another in idiom, and indeed between one manuscript of that version and another, numerous though these copies are.

The writer of the General Prologue gives a number of examples of the changes made in revision. From these it emerges that the involvement with the problems of translation had revealed much both generally about the nature of language and more particularly about the peculiarities of English. In crude terms what the translators had come

[30] The Prologue writer's own example (Forshall and Madden (above, n. 2) i. 57) of the last is the rendering of 'Dominum formidabunt adversarij ejus' (1 Sam. 2: 10) as 'the Lord hise aduersaries shulen drede'; in fact this is already an improvement upon the actual Early version translation 'The Lord shulen drede the aduersaries of hym', where only the ending of the auxiliary verb (an ending that would not have been preserved by many fifteenth-century scribes) shows the correct sense.

to observe was that language could not so easily be dismissed as mere *habitus*, as Wyclif had done. They had perceived that two languages are never mirror images of each other, but that what one leaves vague another insists upon specifying, that the range of association carried by a word in one language may differ from those contained in its most obvious rendering in another, that the possibilities for emphasis available in an inflected language by use of word order are hardly transferable into a language that depends upon word order to convey basic meaning. If the Prologue gives insight into the developing theories of the translators, the Later Version itself provides proof of the skill with which they used their insights. The Version is entirely idiomatic, uses Latinate vocabulary only for those words of peculiarly biblical nature that have remained limited tó scriptural occurrence, but keeps as faithfully to the original text as it is possible for a translation to be.

The translation is also entirely uncontroversial, entirely lacking in any Wycliffite slant or polemical twisting.[31] Why then was Arundel so adamant about banning it? Why did Lyndwood's gloss to Arundel's Constitution go even further and imply that any translation, even of short passages of Scripture quoted within an independent frame, was covered by the prohibition?[32] Events of the later fifteenth century make it clear that the Constitution was not merely a pious or, as Lollards saw it, an impious hope: its terms were used to persecute many Lollards and indeed were interpreted so widely that possession of any English work, even of the *Canterbury Tales*, might be used as evidence of heresy.[33] Use or defence of vernacular Scriptures had evidently become the most obvious social mark of the Wycliffite heresy, and was seen as the key to all the other errors of its adherents.

If Wycliffism became in the minds of opponents such as Arundel and Netter a heresy peculiarly associated with the use of the vernacular, it is the more remarkable that Wyclif himself should have refrained from using it in his writings. At what date did his followers realize the importance of English? And at what point did they abandon the use of Latin? Earlier critics of the Lollard movement would hardly have understood these questions, since they assumed that Lollard use

[31] In all the hostility to the Wycliffite Scripture there never ensued any debate upon the rendering of individual words such as marked the appearance of Tyndale's New Testament.

[32] W. Lyndwood, *Provinciale* (Oxford, 1679), 286 where it is indicated that translation of biblical passages quoted in the fathers is illicit, along with the use in works of English origin of any scriptural text.

[33] For this example see Lincoln register Chedworth fo. 62ᵛ, a case in 1464.

of the vernacular was the unavoidable result of the heretics' ignorance of Latin, that no conscious choice was therefore available. The summary above of the processes involved in the translation of the Bible should make it clear that dismissal of the topic along those lines is unconvincing. The answer to the first question is to be found if anywhere back in Wyclif's lifetime. Though the three sets of sermons which Wyclif put together at Lutterworth, described by him as *sermones rudes ad populum*, are all in Latin,[34] his Oxford followers Philip Repingdon and Nicholas Hereford preached in the vernacular to appreciative congregations of secular as well as clerical persons in May and June 1382 in St Frideswide's churchyard in Oxford.[35] Repingdon's sermon was on Corpus Christi day, and he apparently used the occasion to praise Wyclif and his teaching.[36] Of Hereford's earlier Ascension Day sermon there is a fuller notarial account made on the instructions of Archbishop Courtenay.[37] After deploring the extent of clerical wealth in England, the litigious quarrels of the clergy that endowment fostered and the increasing preoccupation of the Church with wealth, Hereford went on to urge that the possessioners should be disinherited, the friars not allowed to beg, and that the king should confiscate temporalities and so satisfy his need for taxes. Although the sermons were given at the invitation of Robert Rygge, chancellor of the university,[38] they were an evident bid for popular support. Hereford's sermon concluded with an appeal to the laity to take action against the Church's temporalities if the king hesitated and there is some evidence that Repingdon repeated this appeal.[39] Hereford certainly, and Repingdon probably, used English for his inflammatory discourse. When these two and a third Oxford disciple, John Aston, were called to London to the Blackfriars' Council to answer for their opinions to the archbishop and his subordinates, all three again provocatively used the vernacular. Courtenay in the course of questions to Aston about his views on the Eucharist demanded that Aston should use Latin, because of the presence of lay persons–to whom his opinions would presumably cause scandal. Aston impertinently prevaricated, distributing the subsequent explanation of his views in leaflet form though the streets and squares of London in English.[40] Repingdon and Hereford similarly appealed

---

[34] *Sermones*, i. Preface.   [35] Of these events a fuller account is given in chapter 4.
[36] *FZ*, 296-7.   [37] MS Bodley 240, pp. 848-50.
[38] *FZ*, 306.   [39] MS Bodley 240, p. 850; *FZ*, 299.
[40] *FZ*, 329-33, Lambeth reg. Courtenay fo. 29ʳ⁻ᵛ in Wilkins (above, n. 12), iii. 163-4.

against the sentence of Courtenay against them, nailing their objections to it on schedules to the doors of St Mary's and St Paul's in London.[41] The eventual recantation of both Hereford and Repingdon, a betrayal that was particularly hasty in the case of the latter, has, I would suggest, obscured the importance of both to the subsequent Wycliffite movement. Hereford in particular was perceptibly more radical than his master: his call for disendowment was more extreme than anything that Wyclif himself expressed; his incitement of the laity to revolutionary action, coming less than a year after the Peasants' Revolt, stands in striking contrast to Wyclif's guarded comments on that event; his use of English was consciously an acknowledgement that Wyclif's ideas could not be confined within Latin-speaking academia if they were to be put into practice.

Though this makes it clear that Wyclif's academic disciples had realized well before Wyclif's own death the necessity of using English, it is equally plain that a complete switch to the vernacular took a good deal longer. Many of the earliest datable Wycliffite texts are still in Latin, even though some of them were declaredly intended for the benefit of those far from the university. The long commentary on the Apocalypse, known from its first words as the *Opus Arduum*, was composed in Latin between Christmas 1389 and Easter 1390 whilst the author was imprisoned by the bishops on charges of adherence to Lollardy.[42] The text itself reflects academic methods of discussion and shows familiarity with a wide body of texts; its author's declared support for vernacular translations and his glee at the replacement of confiscated English sermons by others *ipse multo forciores* did not lead him to compose his own tract for the times in the native language.[43] Nor is there any trace of an English translation of it or of debt to the text in later Lollard works; its legacy, as its preservation, was entirely in Hussite circles.[44]

More overtly directed towards the propagation of Wycliffite doctrines is the *Floretum*, an alphabetical set of *distinctiones*, using biblical, patristic, and canonistic sources along with Wyclif's own writings, on a number of theological, ecclesiastical, and moral topics.[45] The prologue to this vast compilation explains its purpose:

---

[41] *FZ*, 318-28, Knighton (above, n. 8), ii. 170-1 and MS Bodley 647, fo. 70[r].

[42] For this text and Hereford's possible authorship of it see my paper 'A Neglected Wycliffite Text', *Journal of Ecclesiastical History* 29 (1978), 257-79.

[43] Brno University Library MS Mk 28, fos. 136[r], 161[v], 166[v], 174[v].

[44] A fragment of a Czech version of the text survives: see B. Ryba, 'Strahovské Zjevenie, Český husitský výklad na Apokalypsu . . .', *Strahovská knihovna* 1 (1966), 7-29.

[*See opposite page for n. 45*]

to provide poor preachers, who lack money and also lack access to books because the friars and monks have shut up all the necessary volumes in their own libraries, with a single tool to aid their preaching of the gospel. Yet interestingly the language used is still Latin, the date of composition some time between 1384 and 1396. The method of the work is again entirely academic: references to authorities are given in full detail, of book, chapter, and alphabetical division within chapter, or for canon law in traditional form with division, section, and the *incipit* of the chapter. The surviving eight English manuscripts of the *Floretum* are all in Latin; so are all but one of the fifteen copies of the abbreviated form of the text known as the *Rosarium*. Significantly, a vernacular translation of this abbreviation survives in a single copy, testimony to the realization that times for the Lollard preacher were changing.

The third extensive Latin Lollard work is a long set of sermons identified by Christina von Nolcken and now known to have survived in six manuscripts.[46] The date of these sermons is unfortunately far from clear, though the absence of specific mention of execution for heresy suggests a date before 1401. Again, as with the *Opus Arduum*, the writer's advocacy of vernacular Scriptures and his outrage that Antichrist, and particularly the false friars, should deplore the laity's interest in the Bible and their desire for teaching in their own language, did not lead him to the apparently logical conclusion, the composition of his own sermons in English.[47] This writer seems to have shared Wyclif's optimistic outlook on language: he observed, 'Although idioms are various, nonetheless the articles of faith and the truths of the gospel remain the same everywhere even if language is changed. Therefore the gospel can be written and spoken in Latin and in Greek, in French, in English, and in every spoken language.'[48] One might guess that this preacher, despite his enthusiasm for vernacular Scriptures, had probably not participated in the actual work of translation, or he would hardly have dismissed the problems so cursorily.

[45] For the text and its abbreviated form see A. Hudson, 'A Lollard Compilation and the Dissemination of Wycliffite Thought', *Journal of Theological Studies* NS 23 (1972), 65-81; 'A Lollard Compilation in England and Bohemia', *Journal of Theological Studies* NS 25 (1974), 129-40; C. von Nolcken, *The Middle English Translation of the 'Rosarium Theologie'* (Heidelberg Middle English Texts x, 1979).

[46] Her paper, entitled 'An Unremarked Group of Wycliffite Sermons in Latin', is published in *Modern Philology* 83, 233-49. The most complete form of the sermons known is that in Bodleian Library MS Laud Misc. 200.

[47] MS Laud Misc. 200, fos. 19^v-20^r, 24^v-25^r, 32^v, 41^v, 66^r-67^v, 92^{r-v}, 134^v.

[48] MS Laud Misc. 200, fo. 201.

In 1391 Walter Brut was brought before Bishop Trefnant of Hereford, accused of heresy.[49] Brut was a layman, such is specified repeatedly, but he was, albeit called at one point *laycus agricola*, also clearly *laicus literatus*. Brut stated that he had been required to write his answer to the charges brought against him in Latin; this task he performed, as the episcopal register shows, with complete competence and at great length.[50] So erudite were his answers felt to be that lengthy refutations were prepared for them by the orthodox side, again in Latin.[51] The first edict against Wyclif and his followers that specifically mentions writings in English seems to be in 1388.[52] So three years before Brut's trial, the significance of the vernacular was beginning to be perceived by the authorities. But it is, I think, important to remember two points. In the first place, the heretics' transference of material from Latin to English was not regularly accompanied by any popularization of the subject matter of that material or of its methods of procedure–the sole change was the 'accident' of language. Secondly, it seems that this transference of language was an accommodation to the audience, and not for some long time a necessity because of the ignorance of the writers–in other words, the Lollard authors remained for many years after 1388 fully capable of writing and of reading in Latin, even if they chose to put out their works in English.

As evidence of the continuing erudition of Wycliffite writings, even when the medium was English, the so-called *Glossed Gospels* may be taken as an example. These aimed to foster understanding of the evangelical message by the provision of commentaries on each of the four Gospels; the four commentaries differ somewhat in their surviving forms, but that on Luke may be taken as typical.[53] Instructions given to

[49] The case is recorded at length in *Registrum Johannis Trefnant*, ed. W. W. Capes (London, 1916), 278-365. A brief biography of Brut is given by Emden, *Oxford*, 270-1, though Emden apparently regarded his chief claim to inclusion to be the erudition of the replies mentioned here.

[50] *Trefnant Register*, 285-358.

[51] For some of them see *Trefnant Register* 368-94 (wrongly marked in the edition as replies to Swynderby); others are in British Library MSS Harley 31, fos. 194ᵛ-205ʳ, 216ʳ-218ʳ and Royal 7 B. iii, fos. 1ʳ-4ᵛ. See M. Aston, 'Lollard Women Priests?', *Journal of Ecclesiastical History* 31 (1980), 445-51.

[52] *Calendar of Patent Rolls 1385-1389* (London, 1900), 448, 468, 536; all of these relate to the same series of mandates. Cf. Knighton (above, n. 8), ii. 263 who mentions under 1388 a measure that 'librosque eorum Anglicos plenius examinarent'.

[53] The best recent account of these is to be found in H. Hargreaves, 'Popularising Biblical Scholarship: the Role of the Wycliffite *Glossed Gospels*', in *The Bible and Medieval Culture*, ed. W. Lourdaux and D. Verhelst (Louvain, 1979), 171-89.

the workers who actually compiled this commentary must have run along these lines: divide each chapter into groups of verses that belong together and use as translation of each group the Early Version (in a slightly revised form); for commentary go to Ambrose and Bede on Luke and translate the whole of their exegesis, omitting one only if there is substantial overlap; note where either, and particularly Bede, is repeating the view of an earlier authority; go to Aquinas's *Catena Aurea* for passages from the Greek fathers and use that assemblage to trace other fathers who commented on Luke–do not just copy from the *Catena* but go back to the originals and make sure that the whole discussion is translated, not just the bit that Aquinas thought relevant; check a harmony of the Gospels and use the commentaries on parallel passages from the other three Gospels for amplification; add in Bernard and Grosseteste, particularly where the biblical material offers any opportunity for criticism of the clergy; in translating, include the origin of each author's comment, the work and the chapter, and indicate whether the author was directly observing on the verse in question or whether he was talking more generally. The scribes who copied out the commentaries must have been given equally detailed instructions: the biblical translation should be engrossed and rubricated, the individual words that are the subject of comment should be similarly rubricated, the names of the authorities underlined–in this fashion the reader can readily perceive the degree of authority he should attach to any word.[54] These instructions, to compilers and to scribes, were to be observed meticulously; and no word of comment was added by these fourteenth-century workers. This description, even if it appears rather frivolous, may give some idea of the enormity of this undertaking, both in scope and in scholarly impetus.

Here erudition is dominant, and the individual viewpoint, whether heterodox or not, only emerges through the selection of other men's words. That the technique was deliberate is clear from numerous Lollard writings where the author is more outspoken: even the ecclesiastical authorities, even Courtenay or Arundel, could not impugn the words of Augustine or Gregory; yet Augustine and Gregory, or even canon law, can be found to support a Wycliffite

---

[54] These instructions can be deduced from the format of most of the surviving manuscripts of the commentaries, MSS Bodley 143, 243, Laud Misc. 235, British Library Additional 41175, Additional 28026 (though this is less handsomely presented), Cambridge University Library Kk. 2. 9 and Edinburgh, National Library of Scotland 6124.

standpoint.[55] The *Thirty-Seven Conclusions of the Lollards* is a far more controversial text than the *Glossed Gospels*; here, however, the interest is not the author's heresies, but his method. Each conclusion is divided into corollaries and the main manner of demonstration is by a manipulation of carefully chosen extracts from Scripture and canon law. Thus the proposition that ministers of religion should be satisfied with modest provision of the necessaries of life is supported by various scriptural citations; the first corollary is less uncontentious, that tithes and offerings may be withheld from prelates or curates habitually failing in their spiritual duty. This is backed up by four references to canon law, which, it is admitted, deal with the case of a priest known to be a fornicator. But this is countered by the claim that avarice is a worse sin than lechery and therefore it is even more necessary that tithes be withheld for this more grievous sin; two commentators, Innocent IV and Hostiensis, are advanced in support of this claim. These references are very precise: that to Innocent '*de restoracione spoliatorum* capitulo "In literis" in 1 colum in þe ende', that to Hostiensis 'in *Summa de decimis* in þe paraf "Quid si clericus" '.[56]

It might be objected that the *Conclusions* are by their nature designed to confront the opposition and that therefore this display of learning is intended not for the ordinary Lollard but for the orthodox academic. This can, however, by no means explain all the English texts. I have described elsewhere the erudition, perhaps even pedantry, of a Lollard author of two long texts written between 1407 and 1414.[57] The text of his sermon, the author says, is to be left with the congregation for them to discuss at leisure; he will answer questions on his next visit and will then deal with any objections that may have been raised against it by any opponents. Yet here, and in his longer tract, the writer translates numerous pasages from the fathers and canon law, considers various understandings of the words *hoc* and *est* in the words of Eucharistic consecration, and uses the language of

---

[55] As *The Apology for Lollard Doctrines* (ed. J. H. Todd (London, 1842)), 46 observes, having cited Augustine and canon law, 'And syn þer wordis are canoniȝed and approuid of holi kirk, oiþer behouiþ to graunt þer wordis or to denay þe canoniȝing and aprouing of þe kirk.'

[56] *Remonstrance* (above n. 14), 12-15; the citations of canon law are in *Corpus Iuris Canonici*, ed. E. Friedberg, 2 vols. (Leipzig, 1879-81), i. 117, 284, ii. 455, 457; for Innocent see the edition (Venice, 1578), fos. 94-5, and for Hostiensis his *Summa Aurea* (Lyons, 1597), fos. 209-10.

[57] 'A Wycliffite Scholar of the Early Fifteenth Century', in *The Bible in the Medieval World: Essays in Memory of Beryl Smalley*, ed. K. Walsh and D. Wood (*Studies in Church History*, Subsidia 4 (1985)), 301-15.

grammar and logic. He alludes to differences of view amongst the ancients concerning the continuum, a piece of erudition that is entirely outside the main argument, but one that the writer apparently thought his audience could comprehend without full explanation.[58] Alongside these two works it is worth placing one further Lollard text, the *Lanterne of Li3t* written between 1407 and 1415; the interest of this text lies in the fact that we know something about at least one member of its actual audience.[59] The case for heresy against the London skinner John Claydon in 1415 was based largely upon his ownership of this text and his affirmed agreement with the many unorthodoxies it contained. Claydon, it is said, was illiterate; but he had commissioned the writing of a copy, had presided over the two-day checking of the text by his literate servant and the scribe, had then paid to have it handsomely bound, and ordered it to be read to him repeatedly.[60] Yet the *Lanterne* quotes numerous patristic sources, as well as biblical and canonistic ones; more remarkably, each quotation is given in Latin first and only then in English translation.

These few examples may serve to illustrate the sophisticated nature of Lollard writing. The second claim, that the Lollard preference for English was a deliberate rather than a forced choice, is to a fair degree substantiated by the evidence given for the first. The opposition to Lollardy reinforces this. Netter's *Doctrinale* was written in the 1420s and was unfinished at the time of its author's death in 1430.[61] It is worth asking what Netter thought he was doing in this inordinately long and detailed work. To a certain extent the *Doctrinale* was a propaganda exercise: if England had produced the heresiarch Wyclif, whose disciples were troubling not only his native country but also Bohemia, then England could also provide a refutation of Wyclif, a refutation at erudite length. This purpose is plain in the dedicatory epistles to Pope Martin V,[62] and its success is attested by the circulation of the *Doctrinale* on the Continent. But Netter had at least one other audience nearer home. The surviving copies in England of monastic and fraternal origin reveal that the text was used to bolster the resolve of those most hostile to Wyclif's views.[63] The *Doctrinale*,

---

[58] The writer was, like Wyclif, an indivisibilist; see above pp. 31-66.

[59] The text was edited by L. M. Swinburn, EETS OS 151 (1917).

[60] *The Register of Henry Chichele, Archbishop of Canterbury 1414–1443*, ed. E. F. Jacob, 4 vols. (Oxford, 1938-47), iv. 132-8.

[61] The date of the various books is sorted out by M. Aston in a note to her paper 'William White's Lollard Followers', *Catholic Historical Review* 68 (1982), 474 n. 22.

[62] *Doctrinale* i. 3-4, ii. 2.

[*See p. 102 for n. 63*]

however, is not only concerned with Wyclif's views of predestination
and the nature of the Church, or of the Eucharist, but also with the
Wycliffites' regrettable advocacy of women preachers, with Lollard
iconoclasm, with the notion of the suspects investigated by Bishop
Alnwick of Norwich that children born to Christian parents needed no
baptism, or with William Taylor's views on the illegitimacy of prayers
to the saints.[64] Hardly topics, one would have thought, on which other
Carmelites needed instruction. Yet, if the *Doctrinale* were (on the usual
assumptions) to reach its Lollard target, it would have had to be translated into English, of which there is no sign and for which Netter
would have had unmitigated abhorrence, or those Lollards–at least
some of them–would have had to be able to read Latin. Perhaps
Netter was over-optimistic in thinking that any Lollard would read
through the vast length of his complete work; but it seems that he may
not have been entirely unrealistic in envisaging that some Lollards
could still understand its language.[65]

It is in the light of all this evidence, complex and even conflicting
as some of it is, that the question of Wyclif and the English language
should be considered. Whether any word of Wyclif's in English survives seems to me properly a matter of indifference. What is important, I would suggest, is the impetus he gave towards the use of the
vernacular, but use for purposes and with methods that involved
little diminution of scholarly enquiry. The one text whose title
enshrines the name of the man, *Wyclif's Wicket*, may serve as an
epitome of the situation: the text survives only in prints of the
Reformation period and not at all in medieval manuscripts, it is mentioned by name only from the very end of the fifteenth century, but it
sets out in English some of the ideas on the Eucharist that Wyclif

---

[63] Of the extant English manuscripts, British Library Royal 8 G. x and Worcester
College Oxford 233 were given by Abbot Whethamstede of St Albans to Gloucester
College Oxford; the scribes of Cambridge University Library Dd. 8. 17, Magdalen
College Oxford 153, and Merton College 319 were Carmelites; Lincoln College
Oxford 106 was a Carmelite production given to the College by its founder Richard
Flemyng.

[64] For these latter topics see *Doctrinale* i. 619, 637-8; iii. 902-52; iii. 342; iii. 729-31,
743, 755.

[65] It is worth considering whether Netter's polemic, and indeed that of earlier opponents, may not have had the unintended effect of publicizing Wyclif's views and of providing a convenient access to the heresiarch's voluminous treatises. The modern critic
can certainly use Netter very readily as an index to Wyclif. F. Šmahel has drawn attention to the publicizing effect of condemnations of Hussite views in Bohemia in '"Doctor
Evangelicus super omnes evangelistas": Wyclif's Fortune in Hussite Bohemia', *Bulletin
of the Institute of Historical Research* 43 (1970), 16-34 at 22.

had expressed in Latin in the 1380s.[66] There is little chance that the *Wicket* is actually by Wyclif. But it does confirm Knighton's astonished and outraged comment that the Lollards used the vernacular, the vulgar tongue, because it seemed to the lay people better and more worthy than the Latin language.[67] For this view John Wyclif was responsible.

[66] It was published first in 1546 (STC 25590), and was reprinted several times; for details about these, and references to the text, see my paper '"No newe thyng": The Printing of Medieval Texts in the Early Reformation Period', in *Middle English Studies Presented to Norman Davis*, ed. D. Gray and E. G. Stanley (Oxford, 1983), 153-74 at 157, 172-3. Further investigation and a critical edition of this text are needed.

[67] *Chronicon* ii. 155 the Lollards 'qui mutaverunt evangelium Christi in evangelium aeternum, id est, vulgarem linguam et communem maternam, et sic aeternam, quia laicis reputatur melior et dignior quam lingua Latina'.

6

Wycliff and Hus:
A Doctrinal Comparison

GORDON LEFF

THE relation of Wyclif and Hus is as reformers rather than as thinkers. Despite their common philosophical allegiance to realism, their systems of thought were markedly different. Whereas Wyclif rigidly subordinated all his tenets to a few fundamental notions, Hus cannot strictly be said to have had a system at all. Wyclif's main influence was theoretical–in his teachings; that of Hus was predominantly practical, through his preaching and his martyrdom. They met in their common revulsion against the abuses within the Church, above all amongst its hierarchy and the religious orders. In that sense Wyclif's influence upon Hus was a moral and practical one. It helped to inspire Hus in his demand for a radical reformation of the Church, culminating in Hus's adoption of Wyclif's doctrine of the Church. Extreme though this was, Hus reached it principally through his own experience as an advocate of reform and as the upholder of the native Czech reforming tradition.

Neither Wyclif nor Hus was a voice in the wilderness, even though Wyclif spoke in a language of his own. They were part of a widespread movement, stretching from the later thirteenth century and embracing heretodox and orthodox alike: the Waldensians, the Franciscan dissidents, Dante, Marsilius of Padua, William of Ockham, Dietrich of Niem, Pierre d'Ailly, Henry of Langenstein, Jean Gerson, to mention only some of the more formative influences in the ecclesiology of the later Middle Ages. One stream issued in the extremism of Wyclif and the radicalism of Hus; the other in the Conciliar movement, although they converged at more than one point. Marsilius of Padua was the source for much of Dietrich of Niem's outlook as well as Wyclif's, and yet Dietrich took a leading part in the Council of Constance which declared Wyclif a heretic.[1] Hus was condemned by the same Council

---

[1] Wyclif's works were never condemned in their entirety. 267 articles were censured

for saying what his accusors enacted: namely that an unlawful pope should be disobeyed and deposed.[2] Ockham inspired Conciliarists like d'Ailly as much as Wyclif, while the belief in an original apostolic ideal of primitive simplicity, which had been betrayed by the Donation of Costantine, was common to heretics like the Waldensians, extremists like Marsilius of Padua and Wyclif, and radicals like Dante and many of the Hussite reformers. Accordingly, much of what Wyclif and Hus held was part of the currency of the age. They diverged from orthodoxy by converting it into an outright challenge to the Church, and from one another by the ways in which they did so.

I

Wyclif was the greatest heresiarch of the later Middle Ages. Yet, apart from his immediate Lollard followers, his influence was indirect; the message handed down from his writings was in the main the work of unbeneficed preachers[3] and artisans from whom it lost most of its original doctrinal nuances. Wyclif himself was never the leader of a sect,[4] nor was he condemned as a heretic during his lifetime. To the end he remained convinced of his own orthodoxy, branding the Church hierarchy as Antichrist for having betrayed Christ. But unlike Hus he was an extremist building upon neither a native reforming tradition nor an accepted body of teaching. In consequence, he gradually became isolated, until he was finally compelled to leave Oxford in 1381 following the condemnation of his Eucharistic doctrine by a commission of twelve appointed by the chancellor of the university, William Barton.[5] The writings of the three remaining years of his life at his Lutterworth rectory were the most extreme of his entire career. In contrast to Hus's works and sermons during his exile from Prague,

under Arundel, Archbishop of Canterbury, in 1411 and sent to Rome; in 1413 some of Wyclif's works were burned at a Lateran Council in Rome. Previously 45 articles, some of dubious authenticity, said to have been extracted from his works, were condemned at Prague in 1403 and again proscribed at the Council of Constance in 1415. See my *Heresy in the Later Middle Ages* (Manchester, 1967), ii. 498.

[2] The Council deposed John XXIII on 29 March 1415, on 72 counts; a week later, on 6 April, the superiority of a General Council over a pope was proclaimed (H. Finke, *Acta Concilii Constantiensis*, iii (Constance, 1907-28), 156-209).

[3] See K. B. McFarlane, *John Wycliffe and the Beginnings of English Nonconformity* (London, 1952), ch. 5.

[4] There is no foundation for the older belief that Wyclif organized a band of poor preachers.

[5] *Fasciculi Zizaniorum*, ed. W. W. Shirley (Rolls Series, London, 1858), pp. 105-14.

between 1312 and 1314, they offered no basis for the kind of movement which arose in Bohemia thirty years later, after Hus's burning. The difference is of fundamental importance. Wyclif, for all his intellectual eminence, was a solitary figure; most of his life was lived in the academic milieu of Oxford, apart from his unsuccessful brief excursion into politics in the service of John of Gaunt in the 1370s. Once his immediate following among his Oxford disciples—Nicholas of Hereford, Philip Repingdon, and John Aston—had been routed in 1381 by William Courtenay, archbishop of Canterbury, Lollardy became a purely clandestine movement. Any initial support it might have had from influential laymen was irrevocably lost after the abortive rising by Sir John Oldcastle in 1414.[6] Lollardy became synonymous with subversion and suffered prosecution by the State as well as by the Church.

However remotely Wyclif may have inspired the reformers of the sixteenth century, there can be no doubt that his main influence was upon Hus and the formation of the Hussite movement. The form that it took is the subject of this paper.

It has long been recognized that Hus belonged to an independent native tradition which was doctrinally widely separated from Wycliffism. Loserth's attempt to prove,[7] by means of parallel passages, that Hus merely plagiarized all his main tenets from Wyclif has been shown to be untenable.[8] Not only did they diverge on crucial matters of doctrine, such as the Eucharist and sinful priests, as we shall see, but Hus frequently gave a different import to his undeniably verbatim citations from Wyclif. Wyclif's significance for Hus lay above all in being a rallying point against the attacks of his enemies. He defended Wyclif according to his own interpretation of him as a reformer rather than a theologian. The modifications in Wyclif's doctrines to which this led will become apparent.

Wyclif's writings fall into two clear divisions.[9] Before 1376 they were mainly philosophical; after that date they became almost exclusively ecclesiological and theological. Moreover, they changed in tone, a change directly related to his political activities. Having gone on a diplomatic mission to Bruges in 1374 to negotiate a

---

[6] See McFarlane (above, n. 3).

[7] J. Loserth, Hus and Wiclif (Leipzig, 1884 (1st edn.) and Berlin, 1925 (2nd edn.)), as well as introductions to the various editions of Wyclif's works which he edited for the Wyclif Society.

[8] Especially by the Czech scholars V. Novotný, J. Sedlák, V. Kybal, V. Flasjšhans, F. M. Bartoš.

[9] For an account see my Heresy in the Later Middle Ages, ii. 496-7.

financial settlement on payments to the pope, in 1376 Wyclif took a leading part in John of Gaunt's attack on William of Wykeham. His preaching and other activities against him in the London pulpits caused William Courtenay, then bishop of London, to summon him in February 1377. Although Wyclif escaped punishment through the presence of John of Gaunt, extracts from his writings on lordship and ecclesiastical power in *De Civili Dominio* were sent to the pope, Gregory XI. This led to papal censure of Wyclif's opinions in eighteen articles, and marked a turning point in Wyclif's thinking. Over the next five years, Wyclif reached the furthermost extreme of anti-sacerdotalism, far surpassing anything which he had written in *De civili dominio*. As I have suggested elsewhere[10] his doctrines of the Church, the papacy, royal power, and the Eucharist largely superseded and out-weighed in importance his earlier views on lordship, which Gregory XI's condemnation tended to magnify. Similarly, his view of the Bible only takes on its full significance when set against his subsequent teaching on the Church and the Eucharist. His formulation of his doctrine of the Eucharist in *De Apostasia* and *De Eucharistia*, both written in 1379, acted as a catalyst. It lost him his remaining support among the friars and led two years later to his withdrawal from Oxford. He was now fighting the entire ecclesiastical and religious hierarchy; his sense of isolation is matched by the increasingly bitter invective of the later works, which are for the most part merely a more violent and unsystematic repetition of his existing views, above all his condemnation of the visible Church.

There is, accordingly, a progression in Wyclif's thought which, although closely connected with his own experience, has its own independent logic. It is here that he differs above all from Hus. Wyclif remained throughout his career wedded to a metaphysics which underlay all his main theological positions. It gives them a continuity and provides a comprehensive theoretical framework for his protest against the Church. Together with his dialectical skill and evangelical fervour, it made him the supreme advocate of reform at Oxford and helped to transmit its impulse to Prague.

Philosophically, Wyclif was a realist, but not an extreme realist, as his treatise on universals, published for the first time in 1985, confirms.[11] He believed in the reality of universal concepts, such as genus

---

[10] *Heresy in the Later Middle Ages*, ii. 545 ff.

[11] *De Universalibus* ed. I. Mueller (Oxford, 1985), translated by A. Kenny *On Universals* (Oxford, 1985).

and species, not as self-subsisting entities but as the constituents of individual substances, as an individual man belongs at once to the genus animal and the species humanity. That entailed recognizing the different kinds of being in an individual, including the universal being which everything must share in virtue of existing at all. And beyond those degrees of being there were the external exemplars in God of all possible beings, the highest kind of being, as part of God's own essence. Wyclif accordingly distinguished three main gradations of being: eternal intelligible being in God; essential or universal created being, subdivided into more and less universal causes of particular beings; and finally individual beings as they exist actually in time, coming into and going out of existence. To these can be added a fourth kind of being, the accidental or non-essential properties, such as size or colour, which individual substances have.[12] Wyclif's realism therefore consisted in recognizing the universal character of individual being; for only if universal terms like 'man' and 'animal' corresponded to something real—as opposed to being merely mental or logical and grammatical constructions, the view of his opponents, the Nominalists or terminists—could they be true. They all shared in the same universal being which had its origin in the intelligible being of all possible beings in God. As Wyclif expressed it, 'There cannot be a creature which does not first have a mental or intentional existence in God before it has being in general and secondary being in its created causes . . . And every creature takes its essence from the eternal ideas in God, and thus every creature is a sharing in mental being.'[13]

Except for the manner in which he expressed it, there was nothing remarkable about that conception. Where Wyclif was singular was in associating God's eternal ideas of all possible beings with his own attributes of necessity and eternity as part of his essence rather as objects of his knowledge of what could exist outside him, as Ockham, for example, had held. Despite the contention of John Kenningham, a Carmelite with whom Wyclif disputed while studying in the theological faculty at Oxford, probably between 1372 and 1374, that it would then follow that whatever God knew must also be,[14] Wyclif had already affirmed the compatibility of God's foreknowledge with free will in his treatise on universals, since God freely caused everything.[15]

---

[12] *De Universalibus* ch. 7, 126-8.
[13] Ibid., 130-1: Kenny, 51.
[14] *FZ*, 463-4.
[15] *De Universalibus*, ch. 14.

The consequences of Wyclif's metaphysics lay elsewhere, in the indissoluble unity of everything in the universe, in virtue of having its intelligible being in God. As he was eternal and could not cease to be, neither could the intelligible essence of anything cease to be, as part of his essence. All being was therefore indestructible. That belief in an unchanging and indestructible essence for everything in the world, independently of its temporal manifestations, provided the philosophical foundation of Wyclif's doctrines of the Bible, the Church, and the Eucharist, the three main areas of his theology, which I shall consider here.

The focus of Wyclif's ecclesiology was the relation of the Bible to the Church. This was not, as used to be believed, through upholding a doctrine of *scriptura sola*;[16] but through the essentially metaphysical and historical definition which he gave to each. It is undeniable that Wyclif revered the Bible with an especial veneration as the repository of all truth eternally given. But that alone would hardly have led him to his revolutionary attacks upon the Church, had he not at the same time denied its authority in some aspect. The way in which he did so was in line with much contemporary ecclesiology. During the later thirteenth and the fourteenth centuries, there had been a growing emphasis upon the apostolic age of the Church and its contrast to its present state. Dante, Marsilius of Padua, Ockham, Dietrich of Niem, among many others, had each in different ways invoked the example of the primitive Church against the existing hierarchical and spiritual condition. Their remedy had been a return to the purity of the past, diverse though their means of achieving it were. Certainly Marsilius and Dietrich said most of what Wyclif said against the pope's primacy, while both the Waldensians and Franciscans had long preached possessionlessness as the true state for Christ's apostles. Even in his literal interpretation of the Bible, Wyclif had many forerunners, especially the school of St Victor in the twelfth century. Nor could Wyclif, any more than other exegetes, confine himself to an exclusively literal interpretation. His novelty lay in the combination of an historical and metaphysical treatment of the Bible to discount the authority of the contemporary hierarchy. But many of his arguments as well as his solutions were drawn from a well-stocked armoury which was not of his making.

[16] For recent arguments on this question see M. Hurley, '"Scriptura sola": Wyclif and his critics', *Traditio*, 16 (1960), 175-352, and the reply by Dom. P. de Vooght, 'Wyclif et la "Scriptura sola"', *Ephemerides Theologicae Lovanienses*, 39 (1963), 50-86.

They were reinforced by his metaphysics. On the one hand the Bible as God's Word was true in itself and for all time; on the other hand the Church in its archetypal being was to be sought not in its temporal form but in the essence in which God eternally conceived it– away from this world. The true nature of the Bible and the Church were not therefore contradictory: rather, Wyclif sought to employ the Bible to point to the true nature of the Church. The truth of the Bible was ever-present in its every word, although Wyclif was forced to modify his earlier strictly literal interpretation;[17] every part of it had to be taken without qualification; it contained all that could be known, and it could not be modified in the slightest degree.[18] However, its truths were not all equally accessible; like St Augustine, Wyclif recognized an implicit as well as an explicit meaning in its words. Hence the need for informed exegesis, the principles of which Wyclif founded in a combination of metaphysical truth, the testimony of the saints, and other canonical statements. Together these constituted the *sensus catholicus*.[19] Wyclif accordingly looked to metaphysics and authentic tradition as the means of understanding the Bible. He was not therefore advocating a doctrine of *scriptura sola* or merely exegesis. He regarded the truth as contained within the words of the Bible, to be discovered by a recognition of the true being which they denoted with the aid of those divinely inspired: above all, St Augustine as well as most of the early Fathers and later authorities like Gregory the Great, St Bernard, Hugh of St Victor, and Robert Grosseteste–a sign of his continuing place in the Oxford tradition.[20] Where Wyclif did stress the individual believer's responsibility was in knowing and defending the Bible with such aids against the falsities of the present hierarchy; indeed he should be prepared to adhere to the words of the Bible even if he could not understand them.[21]

It was here in the effective exclusion of the Church from the dialogue that Wyclif went beyond previous scholastics. He was appealing to Scripture over the heads of the hierarchy and at the same time disavowing the Church. If the reason was its betrayal of Christ's teachings, the grounds were metaphysical. Wyclif translated St Augustine's division of the faithful into the two cities of the heavenly and the

[17] *FZ*, 14, 20.
[18] Ibid., 475; *De Veritate Sacre Scripture*, 3 vols. (London, 1905-7), i. 1-2, and *passim*.
[19] Wyclif's *Trialogus* (Oxford, 1869), bk. iii, ch. 31, contains a concise account of his view of Scripture.
[20] *De Veritate Sacre Scripture*, i. 36ff.
[21] Ibid., 61.

earthly into metaphysical terms. Instead of referring the separation of
the damned and saved to the next world, Wyclif made them eternal
and ever-present. Where St Augustine had treated them all as members of the Church in this world, whatever their final destiny, Wyclif
from the outset identified the elect as alone of the Church; the
damned, called by Wyclif the foreknown (*presciti*), were eternally
excluded. The status of each remained the same for eternity. Here the
nature of Wyclif's thought is clearly revealed. Eternally distinct con-
ceptually, saved and damned remained so also ontologically. Each
represented a different kind of being which could not merge, even
temporally.

The effect was to transform the traditional notion of the Church. It
became defined by Wyclif as exclusively the body of the elect (*congre-
gatio predestinatorum*).[22] Those who were truly of it were bound
together eternally by the grace of predestination, enabling them to
remain in a state of election until the end;[23] it gave them immunity
from the consequences of even mortal sin. Here, too, eternal truth
overcame temporal vicissitudes. The Church was outside both space
and time; it was not a physical entity, but in being wherever the elect
were, whether in heaven, purgatory, or on earth.[24] It had thus existed
before the Incarnation, its *esse intelligible*, like that of anything else,
having been for all time.[25] In the same way, the damned equally were
of one congregation with Antichrist at their head and composed of the
three classes of infidels, heretics, and those not chosen. Furthermore,
lacking the grace of election, their grace in this world, however great,
did not suffice for their salvation; they therefore remained in mortal
sin, even though temporally in grace.[26] Each body was therefore eternal and its membership irrevocable.

The overriding consequence of this division was Wyclif's denial of
any visible identity to the Church. In contrast to his insistence upon
the indestructibility of God's Word as given in the Bible, he stressed
that in this world neither the saved nor the damned were known;[27] that
remained a mystery, save for a special revelation. Such an attitude was
utterly disruptive of ecclesiastical authority; for if only those chosen by
God were of the Church, and they could not be known, there was no
reason for accepting any visible priestly authority, or indeed for such

---

[22] *De Ecclesia* (London, 1886), 2, 7. See also *De Civili Dominio*, i. 288.
[23] *De Ecclesia*, 107, 111.   [24] Ibid., 8, 99.
[25] Ibid., 106.   [26] Ibid., 63, 102-3, 139.
[27] Ibid., 251; also *De Civili Dominio*, i. 25 and *Opus Evangelicum*, 2 vols. (London, 1895-
6), iii. 216.

authority at all, since the elect and damned remained what they were regardless of what happened in this world.

Had Wyclif stopped there he would have sufficiently undermined the *raison d'être* of the Church as traditionally conceived. On his definition it required neither priests nor sacraments, merely conformity with God's Word and Catholic tradition, in the sense earlier defined. Yet Wyclif could not entirely abandon himself to the full rigour of his own logic. He neither went the whole way in rejecting the sacraments or the priesthood, nor was he prepared to leave those who violated Christ's law to their future judgement at the hands of God. He intervened with his own condemnation of those whom he regarded as of Antichrist. There was therefore an ambivalence in Wyclif's attitude to the Church directly engendered by his metaphysics. He at once denied that any pope or priest could claim to exercise his office without a special revelation (itself beyond visible proof),[28] and he treated the Bible as evidence to deny most of the attributes of the existing Church—wealth, hierarchy, coercive power, independent jurisdiction, the very existence of offices like that of pope and cardinals—and to anathematize those who upheld them as traitors to Christ.[29] Here Wyclif said little that was new; the novelty lay in the metaphysical and ecclesiological framework within which he applied it. Like Marsilius of Padua and other critics of the Church, he contrasted the virtues of poverty, humility, charity, and equality to the present abuses of worldliness and wealth, and the growth of what he called a 'Caesarian' hierarchy. He also attributed the decline of the Church to the Donation of Constantine by which the Church under Pope Sylvester I had first come to accept endowments and so entered on the path of cupidity and sin.[30] Like the Franciscan Spirituals, he extolled Christ's poverty as the supreme virtue and the height of simplicity and purity. To those who sought to follow Christ it could never be foresworn;[31] and to return to this original apostolic state was the way back to Christ.[32] It should go together with the renunciation of all dominion and civil authority.[33] This remained Wyclif's message for

[28] *De Potestate Pape* (London, 1907), 176; *De Ecclesia*, 31; *De Civili Dominio*, i. 381.

[29] The references here are too numerous to be included, but see, e.g., *Sermones*, 4 vols. (London, 1887–90), ii. 58, iii. 78, 426–9; *Opera Minora*, 255.

[30] *Opera Minora*, 204, 226; *De Blasphemia* (London, 1893), 61; *De Veritate Sacre Scripture*, i. 70; *De Civili Dominio*, iii. 59, 217.

[31] *De Civili Dominio*, iii. 60, 242, 444; *Trialogus*, 302, 378–83.

[32] *De Ecclesia*, 371–2.

[33] *De Civili Dominio*, ii. 145 ff., iii. 60 ff., 445 ff.; *De Potestate Pape*, 83, 200–1; *De Ecclesia*, 184–7, 365.

the reformation of the Church, from *De Civili Dominio* onwards, repeated with increasing vehemence to the end of his life. It went together with an equally growing conviction that all offices save those of priest and deacon, which had alone existed in the primitive Church, were unscriptural and their holders usurpers.[34] It led Wyclif to perhaps his most revolutionary step of rejecting the authority of the Church hierarchy altogether, pope and cardinals first and foremost. Christ alone was head of the Church, its chief abbot.[35] Towards the pope Wyclif's hostility grew after his condemnation by Gregory XI and especially with the outbreak of the Great Schism in 1378. When he came to write *De Potestate Pape* in 1379 he added to his previous metaphysical grounds for not accepting the visible ecclesiastical hierarchy the same arguments, drawn from Scripture, which had been used by Marsilius of Padua sixty years earlier. These followed two main directions. The first was that spiritual power was entirely independent of human agency; hence no man could exercise it or confer it on others.[36] Only if a priest, or pope, acted for God did his sentences of excommunication or absolution carry any power.[37] Wyclif here went beyond Marsilius in adding that since God gave his power without visible sign there was no means of assessing a priest's powers.[38] Although Wyclif did not go so far as openly to deny the role of priests and the sacraments entirely, what he said went far towards depreciating them. He remained ambiguous over the question, unlike Hus, as we shall see. Certainly he attacked auricular confession and absolution as unscriptural, but he never openly counselled refusing to take the sacraments even from a priest of known bad character.[39] At the same time, he stressed the power of the saved layman to hear confessions and give pardons.[40] But the supreme test of a priest's standing was whether or not he preached; to do so was his first duty as Christ's disciple. Any priest who failed to preach failed as a priest.[41] That so many did so fail added to Wyclif's general indictment of the priesthood.

Secondly Wyclif, like Marsilius, appealed directly to Scripture to indict the present hierarchy. In particular, he pointed to the absence

---

[34] *De Potestate Pape*, 35, 372; *De civili Dominio*, i. 380; *Opera Minora*, 142-3, 305; *Trialogus*, 296; *De Simonia* (London, 1898), 43.
[35] *De Civili Dominio*, ii. 166; *De Ecclesia*, 31; *Trialogus*, 263.
[36] *De Potestate Pape*, 14-15.   [37] Ibid., 16, 26-8.
[38] Ibid., 14.   [39] *De Blasphemia*, 140.
[40] Ibid., 140; *De Potestate Pape*, 266.
[41] *De Veritate Sacre Scripture*, ii. 137, 138, 156, 173, 179; *Polemical Works*, 2 vols. (London , 1883), i. 261.

from the Bible of any mention of popes, cardinals, or bishops. Here he followed Marsilius's exegesis of Matthew 16: 18 and 19 to deny the Petrine basis of papal primacy. Both he and Marsilius rejected the claim that the pope had succeeded Peter as head of the Church, taking the rock of the Church to mean Christ instead. Peter's primacy referred to his own personal qualities not powers that had been transmitted to succeeding Bishops of Rome.[42] Peter, however, had not even been Bishop of Rome; Paul had more right to that title. Nor had Rome then been supreme among the local churches: Antioch, Alexandria, and Jerusalem had been at least her equals.[43] Accordingly Wyclif, like Marsilius, with the aid of citations from the chroniclers, concluded that the pope had no claim to be head of the Church. Once again he took the argument further in denying the very *raison d'être* of the pope and other prelates for having no scriptural basis and for violating Christ's teachings. The pope was a mere man where Christ had been God; together with the cardinals he had gained his place by usurpation.[44]

In branding them as Antichrist for acting unscripturally, Wyclif was, of course, being inconsistent with his metaphysical premises that the damned and the saved were unknown. In the writings and sermons of his last five years, he dwelt increasingly upon the Church's visible betrayal of Christ's evangelical life and teaching.[45] Wyclif saw its source in the Church's endowments and the use of force to maintain its privileges together with the crimes which they engendered: these included simony in taking first-fruits, excommunication for non-payment of tithes, litigation, patronage, false indulgences, and so on. Here Wyclif echoed the cry of moral reformers throughout the Middle Ages, as he was in his turn to be re-echoed by Hus and his confrères.

Wyclif, however, did not stop there. He sought the dissolution of the Church as an independent corporation. For this he turned to the king; in appealing to him to return the Church to its archetypal purity, he was also responding to his own theoretical presuppositions of what the Church should be. He was sufficiently convinced of its independent existence, outside all space and time, to countenance its physical

---

[42] *De Potestate Pape*, 76, 97, 135, 173, 178, 218-19, 232.

[43] Ibid., 94, 111, 140-1, 150, 165-79, 195-7, 215.

[44] Ibid., 102-4, 106-7, 108-9.

[45] Wyclif gave ten signs of Antichrist, including seduction from Christ's teachings, the making of human laws which were unscriptural, failure to preach, wordliness, assertion of civil jurisdiction by ecclesiastics, the use of force, arrogance, lack of humility, attacking foes.

dismemberment as in its own interests. Restored to Christ the priesthood would again follow his example of a life of poverty and preaching.[46] To achieve it the king and the lay lords were to expropriate the Church's possessions and withdraw its civil rights.[47] Instead of living on endowments those of its priests who were worthy would be supported by alms; the remainder would have nothing.[48]

Wyclif accordingly looked for palpable means to give effect to a palpable programme; he displayed none of the vague aspirations of the various prophetic sects of Joachists. In his treatise *De Officio Regis* he sought to establish the king's supremacy over all men, including priests. The king's power corresponded to Christ's divinity, whereas that of the priest was to be compared with Christ's humanity.[49] The king, as God's vicar, stood apart from the rest of mankind; to resist him was sinful. Even tyrants were divinely ordained and had to be suffered, provided that God's law was not violated.[50] Like Marsilius, Wyclif maintained that the Church's temporalities were dependent upon the king, who had unchallenged power in his own kingdom.[51] Moreover, it was the king's function to exercise coercive authority, even over the Church: he could correct and banish evil priests, sequestrate Church property, even demolish churches in an emergency and convert them into towers for defence.

Here again Wyclif had gone beyond his original ecclesiological brief; for metaphysically there was no more means of knowing whether a king was damned or saved, and so could licitly exercise power, than a priest. His doctrine of royal power enunciated in *De Officio Regis* thereby effectively superseded his earlier teaching on lordship in *De Civili Dominio*. On the one hand, the Church was excluded from civil and spiritual jurisdiction on metaphysical and biblical grounds. On the other, kings and secular lords to whom it could have applied with most force—namely, that only those in grace could rightly exercise dominion over others—were expressly endowed by Wyclif with scripturally sanctioned authority. His earlier declaration in *De Civili Dominio*, that only grace could confer temporal lordship,[52] which

---

[46] e.g. *De Potestate Pape*, 89 101-2, 198, 341; *De Civili Dominio*, i. 330-1, 450, 469, 470-8, ii. 14, 18, 22, 23, 24, 32, 115, iii. 25; *De Ecclesia*, 190-2, 292, 294, 337-45, 372.

[47] *De Officio Regis*, 210, 211-13; *De Veritate Sacre Scripture*, i. 28, 93.

[48] *De Officio Regis*, 59; *De Civili Dominio*, i. 56, 311-12; *Opera Minora*, 23, 171.

[49] *De Officio Regis*, 13, 16, 137, 143.

[50] Ibid., 4-6, 346; *Opera Minora*, 165-6, 375.

[51] Ibid., 66, 118-20.

[52] *De Civili Dominio*, i. 1.

could not be achieved by conquest or coercion, had little consonance with the doctrine he enunciated three years later in *De Officio Regis* and reiterated in his subsequent works. Even had he not done so, his notion of dominion and grace which he developed from Richard Fitzralph was singularly devoid of immediacy. Like the rest of his treatment of the Church hierarchy Wyclif required more pragmatic means to establish his case.

His doctrine of the Eucharist, on the other hand, was the final development of Wyclif's metaphysics. It largely dominated the thinking of his last five years to the point of obsession. Unlike the notion of dominion and grace, that of the Eucharist grew directly out of his metaphysics. For the previous fifteen years before its final formulation in *De eucharistia* and *De Apostasia* Wyclif had tried various approaches to reconcile the doctrine of transubstantiation with his own conception of being as indestructible.[53] He was not the first to have been concerned with explaining how the bread and wine of the sacrament became Christ's body and blood. Nor did he ever deny that the change took place. What he found it impossible to accept was that the bread and wine were no longer bread and wine after transubstantiation although they continued to appear as bread and wine. For Wyclif, this would have meant that accidents could subsist independently of substance. This he rejected as contrary to the metaphysical truth that being was indestructible. Once in being, bread and wine could not be annihilated. Accordingly, even when transubstantiated their own essences as bread and wine must continue to coexist with the new substance which had been sacramentally engendered. As defined by Wyclif in his later works the Eucharist was 'the body of Christ in the form of bread and wine'.[54] Such a conception came close to what was later to be the doctrine of consubstantiation.

That it could have become the hallmark of Wyclif's heresy is as much an indication of how far Wyclif had become identified with unorthodoxy as of the intrinsic nature of his Eucharistic teaching. Not only did he continue to uphold the sacramental truth of transubstantiation; he also evinced a genuine concern over the blasphemous consequences of the prevailing view. To permit knowledge to be confined to accidents without revealing an underlying substance would put men at the mercy of their senses and mean the end of all true knowledge.[55] It would also mean idolatory since men would then

[53] *FZ*, xv. [54] *Trialogus*, 149.
[55] *De Apostasia* (London, 1889), 120; *De Eucharistia* (London, 1892), 78-80.

be worshipping mere accidents.[56] Similarly, to identify the bread and wine with Christ's body and blood would be blasphemy in identifying him with what was material and corruptible; the priest would then be breaking Christ's body when he broke the bread; and an animal eating the host would be eating Christ.[57] Above all, it would give the priest the power of making Christ's body when he celebrated mass. Accordingly, Wyclif's own solution was to treat the transubstantiation of the host as both natural and supernatural; the bread and the wine remained bread and wine, but the body of Christ was now added to them. The change involved not the destruction of the bread and wine but their coexistence with Christ.[58]

Despite the comparative innocuousness and moderation of his Eucharistic teaching it marked Wyclif's final alienation from the Church—although only among disciples and followers did it become the heresy of remanence.

II

Wyclif's doctrines, then, were part of a total outlook. Even if there were inconsistencies and the parts lacked symmetry, they were united by a set of philosophical presuppositions which gave his thinking continuity if not always coherence. The same cannot be said of Hus. He was first and foremost a reformer in the moral and practical tradition of his Czech forerunners, like Milíč of Kroměříž and Matthew of Janov.[59] The main lines had been formed by the time both Hus, and Wyclif's works, entered upon the scene. Wyclif—whose writings probably became influential at Prague from the last decade of the fourteenth century—came to be treated as a symbol in the dispute between the reformers and their adversaries at Prague. Hus defended the forty-five articles, said to have been extracted from Wyclif's work and condemned at Prague in 1403, as much on principle as for their doctrine; for him as for his confrères Wyclif was the reformer who had expressed the same ideals for which they were struggling. The fact that Wyclif's teachings had been first proscribed by the theological faculty at Prague, then under the influence of the German masters, added point to Hus's defence of them.[60] It stimulated Hus to study Wyclif's works and to embrace his realism in opposition to the prevailing

---

[56] *De Apostasia*, 129; *De Eucharistia*, 14, 63, 284; *Trialogus*, 261, 263, 268, 269.
[57] *De Eucharistia*, 11-13; *Trialogus*, 272.   [58] *De Apostasia*, 210.
[59] See my *Heresy in the Later Middle Ages*, ii. 611-19.   [60] Ibid., 623.

terminism or nominalism of the Germans who dominated the theological faculty. Accordingly, it is important to distinguish between Hus's allegiance to Wyclif as an individual and his doctrinal adherence to Wyclif's teaching. It was in the first respect that Wyclif's influence upon Hus was so profound; in the matter of doctrine their divergences are as striking as their affinities.

To begin with, Hus had neither Wyclif's extremism nor his metaphysics as an intellectual framework, however much he accepted the same brand of realism. Moreover, unlike Wyclif, comparatively little of what he wrote was of an academic or formal nature. Beyond such exercises as his Commentary on the *Sentences* and his various university disputations (*Quodlibeta*)–all strikingly unoriginal works–most of his output was even more than Wyclif's in response to immediate issues. Hus could have said all that he said without the aid of realism; and where it had directly affected Wyclif's Eucharistic doctrine Hus remained markedly orthodox.

Since this was one of the main issues between Hus and his adversaries, both at Prague and later at Constance, the difference is particularly instructive. Hus was accused in 1409 of having preached remanence as early as 1399, a charge he never ceased to deny. His writings support him. From the treatment of the Eucharist in the fourth book of his Commentary on the *Sentences* to his final work on the subject, *De Cena Domini* written in 1415, during his imprisonment at Constance, Hus held to the orthodox position of the transubstantiation of the bread and wine.[61] Where he did seem to lean towards Wyclif was first in emphasizing that the change was due to Christ not to the priest, and second in calling the bread Christ's body: this was characteristic of Hus's flirting with Wyclif's expressions to reach a different conclusion. In this case by bread he stressed that he meant the sacramental bread.[62] He thereby took up Wyclif's theme of distinguishing between the bread in its natural and what he called its 'supersacramental' form. He also seems to have been preoccupied by the same real problem which Wyclif raised, that if the bread and wine no longer remained as bread and wine after consecration, to eat the host would be to eat Christ. To overcome it, Hus distinguished between Christ's form, which was the sacramental bread, and his substance which inhered within it; both were Christ, but when the host was

---

[61] In *Historia et Monumenta Johannis Hus et Hieronymi Pragensis*, 2 vols. (Nuremberg, 1558), i. 40ʳ.
[62] Ibid.

eaten, Christ was not affected.[63] Thus, as so often, Hus performed the delicate act of putting Wyclif's words into an orthodox setting; it was a dangerous game to play, and to malicious tongues it provided powerful ammunition against him which helped to bring about his downfall at Constance.

Next closely allied to remanence was the question of the sacramental powers of sinful priests. Here, Wyclif and Hus were closer together in that, as we have remarked, Wyclif never decisively came down for or against. But, on the other hand, Hus showed none of Wyclif's equivocation. He accepted the distinction, which Wyclif passed over, between the office and the person, itself indicative of a different conception of priestly authority. So far as their office was concerned, all priests could consecrate and administer the sacraments, because their power to do so arose from their office. If, however, a priest was personally unworthy then he would be performing his priestly functions unworthily and equivocally.[64] Moreover, he did so 'to his own prejudice in despising God's name'.[65]

Hus, then, conceived the nature of a true priest in fundamentally different terms from Wyclif. It was moral (owing its inspiration to Matthew of Janov) where Wyclif's was metaphysical. Wyclif's distinction between the saved and the damned meant that anyone not of the elect could *ipso facto* not be a true priest. Hus, on the other hand, began from the traditional position of mortal sin as a personal state which disqualified the individual concerned—as distinct from the nature of the priesthood itself. He maintained that position throughout his trial at Constance, despite his having adopted Wyclif's conception of the Church in his *De Ecclesia* written in 1412: an indication of the unsystematic character of his thought. For Hus a true priest was one who remained true to God. Even in *De Ecclesia* and afterwards he continued to make conformity with Christ's precepts the touchstone. A priest, whatever his personal qualities, remained a priest within the visible Church and was due the respect of his office. Thus, in contrast to Wyclif's equivocation, Hus explicitly acknowledged that there were good and bad priests within the Church who shared their order in common.[66] They were the instruments in bringing God to the faithful.[67] If Hus's own position was equivocal, this came from attempting

[63] *De Corpore Christi* in *Opera Omnia*, ed. V. Flajšhans, 8 vols. (Prague, 1903-7), i. fasc. II, 11.

[64] *Historia et Monumenta*, i. 39ʳ.

[65] Ibid., 39ᵛ.   [66] Ibid., 256ᵛ.

[67] *Posiciones, Recommendaciones, Sermones*, ed. A. Schmidtová (Prague, 1958), 174.

here–as in so much else–to combine Wyclif's metaphysics with his own essentially moral and practical outlook.

The one point at which he himself became irretrievably implicated in Wyclif's heterodoxy was over the nature of the Church, although as we have just mentioned, his own different point of view showed through. His most radical break with tradition was his rejection of the pope as head of the Church. He reached this position in *De Ecclesia*[68] and maintained it henceforth to the end. This work was the crystallization of Hus's own experience in his struggle against ecclesiastical authority. It is as much an *apologia pro vita sua* as a theoretical treatise. Written during his exile from Prague in 1412, it formed the basis of Hus's condemnation at Constance in 1415. It shows clearly the relation between Hus's thinking and that of Wyclif. It is here that its main interest lies, rather than in any intrinsic merits of the treatise itself. Hus was essentially a moralist; his best works were those in which he was denouncing some evil or injustice, as in his polemics against his erstwhile confrères, Stanislav Znojmo or Stephen Páleč,[69] and his attack on simony in the Czech work of that name.[70]

De Ecclesia in its structure illustrates the cleft between the theoretical and moral in Hus's approach. It falls into two parts: the first concerns the nature of the Church; the second the practical issues with which Hus was himself confronted.[71] He began by taking over Wyclif's definition of the Church as the body of all the predestined, past, present, and future. As early as 1405 Hus had put it forward in his synodal sermon of that year; but it had then been only one of three definitions and he had then and later adhered to the traditional view of the Church as the body of all the faithful.[72] In *De Ecclesia* Hus also followed Wyclif in excluding the *presciti* eternally from membership of the Church and making Christ its sole head.

When it came to the practical implications, however, Hus's–or rather Wyclif's–definitions soon tended to break down, and for much the same reasons in both cases. It was logically impossible at once to assert ignorance of who is damned and who is saved and to damn those who betray Christ. To identify the sinners was to know what had been defined as unknowable. Neither Wyclif nor Hus was prepared to

---

[68] *Tractatus de Ecclesia*, ed. H. S. Thomson (Cambridge, 1956).

[69] *Historia et Monumenta*, i. 255ᵛ-264ᵛ, and 265ᵛ-302ᵛ.

[70] Translated by M. Spinka in *Advocates of Reform* (Library of Christian Classics, xiv, London, 1953), 196-278.

[71] It divides at chapter 11.

[72] *Historia et Monumenta*, ii. 28ʳ. See my *Heresy in the Later Middle Ages*, ii. 663.

remain silent on such grounds. In *de Ecclesia*, theory was for all practical purposes left behind once Hus turned to the failings of the pope and the Church hierarchy. The *presciti* became a moral rather than a metaphysical category; rather than only one Church of the elect, Hus tended more towards Matthew of Janov's distinction within the Church between the communion of the elect and the mass of the faithful.[73] Moral purity became their distinguishing mark. In particular Hus diverged from Wyclif over both the distinction between the office of priest and the person and in a less rigorous application of Wyclif's notion of the grace of predestination. Hus seemed prepared to accept any evidence of grace as a sign of predestination.[74] Moreover, Hus explicitly made moral probity the test of a true priest: 'If he is manifestly sinful', he wrote, 'then it should be supposed, from his works, that he is not just, but the enemy of Christ.'[75] This is tantamount, as we have suggested, to applying the test of a true priest in this world and not waiting for the final judgement in the next.

Hus, like Wyclif, was thereby denouncing the present hierarchy on moral grounds, but his attack was at once more moderate and more personal. Following his distinction between the office and the person, Hus was prepared to acknowledge that the pope and cardinals were the most dignified part of the Roman Church and that they should be treated as such so long as they remained true to Christ.[76] He did not, however, recognize their headship of the Catholic Church. They could sin and err, as the egregious example of Pope Agnes–who had reigned as John VIII for two years, five months, until her sex had been revealed–showed.[77] Again, Hus followed Wyclif and Marsilius in denying that Christ's commission to Peter had given the Bishop of Rome primacy over the rest of the Church.[78] Christ alone was head of the Church and the universal Church alone infallible. To put the pope and cardinals in his place was to put man before God.[79] For Hus, as for Wyclif, the papacy was a human institution, the creation of the emperor Constantine; the word pope was not in the Bible.[80] For that reason it could be dispensed with.[81]

Although Hus did not set up the same opposition between the present hierarchy and the Bible, he, too, made the Scriptures the touchstone of canonical authority. Papal decrees were the work of

---

[73] *Heresy in the Later Middle Ages*, ii. 617-18.
[74] e.g. *De Ecclesia*, 39.   [75] Ibid., 38.
[76] Ibid., 48.   [77] Ibid., 48, 103, 107, 141, 233.
[78] Ibid., 48, 57-62, 66.   [79] Ibid., 51-2.
[80] Ibid., 101 ff.   [81] Ibid., 172-3.

fallible men, and had none of the imperative obligation of the Bible as the word of God.[82] In his Commentary on the *Sentences* Hus called the Bible 'the most certain, profound and worthy' source of all knowledge because its subject was the divine.[83] He rejected Páleč's description of the Bible as something inanimate; it was, on the contrary, the book of life, indispensable to the true Christian.[84] Indeed, to a greater degree than Wyclif Hus based himself upon its authority for his argument together with citations above all from the Fathers. Like Wyclif he placed St Augustine as supreme among them.[85] Hus particularly stressed the importance of such authorities in helping to understand the Bible.[86] This sense of being on the side of true Catholic tradition enabled him to confront the hierarchy and ultimately disobey it in the name of Christian truth. He especially attacked simony and failure to preach God's word as the marks of Antichrist: the category extended to a pope who was guilty of such failings.[87] He regarded simony as any payment for spiritual ministrations, including those made to the pope and papal reservations.[88] Hus also believed with Wyclif that the remedy for the Church's ills lay in a return to its primitive state of apostolic simplicity; but unlike Wyclif he did not advocate wholesale expropriation by the temporal powers as the means to achieve it. Priests who persisted in living sinful lives should be shunned by the faithful and tithes withheld from them.[89] Where revenues were excessive lay lords should have power of confiscation and in the case of simoniacs suppression.[90] To eliminate simony Hus counselled the revival of the ancient practice of election to spiritual offices in the presence of the people.[91] Correspondingly preaching should be made obligatory. Nothing should be allowed to stand in its way, not even the bans of superiors.[92] How important Hus regarded preaching may be gauged from his public defence in 1412 of two of Wyclif's condemned 45 articles on the subject. Article 14 had stated that those failing to hear or preach God's word because of excommunication were traitors to Christ. Article 15 had maintained that any priest or deacon could preach without papal or episcopal permission. In support of these

---

[82] Ibid., 56, 106, and *Historia et Monumenta* i. 262ʳ.   [83] *De Ecclesia*, 20.
[84] *Historia et Monumenta*, i. 262ʳ.   [85] *De Ecclesia*, 121.
[86] e.g. his letter written from Constance to his disciple Martin, in F. Palacký, *Documenta Mag. Johannis Hus* (Prague, 1869), 119-20.
[87] *Historia et Monumenta*, i. 258ʳ⁻ᵛ; *De Ecclesia*, 103, 140, 167.
[88] *On Simony*, 208, 213 ff.; *De Ecclesia*, 104-5, 113.
[89] *On Simony*, 252, 273.   [90] Ibid., 272, 275.
[91] Ibid., 268, 270.   [92] *De Ecclesia*, 190.

Hus declared that preaching was the way of combating Antichrist.[93] It was therefore one of the indispensable tests of a true priest.

In his attitude to laymen Hus did not go so far as Wyclif in making every member of the elect a true priest who could act as such. He was, however, prepared to allow that laymen could judge their spiritual superiors and, if found wanting, refuse them recognition. This was mainly to take the form of withholding tithes, as we have already mentioned. Hus, in his defence of six of Wyclif's condemned articles in 1412, had argued that tithes were pure alms and as freely given could be freely withheld; and those priests who lived contrary to Christ could have their temporalities withdrawn by laymen.[94] Hus refused the priesthood an inherent superiority to laymen; office, he said in reply to a preacher from Pilsen who had asserted the contrary view, was not superior to merit.[95] Although at one point Hus did go so far as to say that every good layman was a priest he neither founded it on Wyclif's metaphysical distinction between the saved and the damned nor did he conclude that the layman could thereby perform the office of priest. He confined himself to the moral that it was better to be a good Christian than a wicked pope or prelate.[96]

So far as the civil role of the Church was concerned, Hus invoked the by now common arguments which had grown up against spiritual involvement in temporal affairs. Christ had barred priests from all litigation and secular authority; this included fighting crusades to gain the submission of other Christians, and all sentences of excommunication and granting of indulgences which had not first come from God.[97] It was on these grounds that Hus opposed the papal bull by John XXIII on indulgences which led directly to his excommunication.[98] The pope had no power to remit sins for a period of time unless God had done so first.[99]

Ultimately, then, Hus based his position upon loyalty to Christ. He defended all his acts of disobedience to his superiors in the name of obedience to God. He owed little to Wyclif's actual metaphysics on the great moral issues of the time–the status of sinful priests, simony, and the other abuses which came from ecclesiastical wealth, worldliness, and pride. This was made apparent to his accusers at Constance

---

[93] *De Ecclesia*, 158; *Historia et Monumenta*, i. 110^v-134^v.

[94] *Historia et Monumenta*, i. 118^r-125^v.   [95] Ibid., 146^v.

[96] See *Heresy in Later Middle Ages*, ii. 671-2.

[97] *De Ecclesia*, 77-8, 82, 183, 189, 208-16; *Historia et Monumenta*, i. 174^v-175^v.

[98] *Historia et Monumenta*, 174^v-189^r.

[99] Ibid.

when, having confidently presented Wyclif's forty-five condemned articles for his comments and anticipated endorsement, they were surprised to find that Hus gave only qualified assent to four of them, hedged on another five, and explicitly rejected the remaining thirty-six.[100] Those which he accepted concerned excommunication, preaching, sinful prelates, and obedience to superiors. That is to say those on moral issues and matters of authority. It was on these questions that the consonance of his outlook with Wyclif's outlook lay. Doctrinally, it led to his embracing the same definition of the Church as the body of the saved. Although, as we have seen, he was perfunctory and inconsistent in its application, he stood by it from the time of *De Ecclesia* onwards, and on it he was ultimately condemned. If Hus was a heretic, it was in this that his heresy lay, even though he shared its practical outcome–the deposition of Pope John XXIII–with his accusers. His successors in the Hussite movement ultimately laid the foundations of the Reformation upon his resistance to papal authority.

The importance of Wyclif and Hus, then, was as forces for reform. They were united less by metaphysics than the conviction that the Church must be restored to Christ. If that led Hus into embracing Wyclif's doctrine of the Church, their outlook nevertheless remained distinctive as did the movements which they inspired. Even Hus's accusers had finally to recognize that Hus was not a Wycliffite.

---

[100] In J. Sedlák, *M. Jan Hus*, ii (Prague, 1915), 305*-10*. See also my *Heresy in the Later Middle Ages*, ii. 676 ff.

7

The Influence of Wyclif

MAURICE KEEN

THE measure of the influence that Wyclif exerted has long been controversial. There are many reasons for this, some of them historiographical; English Protestant historians between the sixteenth and nineteenth centuries so exaggerated his significance as to make it difficult for anyone coming after to achieve a just balance. Among the most important sources of difficulty, though, is quite simply the kind of man that Wyclif was. He was a man of the schools, an Oxford don. Like many of that breed, he seems to have been more at home with ideas than with men. The call to which he responded was the call to study, not the call to action. There is no evidence that he had any special gifts for organization or for administration and his brief forays into public life admitted him only to the corridors of power, and that momentarily, never to the inner *sancta*. He was not a practical reformer: he called on the clergy to evangelize, but he did not evangelize much himself. He never had to face real persecution or the threat of martyrdom. Oxford was his true home, and when he was silenced there he did not seek actively, as one or two of his closest Oxford disciples did, to take his cause to the people. He withdrew to his rectory at Lutterworth. He probably preached in his church there and no doubt he celebrated mass, but he did not make his parish into a nest of heresy. Rather, he wrote voluminously in the academic Latin which had become his natural medium of communication. The products of his pen, from this period and before, bear witness to his mental energy and to the strength of his feelings on religious and political issues, but there is no way in which the path of life that he chose can be cast into a heroic mould. He was a thinker, not a doer.

The consequence of this is that the influence of Wyclif has to be measured, in large part, not in terms of his direct personal influence on given individuals but in terms of the impact of his ideas, as set out in his written works. Though we are assured that at one time he had a higher reputation in the Oxford Schools than any other contemporary teacher, only three of the known early leaders of Lollardy in England had come into really close contact with him, Aston, Hereford, and Purvey (and the last was not an Oxford man). In consequence we are presented with a problem that always arises when we seek to measure influence through the reading of books rather than of men (as Hobbes put it in a different context), that that influence is presented to us through the distorting lens of the minds of others. If those others are insufficiently equipped to absorb the original ideas then these will appear distorted, debased, or misunderstood; alternatively, the ideas will be taken up by minds on which other influences are simultaneously at play and by men who themselves are seeking to make their own independent contribution. This second problem arises clearly with Wyclif himself: how do we draw the balance between his originality and the influences upon him of the ideas of such as Bradwardine, Fitzralph, and Grosseteste? In the particular case of Wyclif's influence on his greatest 'disciple', John Hus, it becomes acute: indeed I have to put the word disciple in inverted commas because it is in itself a tendentious description.

Naming Hus brings us up against another of the great problems about the measuring of Wyclif's influence. Wyclif's thought cast its shadow across the history of two countries, England and Bohemia, which were separated by long distance and whose social and political conditions, at the end of the fourteenth century, were very different. There is a natural tendency to treat the two parts of the story as separate. Indeed this course becomes very nearly inescapable for those English historians who like myself are ignorant of the Czech language. On the other side, it is only natural that Czech historians, immersed in the history of their great national revolution in the late Middle Ages, should not concern themselves over much with the history of English Lollardy, which by any reasonable standard of historical significance was by comparison a side-show. Each history, moreover, presents its own intrinsic and very different problems when it comes to assessing Wyclif's influence.

In England, partly in consequence of the sociological bias of much modern historical writing, attention has tended to focus on proletarian or lower middle-class Lollardy, on the humble Bible men of Lollard congregations in the Chilterns, in East Anglia, and in such towns as Bristol and London, whom McFarlane splendidly epitomized as 'solemn if well meaning bumpkins'.[1] Here the significance of Wyclif's

[See opposite page for n. 1]

influence can clearly be challenged on the ground that the intellectual refinements of his thought were beyond the apprehension of such followers. Criticism of the papacy and of the mendicants, questioning of the rights of the possessionate clergy and grumbling about tithes were matters generally in the air in the English autumn of the Middle Ages, in no way identifiably Wycliffite. Can Wyclif be said to have done much more here than provide a great name that let him pass as a father-figure for a certain brand of alehouse anticlericalism?

In Bohemia the problem is very different, for it is the other kind of distortion that comes into question. Loserth long ago demonstrated that very substantial passage in Hus's writings were borrowed directly from Wyclif, often word for word;[2] but is that enough, patriotic Czech historians have cogently asked, to impugn the originality and independence of their national hero? It is quite clear that on central questions, such as the Eucharist, Hus and Wyclif held quite different views and it is also clear that Hus had been influenced, early and profoundly, by the thought of a previous generation of Czech religious thinkers whose ideas were akin to Wyclif's in some ways but independent of him. Besides, though Hus and Wyclif were both scholars, in other ways Hus was all that Wyclif was not, a man at the centre of ecclesiastical politics, a great and eloquent popular evangelist, and ultimately a martyr for his views. These separate problems facing the historians of Wyclif's influence respectively in England and Bohemia inevitably deflect attention from a third matter, how far the two histories really are separable; or to put it the other way round, what degree of interdependence was there between Wycliffite influences in the two countries in question? In what follows I shall try to take a look at each of those three matters in turn, though it is the third that seems to me the most interesting in the light of present knowledge and current research.

Among English historians of Lollardy, as I have said, interest has tended (at least until very recently) to focus on lower class Lollardy, partly because it seems to have survived so long, partly on account of an inclination to approach heresy in social terms, and also because it is the kind of Lollardy well illustrated in the most plentiful and readily available record sources, the accounts of the examinations of

---

[1] K. B. McFarlane, *John Wycliffe and the Beginnings of English Nonconformity* (London, 1952), 184.

[2] J. Loserth, *Wyclif and Hus*, tr. M. J. Evans (London, 1884). Book ii sets out key related passages in parallel columns.

suspected heretics in bishops' registers. This approach is one that is
almost inevitably lopsided in a particular respect: it concentrates
attention too much on the taught and too little on the teachers. An
example, which has been beautifully elucidated by Mrs Aston, may
make the point clearer.[3] Between 1428 and 1431 Bishop Alnwick of
Norwich conducted a series of investigations into the heresy of a
series of East Anglian Lollard groups, whose principal evangelist
was the noted heretic missionary, William White. He and his
followers were examined on a series of articles concerning their
views on such matters as the payment of tithes, the adoration of
relics and images, respect for St Thomas of Canterbury, the right of
the faithful to preach—and on the sacrament of the altar. From the
answers of White's followers one would certainly conclude that there
was some distant Wycliffite influence at work (though even this
might be unsure without the last item), but it would appear to have
suffered a great deal of simplification and of 'embroidery and eccentric variation' as Mrs Aston puts it. But when we come to the
opinion of White in the matter of the mass we are clearly up against
something a good deal more precise and closer to Wyclif. Where his
Beccles disciples put the crude point that 'after the sacramental
words said of any priest at Mass, there remains nothing but only a
cake of material bread',[4] he declared that the bread did not cease to
be bread, remaining *verus panis in natura*; but not merely bread, being
simultaneously the flesh of Christ and the substance of bread.[5] To
quote Mrs Aston again, we 'here observe heresy that was academic,
more or less, in origin, passing through active proselytising . . . into
the sometimes limited intelligences of glovers and skinners, and into
the domestic talk of enthusiastic women. As it did so, its content
changed—and moved immeasurably further from Wyclif.'[6] But as she
rightly stresses, if it had not been for William White there would not
have been such a nest of Lollardy, crude or otherwise, as Bishop
Alnwick uncovered in East Anglia, and the central figure in the story
was an educated priest who had some understanding at least of
Wyclif's doctrinal view on the Eucharist. The moral is clear: to

---

[3] M. Aston, 'William White's Lollard Followers', in her *Lollards and Reformers*
(London, 1984), 71-100.

[4] N. Tanner (ed.), *Heresy Trials in the diocese of Norwich* (Camden Soc., 4th series,
vol. xx, 1977), 115.

[5] *Fasciculi Zizaniorum*, ed. W. W. Shirley (Rolls Series, 1858; henceforward = *FZ*),
424, 418.

[6] Aston (above, n. 3), 99.

redress what threatens to be an imbalance we need to look more at the teachers and less at the taught.

This, of course, is easier said than done. Aside from those direct disciples of Wyclif who were called before the Earthquake Council in 1382, William White was one of only a very few leading Lollard teachers who were successfully laid by the heels and whose examinations we can follow (the other principal ones were John Purvey, who abjured a series of errors after a trial in 1401, and William Taylor, who was examined in 1421 and went to the stake).[7] Over and above the records of examinations, sufficient evidence survives for the period between the Earthquake Council and Oldcastle's revolt to offer a tantalizing glimpse of what looks like a network of Lollard teaching and preaching, largely dependent, it would seem, on the patronage of the now celebrated Lollard knights.[8] Sir William Neville used his influence to ease the imprisonment in Nottingham castle between 1387 and 1391 of Nicholas Hereford, Wyclif's one time colleague at Queen's College, Oxford and one of those who worked on the first Lollard Bible translation, and it looks as if he may have helped to ensure that books were made available to him and have connived in the dissemination of his heretical writing.[9] We know that *codices* of Wyclif's own works were preserved at Kemerton and Braybrooke, livings in the gift respectively of the Lollard Knights Sir William Beauchamp and Sir Thomas Latimer, who both presented to them priests with established Lollard leanings.[10] Through the influence of the Cheney family, Thomas Drayton, who was a friend of the university trained Lollard William Taylor, was presented to the living of Drayton Beauchamp in the Chilterns. And the story of the greatest of all the Lollard Knights, Sir John Oldcastle, records a sufficient series of connections to suggest that the description of him in the *Gesta Henrici quinti* as the *dux et capitaneus* of the sect was not without some justification.[11] He was an acquaintance of Richard Wyche, another university-trained Lollard; he received Lollard preachers in his castle at Cooling in Kent; and his patrimonial estates at Almeley in Herefordshire marched with lands of

---

[7] Wilkins, *Concilia Magnae Britanniae*, iii. 255-60; *FZ*, 400-7; *The Register of Henry Chichele 1441-43*, ed. E. F. Jacob (Oxford, 1938-47), iii. 167-8.

[8] On the Lollard knights, see K. B. McFarlane, *Lancastrian Kings and Lollard Knights* (Oxford, 1972), 137-227.

[9] Ibid., 198-9; and see A. Hudson, 'A Neglected Wycliffite Text', in her *Lollards and their Books* (London, 1985), especially 58-61.

[10] Hudson, *Lollards and their Books*, 78-9; *Lollard Knights*, 195-6.

[11] *Gesta Henrici Quinti*, ed. B. Williams (London, 1850), 2.

Sir John Clanvowe, an alleged Lollard Knight and author of the puritanical English homily *Of the Two Ways*.[12] They lay besides in an area where William Swinderby and the most obdurate of Wyclif's Oxford disciples, John Aston, had both been active as evangelists. Oldcastle was also a possessor of Lollard books: indeed it was on the evidence of a book that he had commissioned that Archbishop Arundel commenced proceedings against him in Convocation in 1413.

Suggestive as they are, there is here only a handful of names and connections. As Oldcastle's case and the preservation (and copying) of Wycliffite books at Kemerton and Braybrooke hint and as Dr Anne Hudson's researches have recently begun to make clear,[13] the really telling evidence about Wyclif's influence in England in the late four-teenth and early fifteenth centuries is not so much that of names as that of books—as I hinted at the beginning of this paper. The most obvious evidence of the influence of Wyclif's teaching, until recently almost inexplicably neglected by historians, is the very large corpus of surviving manuscripts of Lollard works written in English and dating from, roughly, *c.*1382 to *c.*1414.[14] There is a wide variety of texts involved here: the Wycliffite Bibles apart they include tracts (some of which do little more than paraphrase and simplify passages from Wyclif, and some of which, like the *Lantern of Light*, are independent compositions), copies of polemical pieces and manifestos like the *Twelve Conclusions of the Lollards* and the *Lollard Disendowment Bill*, and the great Lollard *Sermon Cycle* of two hundred and ninety-four sermons, of which no less than thirty copies survive in whole or in part. None of these English works can safely be ascribed to Wyclif, but many of them are, like the Bible translations, clearly the work of men of some learning, being replete with biblical, patristic, and canonical citations. A good many of the manuscripts, including most of those of the *Sermon Cycle*, are of a high standard of production, carefully corrected and rubricated.[15] In short, these texts imply a degree of

---

[12] W. T. Waugh, 'Sir John Oldcastle', *Eng. Hist. Rev.* 20 (1905), 441; and also see V. J. Sattergood, 'The two ways—an unpublished religious treatise, by Sir John Clanvowe', *English Philological Studies*, 10 (1967), 33-56.

[13] Hudson, 'Some Aspects of Lollard Book Production', in *Lollards and their Books*, 181-91.

[14] There are two substantial collections of these texts, T. Arnold, *Select English Works of Wyclif*, 3 vols. (Oxford, 1869-71) and F. D. Matthew, *The English Works of Wyclif Hitherto Unprinted* (EETS, OS 74, 1880). Dr Hudson has printed a selection with intro-duction and critical apparatus (vital for relating these English works to Wyclif's Latin writings) in her *Selections from English Wycliffite Writings* (Cambridge, 1978).

[*See opposite page for n. 15*]

organization, scholarly involvement, and scribal co-operation in their production (and in the case of the Wycliffite Bible accessibility for the translators to learned works); and also imply the availability of substantial funds to pay for them. When McFarlane wrote his *John Wyclif and the Beginnings of English Nonconformity* in 1952 it seemed safe to say that 'Lollardy had always appealed most strongly to the lower middle class' of artisans–weavers, glovers, butchers, and skinners:[16] but here is evidence of a Lollard public and of Lollard teaching and preaching that will not brook confinement to so humble a level. The implications of the evidence do make sense, on the other hand, in the context of his later revised views on the significance and the real religious unorthodoxy of the Lollard Knights,[17] of a world in which men of position and influence could offer patronage and protection to Lollard writers and scholars, which in turn made possible the instruction of clerics who would teach and preach the views expressed in the vernacular tracts and sermons and expound the English Scriptures to humbler men. There are moreover enough of these texts to suggest that in the rough period 1382 to 1414 there were among the Lollards more of these men of influence and more scholars and teachers than we are now able to name.

With regard to preachers and teachers two Lollard books which are not in the vernacular, and to which Dr Hudson again has drawn attention, are very significant. These are the two Latin works known respectively as the *Floretum* and the *Rosarium Theologie*, the latter being an abridged version of the former with some independent matter added.[18] Dr Hudson describes these two compilations as 'collections of authorities, biblical, patristic, scholastic and canonistic, on a range of moral and ecclesiastical topics; the topics arranged in alphabetical order, with cross references for ease of use by a preacher or tract writer'.[19] The two collections were put together sometime between 1384 and 1396 and are noteworthy for the number and length of the citations that they include from one D.E. or *Doctor Evangelicus*, that is to say Wyclif. In effect they were handbooks of Wycliffite

[15] Hudson, *Lollards and Their Books*, 186-90; id., 'A Lollard Sermon-Cycle and its Implications', *Medium Aevum*, 40 (1971), 142-56, especially 145, 150-2.

[16] McFarlane (above, n. 1), 187.

[17] In his *Lollard Knights*, published in 1972, on the basis of lectures on the knights first delivered in 1957.

[18] On these two works see Hudson, 'A Lollard Compilation and the dissemination of Wycliffite Thought', in *Lollards and their Books*, 13-29.

[19] Hudson, *English Wycliffite Writings*, 7.

thought, and Dr Hudson has found clear evidence that they were used as such.[20] No less than eighteen insular manuscripts survive, and a single manuscript survives of an English translation of the *Rosarium*.[21] What is particularly interesting about these works from my present point of view is that they are clearly products of considerable scholarship. The range of their references to theological and canonistic writers is very wide, and implies access to very ample library facilities, which in turn means that they were almost certainly produced by university men working in Oxford. They thus provide a vital link in the chain of communication whereby the academic teaching that Wyclif had forged in Oxford was passed on, with the aid of university men and probably through those 'schools' of Lollardy to which reference is found from time to time in bishops' registers,[22] to the preachers and teachers who ministered to the humble Lollards of local congregations and conventicles.

I must here stress the importance of Oxford. When McFarlane wrote in 1952 it seemed to him that Archbishop Courtenay's firm action in 1382–the condemnation of Wyclif's errors in the Earthquake Council at Blackfriars and the activity of the Convocation held in Oxford that November–had 'utterly routed' the Wycliffite heresy in its principal stronghold, and that meant that 'once the first generation of academic Lollards had died out, the movement would ultimately cease to be Wycliffite'.[23] The compilation of the *Floretum* and the *Rosarium* shows how this was not inevitable, providing as they did the means whereby the teacher of humbler Lollards could be brought in touch with learning with a Wycliffite slant; and since they were compiled between 1384 (the *Floretum* includes substantial quotations from the *Opus Evangelicum*, written in that year) and 1396 (the date given by a colophon in a manuscript) they also call in question whether Lollardy really was routed in the university after 1382. Dr Hudson's suggestion that these works were put together in Oxford is of course only a hypothesis, though a most plausible one: fortunately there is other evidence that makes it clear that after 1382 interest in and active discussion of Wyclif's views was by no means scotched in the university.

Once again, the evidence of books is very significant. For instance,

---

[20] Hudson, *Lollards and their Books*, 25-6.
[21] Ibid., 24-5; the text is in Gonville and Caius MS 354/581.
[22] Hudson, *Lollards and their Books*, 28.
[23] McFarlane (above, n. 1), 113.

the Bodleian manuscript of Wyclif's *Postilla* on the New Testament was, as Miss Smalley showed, written in Oxford in 1403,[24] the original scribe making no bones about the author's name, which was subsequently erased. Queen's College, in 1401, paid out money for a copy of Wyclif's *De Mandatis*.[25] The Gonville and Caius manuscript which is one of the most important surviving English manuscripts of Wyclif's writing and which includes the only insular copy of the *De Dominio Divino*, was in 1403 in the hands of Henry Bryt, a fellow of Queen's and John Mychel of Exeter College.[26] It was in Oxford, again, that in 1407 the Bohemian scholars, Nicholas Faulfiš and George Knehnic, corrected the copy they had made at Braybrook of Wyclif's *De Veritate Sacre Scripture*.[27] To this list of books we can add a series of names of known Oxford Wycliffites of this period. One is that of Robert Lychlade, expelled for teaching heresy in 1395, but restored in 1399 and in 1402 presented to the living of Kemerton by the Lollard Knight Sir William Beauchamp[28] (where the same two Bohemians made a copy of Wyclif's *De Ecclesia*). Others include William James, a fellow of Merton and John Mybbe, the principal of Cuthbert Hall who became involved in Oldcastle's rising and, most important of all, the two successive Lollard principals of St Edmund Hall, William Taylor and Peter Payne,[29] of whom more hereafter.

There were clearly more Wycliffites in Oxford between c.1380 and c.1410 than just this list of names and it is also clear, more importantly, that they were not silent. A note in a Corpus manuscript, dated to between 1390 and 1410, refers to the opinions that the *fautores* of Wyclif in the university *assert*, using the present tense.[30] In 1395 Lychlade was publicly maintaining Wycliffite views, and in 1397 a group of petitioners from the university complained to the Convocation of the continued teaching of Wyclif's doctrines in the schools.[31] Wyclif's

[24] B. Smalley, 'John Wyclif's *Postilla super totam Bibliam*', *Bodleian Library Quarterly*, 4 (1953), 188.

[25] Hudson, *Lollards and their Books*, 78.

[26] Ibid., 79; there is evidence which supports the suggestion that this may be the actual copy from which the Bohemian scholars Faulfiš and Knehnic copied this text, though it is not absolutely conclusive.

[27] A. B. Emden, *A Biographical Register of the University of Oxford* (Oxford, 1957-74) ii. 670-1.

[28] Ibid., ii. 1184.

[29] See A. B. Emden, *An Oxford Hall in Medieval Times* (Oxford, rev. edn. 1968), 125-61 (chapter 7, 'Two Lollard Principals').

[30] Corpus Christi (Oxon) MS 116, fo. 50ᵛ, quoted by J. A. Robson, *Wyclif and the Oxford Schools* (Cambridge, 1961), 229 n. 1.

[31] H. B. Workman, *John Wyclif* (Oxford, 1926), ii. 343.

opinions were clearly in the background of the debate in Oxford on Bible translation in 1401;[32] and Netter in his *Doctrinale* refers to a debate in Oxford between himself and Peter Payne, though the precise date is not clear.[33] Most telling of all, of course, is the obvious anxiety of Archbishop Arundel about the state of the university and the support to be found within it for Wyclif's views: which led first to his constitutions of 1407 inhibiting the reading of Wyclif's polemical works in the university (as well as prohibiting the translation of Scripture); then to his appointment in 1409 of a committee of twelve to search Wyclif's work for errors and heresies; and finally to his visitation of the university in 1411 and the imposition of a new oath on all incepting as masters, that they would not uphold any of the two hundred and sixty-seven errors and heresies that the committee had uncovered in the writings of the heresiarch.[34]

I have deliberately laboured the evidence of the continued interest in Wyclif's ideas and writings in Oxford. Wyclif was a man of ideas and ideas lose their force and go stale if they are not subjected to discussion: debate is their oxygen. After 1411 and after the fiasco of Old-castle's revolt in 1414 Lollardy did lose touch with *academia* (and with knightly patronage too), and the fire in its belly slowly went out. But down to the end of the first decade of the fifteenth century it was by no means extinguished: Wyclif's views remained a lively subject of discussion in the university among both his supporters and his critics, and among the former, as the compilation of the *Floretum* and the *Rosarium* suggest, there were those who were determined to make sure that they were disseminated accurately to a wider audience. Most important of all, as I hope to suggest, in this period the vigour and confidence of Wyclif's *fautores* in Oxford and elsewhere in England helped to secure that his writing and opinions made the powerful impact that they did in Bohemia. But for their continued activity and activism that influence would not have been so sharp and the course of the history of the Czech religious upheaval would probably have been considerably different.

It would be impertinent for one to whom the extensive Czech literature on the subject is a closed book to attempt a precise estimate

---

[32] See Hudson, 'The Debate on Bible Translation, Oxford 1401', in *Lollards and their Books*, 67-84.

[33] T. Netter, *Doctrinale* (Venice, 1571), i, cols. 7-8.

[34] For an effective review of Arundel's various proceedings see Emden, *An Oxford Hall*, 143-9.

of the debt of Hus and his school to the teaching of Wyclif. I will therefore try to be brief on this matter and confine myself to points that do
not seem to me to be very controversial. But I cannot pass the subject
by, because it seems to me undeniable that Wyclif's influence in Hussite Bohemia was profound and important, and that therefore there is
no way of glossing over it in any attempt to do justice to the significance of his work in his own age.[35]

Wyclif's philosophical views were what originally drew the attention of Prague scholars. Work of his was known there as early as 1381,[36]
but we have no evidence that he made any very strong impression
before the 1390s. Then his teaching began to take root. It is not surprising that it did so; there was a strong realist strain in the thinking of
great Czech teachers like Milic and more especially Mathias of Janov,
so the seed fell in a soil that was in a measure prepared for it and
flourished naturally. John Hus himself enthusiastically copied and
glossed the *Materia et Forma*, the *De Ideis*, and the *De Universalibus* in
1398.[37] The early philosophical tracts of Stanislav Znojmo and Stephan
Palec, composed in the same general period, were so penetrated with
Wyclif's thought that two of them have been attributed by modern
editors to the master himself.[38] Wyclif was thus first impressive to the
Czechs because he presented a more coherent and comprehensive up-
to-date statement than any other that they had met of the realist
position, with which their revered masters of the previous generation
seemed to be in sympathy. It was natural that this interest should lead
forward to an interest in his controversial theological works which,
with their strong emphasis on the Bible and on the example of the
primitive Church, proved also to have a sympathy of theme with the
teachings of Milic and Mathias. Soon the whole gamut of Wyclif's
views was under debate. Already in 1400, apparently, certain Czech
masters were discussing with the lay preacher Thomas Stitny Wyclif's
opinions on the Eucharist;[39] and in 1405 Stanislav of Znojmo was
charged with publicly upholding in the schools the doctrine of
remanence, on the same metaphysical ground on which Wyclif had

[35] In what follows, I must acknowledge my profound indebtedness to the masterly
article of F. Smahel, ' "Doctor Evangelicus super omnes evangelistas"; Wyclif's
Fortunes in Hussite Bohemia', *Bull. Inst. Hist. Res.*, 43 (1970), 16-34.

[36] D. Trapp, 'Unchristened Nominalism and Wyclifite Realism in Prague in 1381',
Recherches de théologie ancienne et médiévale, 24 (1957), 320-60.

[37] R. R. Betts, *Essays in Czech History* (Oxford, 1969), 141.

[38] A. H. Thompson, 'Some Latin Works erroneously Ascribed to Wyclif', *Speculum*, 3
(1928), 382-91.

[39] Loserth (above, n. 2), 75.

denied the possibility of annihilation.[40] Stanislav was later to retract this view, it is true, and Hus himself never adopted Wyclif's view on the sacrament of the altar, remaining thoroughly orthodox in this matter: but his friend and colleague Jacobellus of Stribro adopted remanence and so later did most of the Taborite theologians.

It must be stressed, though, that Wyclif's realism and his emphasis on biblical study and the example of the early Church were not the only reasons why the Czech masters were attracted to his way of thinking. There were other less reputable and less rational forces at work. 'Germans, haha; out, out!'–so runs a marginal note to the philosophical tracts that the young Hus copied out in 1398.[41] In Prague Wyclif's influence became caught up quite early in the quarrels of the constituent nations of the University of Prague and in particular of the Czech and German nations, which for long were pursued even more ruthlessly than the perennial dispute between nominalists and realists. The two quarrels were not separate. Though it would of course be ridiculous to identify all Czech masters as realists and all Germans with the rival nominalist school, there were real and sharp contrasts between their native traditions of thought in these matters, and certain events tended to polarize the situation. Very important was the condemnation of forty-five articles from Wyclif's works which the Silesian John Hübner secured from the university in May 1403, with the support of the cathedral chapter.[42] The result of this condemnation, which was regarded as a national affront by a number of Czech masters, was merely to strengthen the determination of a group among them, who if outnumbered were influential, to defend Wyclif's teachings. It was in the wake of this condemnation that in 1405 Stanislas defended Wyclif's doctrine of remanence and called down upon himself the wrath of Archbishop Zbynek: and though he recanted on the point others took up the cudgels on different issues.[43] In ensuing and increasingly intemperate debates and confrontations the Czech realists came more and more to identify their defence of Wyclif with the rights in the university of the 'holy Czech nation', and their opponents to take their stand on the identity of views between the Prague realists and the formally condemned heretic, Wyclif. As the war of words was carried outside the schools into the pulpits of Prague city

[40] Loserth (above, n. 2), 98. Stanislav's tract *De Romanentia Panis* does not appear to have survived.

[41] Smahel (above, n. 35), 19.

[42] Ibid., 22; Loserth (above, n. 2), 97.

[43] M. Spinka, *John Hus at the Council of Constance* (Columbia, 1965), 33-4.

the language of the dispute became more violent and scurrilous, and names came to count for more and thought for less.[44] Because the archbishop and the majority of the higher clergy had been drawn into the struggle on the anti-Wycliffite side (being, like many of the Germans, supporters of Gregory XII, whereas Hus and his friends were enthusiasts of a Council), the decree of Kutna Hora of 1409, which secured to the Czech nation a controlling voice in the university,[45] changed nothing. A large number of Germans and other aliens left the university; but in the next year the old battle lines were essentially the same when Zbynek ordered all copies of Wyclif's works to be impounded and had them burned–it was Hus versus the hierarchy, Hussites who defended Wyclif along with all they deemed especially holy and good in the national Czech reform movement against the Germans, the local ecclesiastical establishment, and the transmontane papacy.[46] The end of this sad road was reached when Hus at Constance found himself accused for holding opinions put together by his enemies not from his works but from Wyclif's, most of which he had never upheld, and was burned because he would not reject quite all of them or denounce Wyclif without reservation.

The moral of this story is not that Wyclif's thought had been lost sight of in the ethnic and ecclesiastical confrontations in Bohemia and Prague, that he had been mytholoziged into a name that one party could hail as that of the fifth evangelist and the other denounce as that of the devil's first son.[47] The men who became most prominently involved in the debates in the university and the city of Prague in the first decade of the fifteenth century were for the most part university masters, men of agile mind and extensive learning who could not help being concerned, not just for names that were being bandied about, but for the intellectual ideas for which those names stood, and who fully understood their implications. Jerome of Prague made himself the most ardent and evangelistic propagator of realist ideas of his generation; he was prepared to tell almost anyone from King Sigismund of Hungary downwards that there was a 'universal ass', and bought himself much trouble by doing so intemperately.[48] Hus's own stance was different from Wyclif's and independent, for he was a reformer first and a thinker second, but he had drunk deep at the fount

[44] See Smahel (above, n. 35), 23-4.
[45] Spinka (above, n. 43), 35, and references there cited.
[46] Ibid., 37-8; Smahel, 23; Betts (above, n. 37), 75.
[47] Smahel, 24, 25.
[48] Betts (above, n. 37), 207, 209.

nevertheless. His bitter jibe at Stanislav and Palec after they recanted their old views, that they had flushed their realism down the loo (*ad cloacas*),[49] shows his awareness of the importance of the philosophical stance to which Wyclif had helped him. His *de Ecclesia*, written in 1412 and one of his most important works, is also one deeply indebted to Wyclif and underpinned by Wyclif's teaching on predestination—which in turn stemmed from his realist metaphysics. Some of Hus's more significant colleagues were, moreover, more deeply touched by Wyclif than he, notably Jacobellus of Stribro, the original protagonist of the administration of communion in both kinds to the laity. Wyclif did become a name that was bandied about in Bohemia by men who did not know or understand what he said, but only because it was simultaneously being bandied about by men who very thoroughly understood his philosophical and evangelical teaching, a great many of whom warmly approved of most of what he had written.

Once again, books are perhaps the most telling evidence. We shall in a moment need to look at what is known about the transmission of particular texts from England to Bohemia, but it is perfectly clear that what we can now see there is only the tip of the iceberg. As the briefest glance at Williel Thomson's catalogue of *The Latin Writings of John Wyclyf* will show,[50] far more texts of Wyclif's works have survived in continental Bohemian copies than in insular ones, and a number only survive in continental manuscripts. The sheer number of copies of Wyclif's works that were made in Bohemia, the preparation there of indices to them to aid the reader, the evidence that survives of the organization of production, all tell the same story.[51] So does the determination of some of the Hussites to make sure that their less scholarly compatriots should get a taste of the authentic Wyclif. Jacobellus produced a version of Wyclif's *Dialogus* in Czech in 1415: and the *Trialogus* and the *De Civili Dominio* were also translated at much the same time.[52] As Hus put it in 1411, Wyclif had 'tried with all his power to bring back to the law of Christ all people and especially the clergy, so that leaving the pomp of the world they might live like apostles the life of Christ'.[53] He and his fellows in consequence saw the evangelical doctor as one whose works were worth copying, reading, pondering,

---

[49] Smahel, 21.
[50] W. Thomson, *The Latin Writings of John Wyclyf* (Toronto, 1983).
[51] Hudson, *Lollards and their books*, 38-40.
[52] Smahel, 26.
[53] Ibid., 28.

and making available to a wider audience: and they made sure that his books were plentifully reproduced.

Just as in England the best evidence of the continued and active interest in Wyclif's teaching after his death resides in books, so it is with Bohemia. There too books are cumulatively the most powerful evidence, and the two cases are related since the exemplars of Bohemian books came from England and, above all (without much doubt) from Oxford.

As we have seen, some of Wyclif's works reached Prague in his lifetime, as early as 1381. This is not as surprising as it may seem at first. Prague was a relatively new university and new universities, in the fourteenth as in the twentieth century, had to build up their libraries; and scholars visiting overseas universities (and especially Paris and Oxford) were therefore encouraged to copy out codices of important works. In the 1370s Wyclif's fame in the schools of Oxford stood high: to bring to Prague something of his work that would offer an insight into the state of up-to-the-minute discussion in an ancient and revered centre of learning was a quite natural thing to do. The first reaction to him that we know of, from the Prague realist Biceps, was unexcited and critical.[54] It was however natural in this case that on closer acquaintance it should become apparent that there was a sympathy between Wyclif's views and those of native Czech realists, and that this in turn should have stirred among a group of scholars themselves deeply committed to the cause of radical religious reform an interest in the more controversial theological work. Hussite tradition has it that one Maurice Rvacka (who was later to become a severe critic of Hus and Wyclif) was the first to be encouraged to obtain copies of these more polemical works from Oxford,[55] sometime in the 1390s. In 1400/1 Jerome of Prague during his stay there copied the *Dialogus* and the *Trialogus* (both works of Wyclif's Lutterworth period:[56] clearly Oxford was the place to look for these as well as for works he had written while still teaching in the university). It was in order to copy and collate Wyclif texts that in 1407 Nicholas Faulfiš and George Knehnic visited Oxford, Kemerton, and Braybrook, and clearly by that time a good many other copyists had been at work.[57] When in 1410

---

[54] Ibid., 18.
[55] Ibid., 20.
[56] Betts (above, n. 37), 197-8.
[57] Hudson, *Lollards and their Books*, 78-9.

Archbishop Zbynek impounded copies of Wyclif's books and had them burnt we are told that no less than two hundred codices were consumed[58]–and we know there were others, that did not perish in that pyre.

It will now be clear why it was that I suggested earlier that the continued interest in Wyclif at Oxford and the activity of his *fautores* there in the period between *c.*1380 and *c.*1410 was important from the point of view of Wyclif's influence not just in England but in Bohemia as well. It is not possible to gauge precisely what proportion of the Wyclif texts that reached Bohemia in the early fifteenth century came direct from Oxford, but it is reasonable to think it was the principal source, at least down to 1407. The Bohemians were clearly aware that Oxford was a place where they could expect to find the books they wanted and to meet English followers of the heresiarch. The open letter, bearing the Oxford University seal and dated 5 October 1406 and testifying to the esteem in which Wyclif was there held, was carried to Prague (perhaps by Faulfiš) and made a considerable stir there. Hus read its contents publicly and referred to it later in the course of his controversy with the Englishman Stokes in 1411: 'he says that Master JW in England is counted for a heretic: this seemeth false by the letter testimonial of the University of Oxford, to which there is more credit to be given than unto him.'[59] Jerome of Prague read the same letter aloud at the end of a *quodlibet* in 1409.[60] Hus's accusers came back in 1415 to the question of this 'forged' letter, which Arundel himself admitted had brought great scandal and embarrassment to the English Church:[61] clearly, it was on all sides regarded as significant. Whether, as Gascoigne believed, Peter Payne stole the seal of the university and appended it to the letter,[62] or whether (as is more likely) it was the genuine record of a snap vote in a hurried congregation held in the long vacation, is not clear. The Bohemians however clearly took it to be genuine and set store by it as a witness to the esteem in which Wyclif was held in the second university of Europe after Paris.

Hus and his party in early fifteenth-century Bohemia were not only interested in the works of Wyclif, but also in those of his English

---

[58] O. Odlozilik, 'Wycliffe's influence upon Central and Eastern Europe', *Slavonic and East European Review*, 7 (1928), 640.

[59] Foxe, *Acts and Monuments of the English Church* (1871 edn.), iii. 59.

[60] Betts, 197-8.

[61] F. Palacký (ed.), *Documenta Mag. Johannis Hus* (Prague, 1869), 232; Wilkins, *Concilia*, iii. 336.

[62] T. Gascoigne, *Loci e Libro Veritatum*, ed. J. Thorold Rogers (Oxford, 1881), 20.

followers and sympathizers. The *Floretum* and the *Rosarium* both found their way to Prague and were eagerly copied there: so did the *Opus Arduum* which has been ascribed to Nicholas Hereford.[63] Their interest was not confined to academic works: there is a Czech version of Thorpe's autobiographical account of his trial before Archbishop Arundel[64] and also a Czech copy of a satiric Lollard poem in Latin on the Earthquake Council.[65] In 1410 a significant correspondence developed between on the one hand Oldcastle and Richard Wyche and on the other Hus and his secular follower Wok of Waldstein. Hus was so impressed by Wyche's letter that he translated it into Czech and had it read publicly. And the words that he wrote in his reply to Wyche are perhaps the best testimony that survives of the undoubted importance that English Lollardy held in the eyes of the Bohemian leaders: 'I am thankful that Bohemia has under the power of Jesus Christ received so much good from the blessed land of England.'[66]

Though it is in a way a digression, something must be said here briefly of Peter Payne, Master of Arts of Oxford and sometime Principal of St Edmund Hall, because no account of Lollard influence in Bohemia could be adequate without it.[67] Before he left Oxford in 1414, in the aftermath of Oldcastle's revolt, Payne was the most significant Wycliffite left in Oxford and probably had been so for some years. He clearly knew he could expect a welcome among the Czechs and he had a long and important career among them. His fidelity to the memory of his English master Wyclif was deep, and he came to be one of the most determined disseminators of his teachings in Bohemia. He almost certainly brought with him there some of the indexes that had been made in England as guides to Wyclif's writings, and he certainly compiled a number of his own and disseminated them among the Czechs.[68] In the debates in the 1420s with Master John Pribram (who was seeking to distinguish what he claimed to be the orthodox views of Hus from the heretical tenets of Wyclif) he anticipated Loserth by four hundred years in his exposition of Hus's dependence–often word

[63] Hudson, 'A Lollard Compilation in England and Bohemia' and 'A Neglected Wycliffite text' (*Opus Arduum*), in her *Lollards and Their Books*, 31-42, 43-65.

[64] Aston, *Lollards and Reformers*, 226.

[65] Hudson, *Lollards and their Books* m 7.

[66] Odlozilik (above, n. 58), 640.

[67] On Payne, see Betts, 236-46; A. B. Emden, *A Biographical Regiter of the University of Oxford*, iii. 1441-3; I am also much indebted to the unpublished Ph.D. thesis for the University of Cornell of W. R. Cook, 'Peter Payne: Theologian and Diplomat of the Hussite Revolution'.

[68] Cook (above, n. 67), 163-73; Hudson, *Lollards and their Books*, 4-5.

for word–on Wyclif.[69] He probably had much to do with the strong leaning toward Wyclif specifically among the Hussite radicals of Tabor and the Orphans, and at Basle he was the most important spokesman for the radical wing of the movement. One other point about him perhaps deserves mention. It is striking how early on in his Bohemian period Payne, the English Wycliffite, adopted Jacobellus's teaching on the administration of the communion in both kinds to the laity, and how eagerly he espoused the Hussite emphasis on the need for frequent communion.[70] His example is a good demonstration of the way in which Wyclif's doctrine of remanence in no way seemed to detract from the centrality of the mass to those who adhered to it (as it is sometimes supposed to have done). To the Wycliffite Payne the emphasis on the Eucharist as the bulwark of the laity against Antichrist, which derived ultimately from Mathias of Janov, seemed wholly right and natural (as it would have done, I think, to Wyclif himself).

Wyclif's influence on the Hussite movement, as we are here reminded, was not seminal. The original impulse of that movement derived from the reformist and evangelical teaching of the great native religious leaders of the pre-Hussite period, as Milic, Mathias, and Thomas Stitny. Neverthelss, Wyclif's was a profound influence. It owed something of its impact to the way in which the disputes over his teaching became enmeshed in the rivalries of Czechs and Germans in Prague and the confrontation between the university and the hierarchy, but to overemphasize this does injustice not only to Wyclif but also to the Czech scholars whose reading of him was always critical as well as enthusiastic. His ready reception also owed much to the fact that his views on evangelical reform chimed so well with those of the great pre-Hussite teachers and also of Hus himself. But above all, in Prague as in Oxford, what made his impact so powerful, I believe, was the coherence of the realist position that underpinned all his teaching, theological and philosophical, and which gave it a general, systematic basis that was lacking in the teaching of the early Czech leaders. Certainly this was why, once Hus and his disciples had absorbed his philosophy, it was so difficult to shake free of it. When Pribram made his bold and astute intitiative to purge Hussitism of the taint of heresy

[69] Cook, 181, quoting from Payne's unpublished *Posicio contra Pribram* (Vienna National Library, MS 3935, fo. 338 is the authority cited).

[70] Cook, 59-60, quoting Payne's unpublished *Replica* of 1415 (Prague Cathedral Library, MS D 109/2 fo. 199ʳ for the passage in question).

(in the interests of reconciliation with the universal Church) by dissociating it from foreign Wycliffism, moderates like Rockycana who sympathized with his aim could not follow him. They were too sharply aware that much more was involved with Wyclif than the Eucharist (on which, because Hus was orthodox, Pribram was concentrating), and that in his philosophical ideas and his concept of the Church Hus so depended on Wyclif that condemnation of the latter must lead to the eventual rejection of the former as well.[71] Realist metaphysic was the key to the profundity of Wyclif's influence in Bohemia, just as it was his realist metaphysic that–because it raised so many and such large issues–kept scholars actively debating him in Oxford long after the so-called rout of 1382; and that sustained interest was in its turn the chief reason why Bohemian contact with Wyclif's thought turned into an extensive cross fertilization of the two movements, Lollard and Hussite, in which much more than metaphysic came to be involved.

Gordon Leff has called Wyclif the 'great heresiarch' of the later Middle Ages. His claim to that title stems from the fact that, despite all his rage and verbosity, he was a thinker of real power, with coherent and wide ranging ideas and stirred by a genuine passion. It is true that both in England and Bohemia it was other men who turned the ideas in his books into an active force for reform, but a generating power came from the ideas and the coherence of their marshalling. Perhaps it is too much to call Wyclif the 'morning star of the Reformation': before that dawn could break much more was needed beyond the metaphysical teaching of an old-style schoolman–a new approach to scriptural texts and a knowledge of Greek that were available in the age of Luther and Erasmus but not in the fourteenth century, and the printing press. But from the point of view of future Protestantism he was certainly a notable and fiery object in the still dark sky, and that is why the early Protestants, when they began to rediscover him, hailed him as a precursor. It is also why, in the late Middle Ages, the words 'Wyclif' and 'Hus' were, after the word 'council', those calculated to send the chilliest tremors down the spines of the captains of orthodoxy and of the hierarchical establishment, and why Catholic writers, even in the sixteenth century, still thought it worthwhile to go about the business of rebutting Wyclif.

[71] J. Palacky, *Geschichte von Böhmen* (Prague, 1844-65) iii. 7. 423-4; Cook, 188-9.

8

The Accursed Memory: The Counter-Reformation Reputation of John Wyclif

ANTHONY KENNY

TWENTY years ago, in a rich article in *Past and Present*, Margaret Aston described how the figure of Wyclif built up by Protestant writers during the Reformation period contained a great deal of myth.[1] It was not only among Protestants, however, that Wyclif acquired a historical ghost: Catholics, too, built up a partly fictional aura round the reformer's memory. But for them, of course, he was not an ancestor to be revered, but an evil spirit to be exorcized. The present essay intends to complement Margaret Aston's study by outlining the history of Wyclif's reputation among Catholics from the middle of the fifteenth to the beginning of the seventeenth century. It will be seen that the Catholic picture of the reformer, like the Protestant one, is related only distantly to his actual life and work. During the Reformation period few of those who wrote about Wyclif, whether to praise or blame him, went to the trouble of reading his works. In the case of the Catholics this was not, perhaps, surprising. They had, after all, been forbidden more than once by the highest authorities to read or quote Wyclif. In libraries outside heretical Bohemia his works were not easily accessible and if they were available at all it was despite official attempts to destroy them. Paradoxically the only writings of his which were widely circulated were the propositions which had been extracted from his works and singled out for condemnation. The official condemnations of Wyclif become the most important single source of information, or misinformation, about him before, during, and after the Reformation.

During his lifetime Wyclif was never personally condemned as

---

[1] Margaret Aston, 'John Wycliffe's Reformation Reputation', *Past and Present*, 30 (1965), 23-51.

a heretic. In 1377 Pope Gregory XI picked out eighteen propositions from the *De Civili Dominio* and wrote to Edward III and others to prosecute him in connection with them; but pope and king both soon died and the bulls became a dead letter.[2] In 1382 a provincial synod at Blackfriars (the 'Earthquake Council') considered twenty-four propositions concerning the Eucharist, the limits of clerical power, the dispensability of the papacy, and the wrongness of Church endowment. The assembled divines censured ten of these as heretical and fourteen as erroneous.[3] Wyclif was not condemned by name; his retirement and swiftly ensuing death allowed the official proceedings to rest for another decade. But the posthumous popularity of his late dialogue, the *Trialogus*, alarmed Archbishop Arundel of Canterbury, and a provincial synod held at St Paul's in 1397 condemned eighteen articles drawn from that work.[4] A reasoned defence of the condemnation of each article was prepared by the Franciscan William Woodford, who had engaged in controversy with Wyclif during his lifetime.[5]

In the first years of the fifteenth century it was not in England but in Bohemia that the debate on Wyclif's doctrines raged most fiercely, mingling with national feeling between Czechs and Germans. In 1403 the twenty-four Blackfriars propositions were condemned in Prague, though only the first four were regarded as heretical. Twenty-one new propositions were added by a German divine to the original list, making a new total of forty-five. The new list contains some which are difficult to trace, in any close approximation, in Wyclif's works; and John Hus is reported to have said that the person who drew up the list deserved to be burnt for fraud. The condemnation was renewed in 1412.[6]

Meanwhile, England had again become concerned about Wyclif. A revival of Lollardy in Oxford led to further inquisition. In 1409 Archbishop Arundel appointed a commission to identify errors in Wyclif's works and to free the university from the infection of heresy. His commission drew up a list of two hundred and sixty-seven suspect propositions, which they forwarded to the archbishop after condemnation by the university. The university's letter to the archbishop says that

---

[2] See Joseph H. Dahmus, *The Prosecution of John Wyclyf* (New Haven, 1952), 49-50.

[3] Text in *FZ*, 275-82.

[4] David Wilkins, *Concilia Magnae Britanniae* ... iii (London, 1737), 229.

[5] Woodford's justification for the condemnation is printed in Gratiu's *Fasciculus Rerum Expetendarum* (Antwerp, 1535).

[6] M. Spinka, *Jan Hus' Concept of the Church* (Princeton, 1966), 397.

twelve masters and doctors have sampled many books, pamphlets, and tracts of Wyclif and marked passages which seemed heretical, erroneous, and contrary to the teachings of the Fathers. 'We have considered them with care and have judged them contrary to sacred doctrine, and all deserving to be burnt.' But, the university goes on, its authority is not taken very seriously by most people, and therefore they are sending the propositions for mature consideration by the archbishop and his colleagues, with the request that they should be sent on to the pope.[7]

The propositions are taken, usually verbatim or with the minimum of paraphrase, from a number of Wyclif's Latin works. In the version printed by Wilkins they are listed, often under slightly confusing titles, as coming from the *Trialogus*, the *Logicae Continuatio*, *De Ordine Christiano*, *De Simonia*, *De Perfectione Statum*, *De Dotatione Ecclesiae*, *De Diabolo et Membris eius*, *Reply to Strode*, *Responsio ad xlv conclusiones*, *De Confessione*, *De Versutia Pseudocleri*, *De Civili Dominio*, *Opus Evangelicum*, and *De Versutiis Antichristi*.[8] The list of propositions was not simply an extension of the previous English condemnations. The articles proscribed by Gregory and the twenty-four condemned at Blackfriars do not occur verbatim; but the eighteen from the *Trialogus* condemned in 1397 figure as numbers 121-4 and 127-40.

Archbishop Arundel and his suffragans, assembled in synod, concurred with the Oxford condemnation and sent on the list of propositions, with their source marked, to the pope, with the request that having made further inquiry into the conclusions he should condemn them (with the books, treatises, and pamphlets from which they came) and also the accursed author and his disciples. They expressly suggest that Wyclif's bones should be exhumed and burnt.[9] The pope who received the letter was John XXIII of the Pisan line, the one of the three popes to which, at this stage of the Great Schism, the English Church had given its allegiance. In February 1412-13 John XXIII held a council in Rome which condemned Wyclif. It did not, however, carry out Arundel's request and condemn the long list of propositions submitted from the Canterbury synod. Instead, the council's synodal decree is directed at Wyclif's books. It condemns the *Dialogus* and

[7] Wilkins, *Concilia*, iii. 346-8.

[8] The attributions to the various works are given by Wilkins, but not always in easily recognizable form. I have followed the identifications given by W. R. Thomson, *The Latin Writings of John Wyclyf* (Toronto, 1983), nos. 47, 2, 414, 35, 426, 48, 430, 386, 384, 38, 376, 420.

[9] Wilkins, *Concilia*, iii. 350-1.

Trialogus by name, saying their noxiousness is notorious; but it condemns also 'all other similar pamphlets and other material bearing the name of John Wyclif, whatever art and faculty it may belong to'. These works are condemned and order is given for them to be publicly burnt: no one must read or expound these books, nor quote them except in refutation. Local bishops are to seek out and destroy all copies. If no one appears within nine months to defend his memory, Wyclif will himself be posthumously condemned as a heretic.[10]

The eventual condemnation took place not at Rome, but at Constance.[11] The main item on the agenda of the council was the ending of the schism which had left the Church with not just two but three claimants to the papacy. But the teaching of Wyclif and his disciples was the second most important item on the agenda. If anyone, following the Roman citation, can be said to have appeared at the council to defend Wyclif's memory it was John Hus, who, relying on the safe conduct he had received from the pope and the Emperor Sigismund, preached a Wycliffite sermon soon after his arrival. Despite the safe conduct, Hus was imprisoned; Pope John, himself under threat from the council fathers, professed himself unable to help. The council, indeed, in its seventh session, began proceedings to depose him; but before this, in its fifth session, it had confirmed his Roman condemnation of Wyclif.[12]

Among those attending the Council of Constance there seems to have been general enthusiasm for the project of condemning Wyclif. The council fathers were not, however, similarly unanimous about which propositions to condemn. Two different sets seem to have been brought to the council by representatives of the different 'nations' of which the council was composed. The English representatives brought with them the list of propositions condemned by the Oxford commissioners. But they arrived later than some of the other parties and the German nation had got in first with the list of forty-five propositions condemned in Prague in 1403. (Bohemia counted, for purposes of the council, as part of the German nation.) This list, as remarked,

---

[10] J. D. Mansi, *Sacrorum Conciliorum Nova et Amplissima Collectio* ... (Venice, 1784), xxvii, 505-6.

[11] The fullest account of the Council's dealings with Wyclif's teaching is Edith C. Tatnall, 'The Condemnation of John Wyclif at the Council of Constance', in G. J. Cuming and Derek Baker, eds., *Councils and Assemblies* (London, 1971). Though full, this account is not entirely accurate.

[12] C. J. Hefele, *Histoire des Conciles* ... French translation by Dom. H. Leclercq, vii (Paris, 1916), 211-13.

began with the twenty-four errors condemned at Blackfriars Council, but then listed another twenty-one which, unlike the Oxford list, are not always easy to trace to their origin in Wyclif's extant works. They are clearly meant to represent, however, the teaching of the *Trialogus*, which had been brought to Bohemia from England in 1402. The course of the condemnation of Wyclif was complicated by the parallel proceedings being taken against Hus. The fifth session, having approved the Roman proscription of Wyclif's books, asked two cardinals, Fillastre and d'Ailly, to investigate the doctrine of Wyclif and Hus and in particular the forty-five articles which are described as 'already condemned in the Universities of Paris and Prague'.[13] From what followed it is clear that the forty-five Prague articles were more familiar to the French delegation than the 267 Oxford ones, about which they complained that they had been given insufficient notice.

More than one commission at Constance seems to have been concerned with Wyclif: perhaps one was a theological commission, to investigate the doctrine contained in the offensive propositions, and the second a canonical commission to conduct the proceedings against the persons of Wyclif and his followers. There was some disagreement between the committees but its nature is obscure. In the sixth session it was decreed that the commission investigating Hus should receive a report from Fillastre and d'Ailly (with whom the canonist Zabarella had now been coupled) on the doctrine of the forty-five articles–to which the Oxford ones are now added.[14]

Among the acts of the Council of Constance preserved by Van der Hardt there are two theological reports on the forty-five propositions.[15] The first is the work of many hands and is brief and pointed, allotting a paragraph of two of objections to each thesis. The second is more discursive, the work of a single author who complains about the lack of books in the place where he is working. Each report attaches to each article a qualification which theologians technically call a 'theological note': that is to say, it states not only that an article is objectionable but assesses the degree of offensiveness: does it deserve the maximum censure as something heretical, or is it merely erroneous or rash or perhaps merely ill-sounding? It is interesting to see that the

---

[13] Mansi (above, n. 10), xxvii. 591.

[14] Ibid., xxvii. 611.

[15] H. Van der Hardt, *Magnum oecumenicum Constantiense concilium* (Berlin, 1697-1700), iii, part 12, 'Theologorum Constantiensium Brevis Censura XLIV articulorum' and part 13 'Diffusa Condemnatio'. Neither report attempts to relate the propositions at issue to their context in Wyclif's own works.

two reports, while they find each several proposition objectionable, disagree considerably about the qualifications to be attached. The shorter report finds only a small minority of the theses actually heretical: numbers 1 and 3 on the Eucharist, number 4 about the sacramental effectiveness of sinful priests, number 7 about the superfluity of confession, number 9 saying that the papacy should be abolished, 21 and 22 and 45 which describe as sinful founding or entering a religious order, 27 affirming determinism, and parts of 14 and 48 concerning unlicensed preaching and the decretals of canon law. The forty-five propositions begin with the ten which were condemned as heretical by the Blackfriars council; the Constance theologians judge only half of these to be heretical. On the other hand they censure 21 and 22 (about religious orders) more severely than the Blackfriars divines, who regard those propositions as no worse than erroneous. The author of the longer report at Constance is more ready to qualify a proposition as heretical: unlike his colleagues, for instance, he thinks it is heresy to say that in the sacrament of the altar the accidents do not remain without a subject.

Considering the atmosphere of the Council of Constance both papers are surprisingly ultramontane: they affirm that there is no salvation outside the Roman Church and they say that it is heretical to think otherwise than as the Roman Church does. But the longer paper is marked as completed shortly after St Lucy's day. It was written, therefore, in December 1414, before the Council had taken on itself to depose the pope who had summoned it and to declare that a General Council was superior to a pope. The longer censure, too, condemns as heretical Wyclif's proposal to abolish the papacy: it does so on the grounds that this would go against the Council of Pisa, which cannot err and which elected Alexander V. Such an argument would not have been used after the council had rejected Alexander's successor, or in later years when the Pisan line had been disowned by Martin V's successors.

The session officially devoted to Wyclif was the eighth session, held on Saturday 4 May in the presence of the emperor under the presidency of the cardinal of Ostia. The procurator Henry Piro asked for Wyclif's followers to be proclaimed contumacious and for Wyclif himself to be declared to have died impenitent: his bones should be exhumed.[16] The forty-five propositions were read out to the council by the archbishop of Genoa, as was a draft decree of condemnation. This

[16] Mansi, xxviii. 629-32; Van der Hardt, iv. 149-52.

had been prepared before 16 February, but had been shelved when the Fathers turned their attention to the possibility of deposing all three popes as a method of ending the Great Schism.[17] The decree, after listing the forty-five propositions continues thus:

Wyclif is also the author of the Dialogue, the Trialogue, and many treatises in which he has set out these errors and many others, and caused great harm to souls and scandal, especially in England and Bohemia. The forty-five propositions, already proscribed academically [*scholastice*] by the universities of Oxford and Prague, have also been condemned by the archbishops of Canterbury, York, and Prague. The latter has also condemned his works to the fire. Finally the pope has recently censured the same writings at the council of Rome .. This present council has had the said articles examined many times by cardinals, bishops, and abbots, masters and doctors of each law, and it has been ascertained that many of them are manifestly heretical, many erroneous, others scandalous, blasphemous, temerarious, and offensive to pious ears. It has also been possible to ascertain that Wyclif's works contain other similar articles. Accordingly the present council confirms the sentences of the archbishops of Canterbury, York, and Prague, and the decree of the Council of Rome, condemns the 45 articles, the Dialogue, the Trialogue, and all other works of Wyclif.

It is the common opinion of historians, and has been believed at least since the Council of Trent, that Wyclif's doctrines were condemned at the eighth session of Constance. But Cardinal Fillastre's diary makes clear that this was not so. 'A decree was read', so we read in the entry for 4 May, 'condemning the forty-five articles and the books and the memory of Wyclif. But after the reading, the Cardinal of St Mark [i.e. Fillastre himself] rose and criticized the decree in several particulars, so it was not decided upon, but the Council was told that it would be amended.'[18]

An attempt was made in this session to include the Oxford articles in the decree of condemnation.[19] The archbishop of Genoa tried to read aloud the complete list, but Fillastre intervened and asked for a postponement. Our sources are confused at this point and various reasons have been given for the opposition to proceeding against them

---

[17] H. Finke and J. Hollsteiner, *Acta Concilii Constanciensis* (Munster, 1896-1928), ii. 19.

[18] 'Non transit in rem iudicatam, sed fuit dictum quod reformaretur' (Finke and Hollsteiner, ii. 19, 34). Hefele, who follows the common opinion that the 45 propositions were condemned in the eighth session, conjectures that the 267 were condemned at the ninth; but a close reading of Fillastre's diary shows that this is incorrect. (It is important to consult the Latin text in Finke, as the English version in Loomis, *The Council of Constance* (Princeton, 1966), is incomplete and sometimes misleading.) See Hefele-Leclercq (above, n. 12), vii. 223-5.

[19] The draft decree condemning them is in Mansi, xxvii. 365.

at the eighth session: was it nationalist preference of the Germans for their list rather than one prepared by the English (there was certainly anti-English feeling at the Council); or was it, as mentioned in the tenth session, that the French delegation felt it had not had time to study them sufficiently; or was it simply, as one writer suggests, that 'the reading of any list of two hundred and sixty theses would have been soporific'?[20] The matter must remain uncertain, but the most likely ground for the objection is given in the diary of Guillaume de la Tour for this day. 'It seemed to the Cardinal of St Mark and some others from the University of Paris that these articles had not been sufficiently studied, at least by the French nation.' Accordingly, the same source tells us, there was a meeting of masters and doctors held on 7 May in the Dominican convent to discuss the articles.[21] There was further discussion of the Oxford articles in a general session on 28 May, but we do not know what was said on that occasion: the council's main attention was elsewhere, for it was the day on which Pope John XXIII was deposed.

It was at the fifteenth session, the session memorable for the execution of Hus, that Wyclif's teaching was finally condemned.[23] Hus was led in and placed on a tribunal, while the Emperor sat crowned on his throne. The priestly vestments for Hus's degradation were already prepared: but before the proceedings began against him he had to listen to the condemnation of Wyclif. First the forty-five propositions were proscribed; then the council proceeded to deal with the theses brought from Oxford by the English nation. The number had now been reduced to two hundred and sixty: a few had been eliminated from the list. There is no record of why this was done or when: presumably at the preliminary hearings on 7 March or 28 May it had been held that these articles were in some sense defensible. One which appears in the original two hundred and sixty-seven but not in the final two hundred and sixty is number 119 of the Oxford list: 'If a prelate prescribes what the law of God does not prescribe, the commandments are to be obeyed and the superior is to be resisted.' The two hundred and sixty propositions were not read out in their entirely. The conciliar decree says that they had been examined and it had been determined that some of them were notoriously heretical and

---

[20] Tatnall (above, n. 11), 218.
[21] Finke and Hollsteiner, ii. 362-3.
[22] Ibid., 40.
[23] Mansi, xxvii. 747; Finke, ii. 48.

long condemned by the holy fathers; that some were blasphemous,
others erroneous, others scandalous, some offensive to pious ears, and
some rash and seditious. No attempt was made to attach theological
notes to particular theses. Fifty-eight only were read out during the
session.[24] But all the articles were condemned:'This sacred synod by
an everlasting decree proscribes and condemns the aforesaid articles
and any or each of them, forbidding each and every Catholic, under
threat of anathema, to dare to preach, teach, put forward or maintain
the said articles or any one of them.'[25] Only after three hundred and
five Wycliffite propositions had been condemned in this way did the
Council move on to the proceedings against Hus. Hus was interro-
gated about his attitude to these condemned articles: he denied that he
had taught Wycliffite error, but said that wherever Wyclif's soul might
now be, he hoped his own soul would join him there. After thirty
articles of his own had been read and condemned, he was degraded,
handed over to the secular arm, and burned that same day.[26]

The condemnation of Hus has long been censured by Protestant
writers as example of cruel perfidy. But the condemnation of Wyclif,
in the form it took, was itself outrageously unfair. Not that he was
innocent of heresy, nor that a more careful judgement would have
been unable to give a precise definition of the heresy. The point is that
it was quite unjust to condemn, under a global anathema, propositions
which many of the council fathers themselves regarded as falling far
short of heresy. It was as if, after a strike in which there had occurred
murders, bodily harm, assaults, obstructions, and insulting behaviour,
the DPP were to announce that anyone who had taken part in the
strike would be prosecuted on a murder charge. The council re-
affirmed the Roman sentence passed in 1412 against Wyclif's books:
no doubt fresh confirmation was thought necessary now that
John XXIII had been deposed. Before the council broke up a new
pope was elected and took the name Martin V: the first pope recognized throughout Christendom since the outbreak of the Great
Schism. One of his first acts was to confirm the council's condemnation of Wyclif in a bull *Inter cunctas* of 22 February 1418. This goes into
great detail in planning the persecution of supporters of Wyclif, going
so far as to lay down the type of manacle with which they should be
fettered. It also sets out a list of thirty-nine questions to be

[24] The list is printed in Hefele-Leclercq (above, n. 12), vii. 308ff.
[25] Mansi, xxvii. 747.
[26] Hefele-Leclercq, vii. 307-50.

put to suspects in the course of inquisition into Wycliffite and Hussite error. Thus the highest authorities in the Church finally proscribed the accursed memory of John Wyclif.[27]

Though the anathemas of Constance do no credit either to the fairness or to the scholarship of the assembled fathers, one of the theologians there present later went some way to making amends. Thomas Netter of Walden, a Carmelite friar who had been a pupil of William Woodford, decided to write a full-length critique of Wyclif's doctrines which would vindicate the decision of the council and do something to redeem the reputation of the English Church from the disgrace in the eyes of Christendom into which it had been brought by the teaching of its foremost theologian. Between 1421 and 1427 he wrote three volumes against the Wycliffites and Hussites.[28] The tone of the work is polemic, though certainly no more so than that of Wyclif's own later works; but the treatment of his opponents by Netter is serious and scholarly. He shows a very detailed knowledge of Wyclif's writings and places the condemned propositions in their context and investigates the sources of Wyclif's ideas. He is aware that not all the propositions condemned at Constance are actually to be found in the reformer's works: he does not, for instance, attempt to locate in his writings the thesis that God should obey the devil.

Netter is a more prolix and less lively writer than Wyclif, but in dealing with the theological issues he can display a dialectical ingenuity very reminiscent of that of his opponent. For instance, he has to reply to the trick Wycliffite question: can you say, pointing to the host, that white round thing is the body of Christ? The answer 'no' appears to be a denial of the real presence, the answer 'yes' to imply that Christ's body is round and white. Netter evades the trap with a counter-question: pointing to the sky on a cloudy summer morning, can you say, 'That round and red thing is the sun in the heavens'? He is also cautious and skilful in dealing with the issues of predestination and free will; but it was not Netter's scholarship and sensitivity that was to shape Catholic reaction to Wyclif, but the crude anathemas of 1415.

A good example of the influence which the Constance condemnations exercised on theology and philosophy can be seen in the

[27] The Bull, given in Mansi, xxvii. 1204 ff., repeatedly uses the phrases 'nefanda memoria' and 'damnata memoria'.

[28] Netter's *Doctrinale Fidei Ecclesiae Cathólicae contra Wiclevistas et Hussitas* was first printed at Venice in 1571; more accessible nowadays is the Venetian edition of 1757 of B. Blanciotti, reprinted Farnborough, 1967. The passages quoted are from ii. 52 and i. 21.

University of Louvain during the half-century after its foundation in 1425. Here, a quarrel between the faculties of theology and arts concerning the implications of the condemnation of Wyclif's doctrine of necessity led to the development of a system of three-valued logic and the eventual prohibition of that system by the pope in 1474.[29] The topic of necessity and contingency is one of the most difficult on which to ascertain Wyclif's true position. In his logical writings and in his *De Universalibus* he presented a careful and nuanced theory, endeavouring by detailed distinctions to reconcile, without paradox, the necessity imposed on the future by divine foreknowledge and omnipotence with the contingency demanded by the moral freedom of human beings. 'All things', he said in the latter treatise, 'will come to pass necessarily by hypothetical necessity, and yet will come to pass most contingently.' Later, in the *Trialogus*, he was prepared to attribute not only hypothetical but absolute necessity to future events, and it seems that he partially recanted his earlier position.[30] But even in the *Trialogus* his necessitarianism is so much hedged about with qualification that it is not at all clear that it conflicts with any Christian conception of freedom. Netter, in treating Wyclif's doctrine of necessity, makes clear that his followers denied that he was a determinist.

At Constance, however, there was condemned a single sentence from the *Trialogus*, truncated and taken out of context: 'all things happen by absolute necessity'. From then on, Wyclif became for theologians the archetypal representative of determinism. The quarrel at Louvain between the theologians and the logicians, which reached its climax in 1469, concerned the future-tensed propositions occurring in prophecies and in the creeds. A faithful Christian must believe these, argued the theologians, therefore they must be true. Not so, replied the logicians; if they are already true, then what they predict cannot but come about and there is no room for contingency. Hence, we must say that at present they are neither true nor false; we must attribute to them some other truth-value, a neutral one between truth and falsehood.

Thus, Peter de Rivo, the spokesman for the arts faculty, wrote as follows: 'Those who maintain that there is determinate truth in propositions about future contingent matters seem to fall into the execrable

---

[29] The story of the Louvain quarrel and the condemnation of Peter de Rivo is told, with a rich collection of contemporary documents, in L. Baudry, *La Querelle des Futurs Contingents (Louvain 1465–1475)* (Paris, 1965).

[30] See *Trialogus*, iii. 8.

heresy of John Wyclif, which was condemned by Pope Martin in the Council of Constance, to this effect: all things happen by absolute necessity.'[31] Peter de Rivo argues thus: if a future event has an antecedent which necessarily entails it and if that antecedent is itself necessary, then the future event is necessary too. But if a future contingent proposition is already determinately true, then its truth is absolutely necessary and it necessarily entails the coming to pass of the future event. Therefore, the future event must be absolutely necessary and not really contingent at all. We reach the conclusion that everything happens of necessity as Wyclif asserted.[32]

De Rivo runs through the customary arguments against this kind of necessitarianism: if Wyclif's heresy were true, God would not be omnipotent or free; the Incarnation of Christ and the prayers of Christians would be pointless; there would be no free will and no point in preaching or advice, praise or blame. 'These absurdities', he says, 'follow from the said heresy of John Wyclif whether he was talking of logical necessity or real necessity.'[33] The only way to avoid Wyclif's heresy was to adopt the Aristotelian view that future contingent propositions were neither true nor false. Indeed, de Rivo could point to a statute of Louvain of 1447 which forbade the teaching of the following proposition: 'Given any pair of contradictory future contingent propositions, one of the two is true and the other false, just as in present and past tensed propositions, and indeed the opposite of this conclusion is inconsistent with the faith.'[34]

The theology professor at Louvain, Henry van Zomeren, led a bitter campaign against Peter de Rivo. But in Louvain itself he made little headway. Not only the arts faculty was against him, but so too, after long hesitation, was the theology faculty, once opinions favourable to de Rivo had been obtained from the theologians of Cologne and Paris. But Zomeren had friends in Rome, including several Cardinals: one of them, Francesco della Rovere, had, in correspondence, showed himself hostile to de Rivo's thesis, which he regarded as only dubiously Aristotelian. So, condemned in his own university, van Zomeren appealed to Rome in 1470.

It was de Rivo's misfortune that before the case had been determined della Rovere succeeded to the papacy in 1471 as Sixtus IV. De Rivo was forced to retract five propositions drawn from his works and to recognize that to deny truth to future-tensed propositions was

[31] Baudry (above, n. 29), 85.   [32] Ibid., 85-6.
[33] Ibid., 86-7.   [34] Ibid., 26, 68.

scandalous and offensive to pious ears.[35] As a way of avoiding the determinism attributed to Wyclif, three-valued logic was henceforth not open to a loyal Catholic.

The Louvain controversy has an interest for historians of logic because of the experiments in semantics which were explored in the course of it. But if one compares the pamphlets in the controversy with the treatment of necessity in Wyclif's *De Universalibus*, one cannot avoid the conclusion that Wyclif's discussion of the paradoxes of free will and determinism operates at a far superior level of sophistication.[36] The decline in intellectual standard is something to which both Wyclif's later polemical hardening and the heavy-handed proceedings of Constance had made their contribution.

As the fifteenth century drew to its end, Wycliffite ideas seemed dead in all the major centres of learning in Christendom. But in the second decade of the sixteenth, as new heresies set Europe ablaze, many thought they could recognize in the new figure of Luther the familiar lineaments of Wyclif.

When Lutheran heresy came to England it was regarded by the orthodox as a revival of Wyclif's teaching. King Henry VIII, in a letter to the Duke of Saxony, claimed that the errors of Luther were 'pure Wyclifism'. When Wolsey in 1521, at the instigation of Pope Leo X, asked the University of Oxford to produce a refutation of Luther, the most substantial work produced by Oxford scholars was entitled *Propugnaculum Summi Sacerdotii Evangelici et Septenarii Sacramentorum adversus Martinum Lutherum fratrem famosum et Wiclefistam*. This was the work of a Welsh Fellow of Oriel, Edward Powell.[37] Powell viewed Luther as the culmination of all previous heresies, but in a special way of the heresies of Wyclif. Luther's downgrading of the papacy was 'most Wyclif-like and stupid'. Luther boasts of his originality, but his heresies are stale; they are drawn 'not from the purity of the evangelical font but from the wicked pits of Wyclif'. Concerning the Eucharist, Luther 'is less than Wyclif in terms of knowledge, but greater in evil'.

At the same time as Edward Powell, Thomas More was writing his own reply to Luther. In the *Responsio ad Lutherum* Wyclif appears

[35] The condemned propositions are given in H. Denzinger and C. Bannwart, *Enchiridion Symbolorum*, Friburg 1952, nos. 719-23.

[36] See my paper, 'Freedom and Necessity in Wyclif's *De Universalibus*', SCH, *Subsidia* 5 (1986).

[37] See G. Fitch Lyttle, 'John Wyclif, Edward Powell, and the Lutheran Reformation', SCH, *Subsidia* 5 (1986).

merely as one of a sequence of heretics from Montanus to Luther.[38] In More's *Dialogue concerning Heresies* Wyclif is called arch-heretic, and a famous passage describes how he retranslated the Bible into English and farced it with evil glosses.[39] In controversy with Tyndale More described Wyclif as 'the first founder of that abominable heresye, that blasphemeth the blessed sacrament' and complains that Tyndale regarded Wyclif as a Jonah sent to warn Nineveh of its sins.[40] But there is no evidence in More's writings that he had ever read a word of Wyclif's own writings.

In 1530 King Henry requested from Oxford University a copy of the articles of Wyclif condemned at Constance. The university replied by sending under its seal a list of the propositions which it had itself condemned in 1410, with a fresh condemnation attached.[41] In the latter part of Henry's reign Wyclif's antipapalism was congenial to those in power, but his Eucharistic doctrine remained anathema.[42] As late as 1546 his English works were prohibited by royal proclamation.[43] On the very same day as Edward Powell was hanged for protesting against the King's rejection of Papal authority, the Lutheran Dr Barnes was burnt for denying transubstantiation.[44]

On the continent as well as in England Wyclif was regarded, by friend and foe alike, as a precursor of the Reformation. At Worms an edition of the *Trialogus* appeared in 1525, the first of Wyclif's works to be printed and the only genuine one until the nineteenth century. In 1528 a Wycliffite commentary on the Apocalypse was printed at Wittenberg with a preface by Luther.[45] On the Catholic side, Bartolomeo Guidiccio, writing to Paul III in 1538 to urge the summoning of a general council to anathematize the errors of the reformers, drew up a list of twenty Lutheran propositions. Nine of these, he claimed, were old errors of Wyclif already condemned at the Council of Constance.[46] But the Wycliffite propositions condemned at Constance had begun

[38] *The Yale Edition of the Complete Works of Sir Thomas More* (New Haven and London, 1963-   , henceforth *MCW*), v. 96.

[39] *MCW* vi. 314-16.   [40] *MCW* viii. 587, 1238.   [41] Lyttle (above, n. 37).

[42] The Bishop of Carlisle quoted Netter against Wyclif in his response to the circular concerning the Bishops' Book in 1537. (Messenger, *The Reformation, the Mass, and the Priesthood* (London, 1966), 282.)

[43] Wyclif's English works were prohibited on 8 July 1546 (*Tudor Royal Proclamations*, ed. P. L. Hughes and J. F. Larkin, 373-6).

[44] Lyttle (above, n. 37).

[45] A. Hudson, *Lollards and their Books* (London, 1985), 46.

[46] *Concilium Tridentinum, Diariorum, Actorum, Epistolarum, Tractatuum Nova Collectio*, ed. Societas Goerresiana, 1896-   (henceforth *CT*), xii. 666.

a new life of their own. A Protestant admirer published a set of 'aphorisms of John Wyclif'. They were none other than the condemned articles.[47]

When the Council of Trent met to codify the Catholic position against the heresies of the Reformation, the anathemas laid upon Wyclif were naturally cited in evidence. This was especially the case when the matter at issue was the theology of the Eucharist. Two Jesuits, Lainez and Salmeron, were instructed to summarize the opinion of theologians on a number of Lutheran articles.[48] They reviewed the thesis that in the Eucharist the body and blood of Christ were present, but so too were the substance of bread and wine, so that rather than transubstantiation there was a substantial union between bread and wine and the body and blood. This error, they said, had been expressly condemned by the Council of Constance, when Wyclif had revived Berengar's theory of the remanence of the substance of bread. They quoted Woodford against Wyclif, and urged that Luther be condemned in similar terms.

When the canons on the Eucharist were presented for consideration at Trent they included the affirmation, to be enforced under anathema, that in the sacrament there remained only the accidents of bread and wine.[49] Had these canons been enacted, the doctrine of Trent would have been, in so many words, the doctrine of Constance. However, after considerable discussion, the word 'accidents' was removed from the canon.[50] In the final version which was approved, this scholastic term did not appear: the non-technical term 'appearances' was used instead. Trent, unlike Constance, did not canonize the scholastic theory which Wyclif had mocked.

Wyclif's teaching on other doctrines was also discussed at Trent. In particular, his theory that the ordination of priests was not a privilege reserved to Bishops was contested when the Council discussed the sacrament of Order. More than once, this view of his was attributed to his own disappointment at not being promoted to the see of Worcester.[51] He was also cited as an enemy of indulgences and as one who had denied the evangelical origin of the mass.[52]

---

[47] Copied from *Fasciculus Rerum Expetendarum*, 133-40.

[48] *CT*, v. 14.

[49] The canons, prepared by Seripando, are in *CT* vi. 131.

[50] The original wording 'remanentibus accidentibus sine subiecto' was replaced by 'manentibus dumtaxat speciebus panis et vini'. The vote between the two formulas was taken on 25 May 1547: *CT* vi. 160.

[51] *CT* v. 162, 45, ix. 9.   [52] *CT* vi. 342, viii. 740.

Most of the references to his work were in fact references to the condemnations of Constance; but one bishop at Trent referred to a proposition of his not condemned there,[53] and several of the Council fathers showed that they had read Woodford and Netter,[54] though no one gave evidence of any first-hand acquaintance with his own writings.

The Council of Trent held its sessions on Eucharistic doctrine in 1547. One year later, on the Protestant side, John Bale, in his catalogue of British writers published at Basle, hailed Wyclif as 'the most strong Elias of his times' and wrote that 'he shone like the morning star in the midst of a cloud, and remained for many days as the faithful witness in the church.' John Foxe, in a Latin Protestant martyrology published at Strasbourg in 1554, gave Wyclif and his followers pride of place among the victims of tyrannical Roman persecution. This martyrology, after Foxe's return to England, grew into the *Acts and Monuments* which forever canonized Wyclif's role as the great English precursor of the Reformation.[55]

During the rest of the sixteenth century, most Catholic writing on Wyclif was written either in reply to Foxe or in reply to Bishop Jewel's *Apologia Ecclesiae Anglicanae* published in 1562. Just as Foxe and Jewel quoted from the condemnations of Wyclif, but hardly at all from Wyclif's own works, so too did the Catholic assailants of Wyclif.

In the battle of the books which ensued on the publication of Jewel's apology, the most eloquent Catholic champion was Thomas Harding. In his book *A Detection of Sundrie Foule Errors*, published in 1568, he is at pains to show that Wyclif held a number of theses which would not be welcome to the Anglicans who claim him as their precursor.[56] He presses into service the fourth and the sixth of the articles condemned at Constance.

Item ... that it is against the Scripture, that Ecclesiastical Ministers should have any temporal possessions. If this be no greater heresie than the reste, M. Iewel, then allowe it, as you allowe the rest. But the gaine is so sweete, you can not brooke it.

Again, Wyclif taught that those who are in sin forfeit all dominion: 'If ye make this no Heresie, then ye denie the Queene to be Queene of England, whensoever she falleth into Mortall sinne.'[57] Lest it should

[53] *CT* ix. 151.   [54] *CT* ix. 52, 161.   [55] See Aston (above, n. 1), 24–7.
[56] *A Detection* ... (Scolar Press Reprint, London, 1974), 82ᵛ.
[57] Ibid.

be thought disrespectful to her Majesty to suggest that she might be in mortal sin, Harding was quick to point out that Protestants rejected the Catholic distinction between venial and mortal sin; and that all Christians agreed that no human being could remain long without sin in this life.

These points made by Harding were made again and again by Counter-Reformation writers, anxious to show that Wyclif was a very unreliable ally for Anglican writers to enlist in their cause.

In Elizabeth's reign the most tireless critic of Wyclif was Nicholas Harpsfield, archdeacon of Canterbury in the days of Pole, who died in 1575 after twelve years' imprisonment and is best known as the biographer of Thomas More. He wrote six dialogues which were published at Antwerp in 1566, pseudonymously attributed to Alan Cope.[58] The dialogues, between an orthodox Englishman Irenaeus and a heretical German Critobulus, are largely a discussion of Bishop Jewel's *Apologia Ecclesiae Anglicanae*. But the sixth dialogue is against pseudomartyrs, with special reference to Foxe. Critobulus hails Wyclif as 'A prince of the purer gospel', a worthy forerunner of Carlstadt, Zwingli, and Calvin.[59] Irenaeus says that Wyclif is an uncomfortable ally for the reformers: Wyclif approved of the worship of relics and images, for instance.[60] Luther, he says, regarded Wyclif as a heretic; and he quotes Melanchthon, writing about the Lord's supper:

I have looked at Wyclif, who makes a great stir on this issue, but I have found in him many other errors, which permit one to judge of his spirit. He did not understand or maintain justification by faith. He naively mixes up politics with the gospel, and did not realise that the gospel allows us to accept the lawful regimes of all nations. He claims that priests are not allowed to possess any private property, and thinks that tithes should be paid only to teachers . . .[61]

Setting Wyclif against the more recent reformers became a standard move of Counter-Reformation apologetic.[62]

[58] *Dialogi Sex . . . ab Alano Copo* (Antwerp, 1566).

[59] Ibid., 429.

[60] The ambiguity of the Wycliffite attitude to image worship became a commonplace of recusant polemic. Thus Matthew Kellison, in *A Reply to Sutcliffe's Answer* (1608), 137, complains that 'Hierom of Prague defiled with ordure the image of Christe, and yet honoured Wicleph's image and crowned it with a diademe'.

[61] Cope (above, n. 58), 824.

[62] It is surprising, however, how comparatively little recusant writers concern themselves with Wyclif at all. A cursory search through the scores of volumes of recusant literature reprinted in facsimile in recent years by the Scolar press has failed to reveal any evidence of first-hand knowledge of Wyclif's writings.

Foxe in later editions of his book of Martyrs replied to some of the taunts of 'Cope', and some fifteen years later Harpsfield returned to the charge. In captivity he wrote a lengthy history of the English Church: to it he added a long appendix, a *Historia Wicleffiana*, a history of English heresy to match the history of English piety.[63] The work must have been written about 1590 but was published only in 1622, at Douai. Though only an appendix to the larger work, the *Historia Wicleffiana* is a substantial treatise in its own right, consisting of nineteen chapters. Harpsfield quotes the chroniclers for the details of the life of Wyclif and the Lollards, but the passages he cites are familiar from Foxe; he devotes a chapter to anti-Wycliffite miracles, and lists Catholic writers against Wyclif's heresies: Woodford, Netter, More, Fisher, Gardner. But he admits that, for lack of books, he has had to rely for his account of Wyclif's doctrines on the work of Netter, 'who detected eight hundred errors in Wyclif's books'. Once only, in the Six Dialogues, Harpsfield appears to make a direct reference to Wyclif himself (to '*tractatus magnus de eucharistia*, c. 9')[64] but here too there may be a tacit use of Netter as a source.

Harpsfield's history combines a chauvinistic pride in the extent of Wyclif's infuence (a single Englishman filling the whole world with his ideas) with a horror at the wickedness of his heresy (no decent Englishman believed a word of Wyclif's teaching until the present pestiferous generation). Readers will find, he says, that Luther borrowed not only his abuse of the Roman Church but all his heresies from Wyclif–except that on the issue of the Eucharist Wyclif is even worse than Luther. He matches Lutheran heresies against the articles condemned at the Council of Constance. But the latter-day disciples of Wyclif disagree with their master about image-worship, celibacy, and pacifism.

Like many another critic of Wyclif, Harpsfield wrestles with his difficult doctrine of predestination.

Among the other accursed doctrines of Wyclif are these: God cannot save the foreknown; God cannot do what he does not do ... and other things of the same flavour. Because all pious ears turn away, he tinctures this absinth with a sweetening draft: God can do these things if he were to will to do so. But who does not see that these contradict and overturn each other: God cannot, and yet can, if he will?[65]

[63] *Historia Anglicanae Ecclesiae* (Douai, 1622).
[64] Cope (above, n. 58), 635.
[65] Harpsfield (above, n. 63), 666.

Harpsfield wrote better in English than in Latin and better in praise than in blame: his life of Thomas More has attracted many readers, his history of Wycliffitism has remained almost entirely unread.

One of the few who did read Harpsfield was the Jesuit Robert Persons, who drew on his work in his own *Treatise of Three Conversions of England from Paganism to Christian Religion* in 1603.[66] Once bursar of Balliol, missionary companion of Edmund Campion, and would-be mentor of Mary Queen of Scots, Persons was in 1603 Rector of the English College in Rome. His book was an elaborate reply to Foxe's *Book of Martyrs* and his heavily annotated copy can still be seen in the English College.[67] Persons mocks at the calendar of Protestant martyrs in which Foxe places Wyclif at the head as martyr of the day for 2 January. Wyclif was no martyr, but died in his bed; and many of the doctrines he held would make a good Protestant blush. To be sure, Foxe had admitted that 'in John Wickliffe's opinions and assertions some blemishes perhaps may be noted: yet such blemishes they be, which rather declare him to be a man that might erre, than which directly did fight against Christ our Savior'. But this is not enough for Persons. Is it all right then to fight indirectly against Christ?[68]

Persons copies from Foxe the list of propositions condemned by the Blackfriars council and then comments:

These articles, though in divers point they concurre with Luther, Swingli and Calvyn his doctrine in these days: yet in other they greatly disagree. And Fox I think will not defend them. As, for example, the fourth article is: That if a bishop or Priest shold give holy orders, or consecrate the Sacrament of the aultar, or minister baptisme, while he is in mortall sin: it were nothing avayleable.[69]

Will yeld to this article, thinke you? For if he do, we may well call in doubt whether ever he were well baptised, and consequently whether he were a christian: seeinge it may be doubted, whether the Priest, that baptized him, were in mortall syn or or no, when he did it.

And again in 9 article is: That it is against Scripture, for any ecclesiastical

---

[66] The *Three Conversions* was reprinted by the Scolar Press in 1966.

[67] A recusant writer who anticipated some of Persons' criticisms of Foxe is William Rainolds, who published his *A Treatise Conteyning the Catholic and Apostolike Faith* in 1593. Wyclif was no martyr, he says, but 'he was both a vile heretike, and as a most pernicious flatterer and parasite, applied his whole learning and gospelising to please the humours of certain noble men his favourers, which gaped for the spoile of the church.' (29.)

[68] Persons (above, n. 66), i. 486.

[69] This was a point already made by Harding and again by Rainolds (above, n. 67, p. 29): since Wyclif's disciples say everyone is always in sin, all their Lord's suppers and orderings are invalid.

ministers to have any temporall possessions at all. This article if Fox will
grant: yet his fellow ministers and his lords the bishops I presume will hardly
yeld thanks, but will pretend scripture to the contrary against Wickliffe.[70]

It is evident, Persons says, from the articles alleged by Fox that Wyclif
held many points of the Catholic religion now disowned by Protestants, such as holy orders, consecration, excommunication, distinction of venial and mortal sins and the like. He concludes, sweepingly,
'Wickliffe, Husse, and other like sectarys did hold many more articles
with us against the protestants, than with them against us'.
Persons's citations of Wyclif seem to come almost entirely from
Foxe's book: there is no evidence of any acquaintance with the
reformer's own works, nor even of browsing in Netter's refutation.
Of all the polemicists of the Counter-Reformation, none was more
intelligent, more learned, more fair-minded, or more courteous than
Cardinal Robert Bellarmine, whose *Controversiae* (in some two million
words) were published in the first decade of the seventeenth century.[71]
Bellarmine accepts the tradition, countenanced in the proceedings of
the Council of Trent, that Wyclif's heresies were due to his ambition.
But none the less he takes his doctrines seriously and argues fairly
against him. In the context of Eucharistic theory, for instance, he is
prepared to agree with Wyclif that annihilation makes no sense; and
he has a long discussion of the Wycliffite puzzle: can you point to the
host and say, 'That round white thing is the body of Christ'?[72] But
here, as elsewhere, he is totally dependent for his knowledge of Wyclif
on the writings of Netter. Had Wyclif's writings been available to him,
there is no doubt that the scholarly Bellarmine would have quoted
them at first hand. But the energies of generations of his predecessors
had ensured that the works of Wyclif were not to be found in the
libraries of Rome.[73]
The level of controversial writing was raised to such a degree by
Bellarmine that it was an embarrassment to his pupils and successors
that the condemnations of Wyclif could not always be justified by
reference to existing texts of his works. Thus the Jesuit Gretser, a few

[70] R. Hooker, *Ecclesiastical Polity*, vii. xxii. 7, condemns Wyclif's error of regarding
clerical endowment sinful, if it is really to be found in him. But, he says 'in his writings I
do not find it'. Another giant of the Reformation era who could not bring himself
actually to read Wyclif's works!
[71] Robert Bellarmine, *Controversiae* . . . (Rome, 1606-66).
[72] Ibid., i. 156.
[73] To this day, only a single MS in the Vatican library contains a few of Wyclif's
opuscules: see Thomson (above, n. 8), p. 315.

years after the publication of Bellarmine's massive work, says that if not all the propositions condemned at Constance are to be found in Wyclif's extant writings, we must believe that the fathers had access to manuscripts now lost.[74]

The writings of Bellarmine and Gretser were quicky imported into England. They were responsible for the first English investigation into Wyclif's own writings since the destructive critique of Netter. Thomas James, the first librarian of the Bodleian library, wrote in 1608 *An Apologie for Iohn Wickliffe, showing his conformitie with the now Church of England*.[75] He took as his target both ill-informed Protestants and ill-willing papists. He announced that his intention was to reply to Wyclif's critics 'out of his own words and works as they are extant in sundray good manuscripts in our so renowned public library'. He takes the reader through a series of topics of reformation controversy: the authority of Scripture, the role of vernacular translations, the authority of tradition, the claims of the papacy, justification by faith, the doctrine of the Eucharist. He has little difficulty in showing that on most of these issues Wyclif's position was closer to that of the Church of England than to that of the Church of Rome. Scripture, for Wyclif, contains all that is necessary for a Christian and should be available in the vernacular; tradition is subservient to Scripture, the pope's power is limited, and popes should not meddle with the affairs of princes. The Church of Rome may err: 'Wickliffe remains, in this point, as in all the former, a resolved, true Catholike English Protestant.'[76] James has some difficulty in making Wyclif a partisan of justification by faith, but claims to find in his writings that faith in Christ is sufficient for salvation and that without faith it is impossible for anyone to please God. 'Thus it may appeare, that Wickliffe did fully understand the point of justification, or else he would never have relied so much upon God's mercie, and so little upon merits.' On the issue of the Eucharist, James denies (unlike the theologians of Trent) that Wyclif held the Lutheran doctrine of consubstantiation.

In all this James's main adversary is the Jesuit Persons, though he also has in his sights Bellarmine and Gretser. Persons is quite wrong to claim that Wyclif retained Catholic doctrines: on the contrary, Wyclif preached against 'pretiosity, speciosity, and miraculositie, and

---

[74] I. Gretser, *Controversiarum Roberti Bellarmini S.R.E. Cardinalis Amplissima Defensio* (Ingolstadt, 1607), 831.
[75] Published at Oxford, 1608.
[76] James, *Apologie*, 2, 10, 145, 25.

sundry such sophistications about images'. James cannot deny that there are passages in Wyclif which display a belief in purgatory and an enthusiasm for prayers to the saints.

I am persuaded that he retracted these opinions in his latter and more learned works. If ever it be God's pleasure, that his works which were cutt and mangled, and scattered worse than Absyrtus' limbes were in the Poet, may be brought forth and set together againe, that we may have the whole bodie of his learned and religious works, and be able to distinguish of the time and order wherin he wrote: then I say we should receave due satisfaction on this point.[77]

In spite of the appeal for research funding with which James concluded his work, the whole body of Wyclif's works remained unpublished until the labours of the Wyclif society in the nineteenth century: some of them, indeed, still await an editor. But with the work of James the historical consideration of Wyclif reaches a new level of sophistication. James was able to consult and quote many of the original works of the reformer and compare them with the caricature current among his admirers and detractors. For the first time since Netter, scholarship takes the place of slander and sycophancy. To be sure, James was partisan: he wanted to prove Wyclif a good Anglican. But he kept his partisanship within the bounds of decency and plausibility. And in his capacity as Bodley's librarian he showed himself an ecumenist in advance of his time. To this day, on the frieze which James commissioned for the upper reading room of the Bodleian library, the visitor may see, side by side in painted harmony, the effigies of Wyclif and Hus–and of Cardinal d'Ailly, who sat in condemnation of both of them at Constance.[78]

---

[77] James, *Apologie*, 66.
[78] On the Bodleian library frieze, see J. N. L. Myres, 'Thomas James and the Painted Friese', *The Bodleian Library Record*, 4 (1952-3), 30-51.

Index

William of Ockham (*cont.*):
38; and papal power 16; in reform movement 105, 106, 110; *Summa Totius Logicae* 9; and Wyclif 2, 109

William of Wykeham 108

Winterton, Dr Thomas 5

Wittgenstein, Ludwig 19

Wodeham, Adam 35, 38

Wok of Waldstein 143

Wolsey, Cardinal Thomas 159

Woodford, William 10, 11, 148; *quattuor Determinationes* 83-4; use of texts by, in Counter-Reformation 161, 162, 164

Workman, H. B. 8, 10, 11, 13

Worms, publication of *Trialogus* at 160

Wyche, Richard 131, 143

Wyclif, John: biographical information on 1-2, 31 n. 1, 67, 83, 107-8, 127; condemnations of, *see* condemnations; influence of, on Hus and Hussites 107, 115, 118-25, 128, 129, 136-45; Oxford testimonial to 77-8, 142; philosophical realism of 2-3, 9-11, 17-29, 108-10, 137; publication of works by 168; and reform movement 105-7; theological motivations of 13, 16, 42-3, 45, 49-51; interest of, in vernacular 86-91, 94-5, 102-3, 167

Wyclif, John (Works): *De Apostasia* 5, 9, 13, 108, 117; *De Blasphemia* 14; *De Civili Dominio* 10, 108, 114, 116, 140, 148, 149; *De Confessione* 149; *De Diabolo et Membrius eius* 149; *Dialogus* 140, 141, 150; *De Dominio Divino* 77, 135; *De Dotacione Ecclesiae* 149; *De Ecclesia* 11, 77, 135; *De Eucharistia* 9, 11, 12, 108, 117; *De Ideis* 137; *De Logica* 40, 42, 46; *Logicae Continuatio* 40-2, 149; *De Mandatis* 135; *Materia et Forma* 137; *De Officio Regis* 116, 117; *Opus Evangelicum* 134, 139; *De Ordine Christiano* 149; *De Perfectione Statuum* 149; *Postilla Super Totam Bibliam* 12, 135; *De Potestate Pape* 5, 11, 114; *Reply to Strode* 149; *Responsio ad xlv conclusiones* 149; *De Simonia* 149; *Summa de Ente* 2, 9; *Tractatus de Logica* 40-2, 63; *Trialogus* 9, 47, 49, 50, 89, 140, 141, 148, 149, 150, 151, 160; *De Universalibus* 17-29, 46 n. 56, 137, 157, 159; *De Versutia Antichristi* 149; *De Veritate Sacre Scripture* 4, 10, 12, 77, 135

Wycliffism: and Lollardy 85-6, 129-36; Netter's critique of 156; and use of vernacular 85, 90-103, 132-3. *See also* Lollard movement

Wycliffite texts 78-83; erudition and scholarship in 96-101, 132-4; in Reformation 160

Wyclif's Wicket 102-3

Zabarella, Canonist Bartolomeo 151

Zbynek of Hasenburg, Archbishop of Prague 138, 139, 142

Zomeren, Henry van 158